THE CONDUCT OF INDUSTRIAL RELATIONS

P D Anthony

Institute of Personnel Management
Central House, Upper Woburn Place, London WC1H 0HX

First published 1977

Printed in Great Britain by Lonsdale Universal Printing Ltd, Bath, Avon

ISBN 0 85292 157 8

CONTENTS

ACKNOWLEDGEMENTS

I should like to thank Professor George Thomason and Dr Tom Keenoy for their contribution to many of the ideas presented here. I should also like to thank Mrs Mair Price for her skill and patience in typing the book

CHAPTER 1

The nature of industrial relations

There is no such thing as a system of industrial relations in Great Britain. If we think of industrial relations as concerned with the determination of terms and conditions of employment and the rules of work, then the manner in which they are settled moves through an almost infinite number of variations between unilateral determination by employers to unilateral determination by workers. If, with an increasing awareness of complexity, we beging to think in terms of various positions on a spectrum of joint regulation between two unilateral extremes, we would be wrong because we would leave out the various ways by which the State powerfully influences the process. If we then decide to think in terms of a tripartite system we next have to remind ourselves that some parts of the system are entirely different from others and that each of the parties is, itself, an enormously complex 'system' open to an infinity of influences. There is little doubt, for example, that the man on the shop floor in a multi-union engineering firm depends more upon the joint shop stewards committee at the plant, for influencing his work environment, than upon his trade union, to which he may also owe less loyalty than to his fellows and their representatives.

There seems to be no purpose in thinking about industrial relations as though it were composed of inter-related parts each influencing the behaviour of the rest in a relatively orderly and predictable manner. There are also great dangers in thinking about industrial relations as a system. Apart from its lack of realism, it carries with it the risk of an ossified conservatism in conceptualizing a 'system' which, once constructed, has to be defended. The habit of thinking about business institutions as though they were social organisms 'is neither necessary nor particularly satisfying. It presents the danger of reifying what is only an analytic construct—the "system".'[1]

Systems thinking may be the explanation for the undoubted conservatism that has characterized attitudes to industrial relations in Britain over the lifetime of present observers. We are all familiar with the popular obsession with the condition of industrial relationships in this country. It does not seem to be related to the actual state of affairs; whether industrial relations are 'worse' or 'better', either in terms of what they were last year or of what they are like in other countries, the public attitude remains the same, a permanent, chronic state of worry, occasionally giving way to despair (that is, when a Commission is established or an Act is passed). It is as though the increase in the habit of international travel has convinced us, at last, that our climate is not really so bad so that we have had to substitute a new source for permanent pessimism, a preoccupation which gives us the mild pleasure of concern about a subject which is sufficiently safe to avoid keeping us awake at nights.

A conservative attitude, a tendency to think of industrial relations in normative terms as orderly and, therefore, as subject to decay or to chaotic tendencies when there are manifestations of disorder, is characteristic of observers who are far more expert about industrial relations than the man in the street. Here is one definition, for example:

> ... industrial relations includes any policy action, pay, condition or agreement within a given concern which

enables the workforce to continue in a cooperative way. Thus, industrial relations have broken down when there is a strike, a go-slow, an overtime ban or work-to-rule or lack of communication.

Such a view of industrial relations must leave the belief in the minds of many practising specialists that they are engaged in industrial relations only when it has stopped! But the definition was not provided by an uninformed or irresponsible group. It was given as written evidence to the Commission on Industrial Relations in the reference on Management's Role in Industrial Relations and by the Institute of Personnel Management, no less.

This restricted view of industrial relations is also characteristic of some academic definitions which, although in more scholarly and sometimes more obscure terms, often share the same conviction that industrial relations is something that is (or ought to be) essentially stable and that it is destroyed when it shows signs of instability. Thus the late Allan Flanders, whose contribution to the study of British industrial relations was enormous, said of it that 'the subject deals with certain regulated or institutionalized relationships in industry. Personal or, in the language of sociology, "unstructured" relationships have their importance for management and workers, but they lie outside the scope of a system of industrial relations.'[2] In *The Reform of Collective Bargaining: From Donovan to Durkheim*, Fox and Flanders described the dangers of disorder and breakdown in industrial relations arising from circumstances in which one group, against the resistance of another, tries to change the procedural norms, or in which tension between prevailing norms and the aspirations of a group provokes challenge, or where the existing regulative system breaks down giving way to a change in the nature of the system and a shift from bilateral to unilateral regulation, when groups with enough power break through in order to impose their own norms.

Both these views of industrial relations seem to share a certain unreality. A 'system of industrial relations' which excludes personal relationships must surely be some sort of abstraction which leaves out of account a great deal of behaviour which anyone associated with the practice of industrial relations is bound to recognize as important. An industrial dispute in September 1973 at Ford Motors began because a line worker was alleged to have threatened a foreman; was the dispute a part of industrial relations while the incident which caused it was not? Again, what Fox and Flanders describe as major sources of disorder in industrial relations, with the implications of pathology that this description suggests, could just as sensibly be regarded as the very essence of industrial relations. The instances which they give of the causes of disorder are almost inseparable from the normal conduct of the parties in industrial relations. If one or other of the parties is *not* concerned with trying to effect some change in procedural norms, or in producing tensions between his aspirations and the prevailing norms, or demanding greater regulation over issues over which new aspirations have developed, then it is quite likely that industrial relations has fallen into a dangerous state of rigidity.

A definition of industrial relations which stresses its institutional character or its bipartisan composition runs the risk of over-simplicity, and a definition which is concerned with its maintenance of a system in stable-equilibrium is likely to be over-rigid. Professor Clegg defines industrial relations in the broadest terms as encompassing 'the rules governing employment together with the ways in which the rules are made and changed and their interpretation and administration.'[3] This is sufficient for our purpose. What we are chiefly concerned with is the ways in which the rules are made and changed rather than with a description of the rules themselves. The content of the rules in British industrial relations has received a great deal more attention than the process by which they are arrived at or amended. The institutions which contribute to their formulation have also been widely described, although there has been a tendency to concentrate upon workers' institutions rather than those of management. This preference is partly explained by the interest and sympathies of some of the researchers, but it also reflects the fact that employers' institutions are discrete organizations while trade unions are more available for public scrutiny.

We are going to be concerned here with the processes by which the rules of employment are made and the influences which affect management and the employer in their contribution to their construction.

When we have said what industrial relations is, we have not got much further in discovering the kind of activity that the subject involves and the kind of behaviour engaged in it by those who are party to it. Let us try to take the matter a little further by discussing the kind of activity and behaviour that seems to feature in the field of industrial relations.

We have already suggested that we cannot exclude from this discussion behaviour of an inter-personal kind. This is often characterized as irrational behaviour (although at whatever level of consciousness it is analysed it rarely seems to lack some purposive quality); while since the popularization of the Hawthorne experiments it has been recognized in management literature as a potent area of influence, it was and still is (see Flanders) rigorously excluded from serious consideration in the field of industrial relations. The reason for this purely academic (and entirely unreal) demarcation lies in some confused squabbles over the nature of industrial conflict and a tendency, amongst management theorists of a human relations persuasion, to treat all industrial disputes as though they were failures of understanding, breakdowns in communication, or ruptures in personal relationships of an emotional kind. In an understandable wish to correct this view, industrial relation specialists have thrown out the baby with the bath water and have either denied the importance of the emotional area or, grudgingly, have consigned it to the attention of management theorists (almost the equivalent of consigning it to the devil). Industrial relations specialists have taken this view partly as a necessary corrective to human relations theory and partly to distinguish their own field of study from that of other academics in order to help to establish the purity of its credentials as an academic discipline.

More will follow in a later chapter about the difference between real and apparent causes of conflict as sources of industrial dispute. Let it suffice for the moment to say that irrationality, and certainly the consequences of irrationality, is characteristic of the behaviour with which the industrial relations specialist has to deal. In so far as this has been recognized it has been acknowledged to a limited extent: it is, for the most part, subordinate labour which is believed to be capable of irrational action and which therefore demands understanding, study and analysis. Managers on the whole believe that managers are rational men whose difficulties are largely imposed by irrational subordinates. The behaviour of managers can appear to be largely unpredictable and partly irrational, however, when viewed from below. Here is De Vos' explanation for the irrationality of superordinate conduct:

> There are two forms of exploitation practised by dominant groups upon the vulnerable lower segments of society. The first of these [is] rationally, goal-directed or 'instrumental' exploitation, the use of subordinates to realize one's own goals or desires . . . [The] second form of social exploitation I term 'expressive' exploitation . . . expressive exploitation is related directly to the irrational and un-

conscious psychological processes characteristic of man's complex mental structure.[4]

De Vos goes on to explain that expressive exploitation results in the institutionalization of inferiority and in scapegoating. Both are aspects of behaviour that are familiar on the shop floor.

One of the problems of industrial relations is that disputes caused by emotional breakdowns have to be handled by a process of conciliation or collective bargaining which is invariably designed for handling rational or instrumental disputes arising from differences of interest. There is no doubt that management and their academic advisers have disgracefully neglected areas of welfare and counselling in industrial relations (or in the wider environment of personnel management), areas which produce considerable conflicts which might be significantly reduced by the application of some old fashioned sense or some new fangled psychotherapy. There is no doubt also that the emotional tensions produced in disputes of interest are often given no opportunity for release in the procedures for their resolution, or by the haste with which grievance procedures are designed to get the dispute away from the shop floor.

There are matters which deserve a little more discussion but we must agree that industrial relations is largely concerned with rational issues and rational disagreements. There is an assumption in any discussion of the behaviour of participants in industrial relations that their behaviour is rational. It is normally directed in a purposive manner at the satisfaction of their interests, the interests of those whom they represent or of those with whom they believe themselves to be closely identified. For this reason it is often believed, because behaviour in industrial relations is self-interested, that it is selfish but this is not necessarily so; it may involve considerable self-sacrifice but the sacrifice, where it occurs, is on behalf of one's group. It is never selfless to the extent that it is designed to damage the interests of one's community.

It is usual for interests in industrial relations to be determined by organizations. The process of defining these interests may take place in a more or less democratic way (as is the case in some trade unions) or in a much more centralized, hierarchical fashion (as perhaps in management organizations). In the process of determining goals in industrial relations there may be a great deal of internal bargaining within the organization, between inhabitants who may value stability or innovation, harmony or conflict. It is likely that the specialist in industrial relations has an important role in this process of internal bargaining. There is no certainty that goals are determined in industrial relations with any precision and their vagueness may partly result from the obvious constraints which surround management decision making in this area.

Management is constrained in the first place by rules which are imposed upon it or in the formulation of which it may have joined. The law regulates management's conduct with increasing severity in industrial relations and, when freed of these influences, management is further constrained by the existence of rules drawn up jointly with trade unions in order to regulate their relationships so as to avoid mutual damage. These are the procedural rules which act as a voluntary constraint upon the parties because the rules are seen as protecting their interests by the mutual regulation of behaviour which they provide. The constraints which procedures give are voluntary in that they are seen to be of advantage but the view of either party may change on the protection which the rules seem to afford and, therefore, in the extent to which they have committed themselves to respect them. At some point before procedural rules become irksome and are abandoned by one party, it may have faced another source of constraint upon its behaviour by vaguer notions concerning what is the ethical way to behave concerning respect for consistency and for patterns of behaviour and values which its opponent may have come to regard as customary. Its respect for such expectations may be a curious blend of morality and hard-headed practical realism because the collective bargaining relationship, however hostile, requires a considerable degree of shared values, expectations and trust between the opposing parties for it to survive.

This degree of mutual dependence is easily obscured by the constraints which the parties impose upon each other. Employers, trade unions and their members depend upon each other but their respective purposes do not coincide. The employment relationship contains elements of essential mutual cooperation: it could not survive without a considerable degree of consensus, support and cooperation. But there are many circumstances in which any one of the parties to the employment relationship becomes an obstacle to the achievement of the purpose of one of the others. Industrial relationships are especially concerned with these circumstances in which different groups are set upon different courses in the pursuit of which one becomes an obstacle to the other. The force, of one kind or another, which can be brought to bear in removing the obstacle and the force with which the obstacle can resist removal, represents the constraints with which management and the unions seek to influence each other's behaviour. The procedures of industrial relations are, for the most part, concerned to protect the parties from inflicting an unacceptable degree of damage upon each other in a relationship which is often hostile. The parties thus seek to control each other's behaviour in two ways: by applying power to prevent the other from getting what he wants and by mutually agreeing to limit the extent and the manner in which power can be so applied. The first level of their relationship is coercive, characterized by a catch-as-catch-can outlook in which power and tactical skill are employed to bring a grudging opponent to accept a conclusion he would prefer to avoid. But this is the competitive aspect of a relationship which is necessarily cooperative and therefore the parties perceive that they must mutually agree to limit the hostility with which it is conducted; it is not in the long-term interests of either party to inflict too much damage on the other. So the second level of the relationship between the parties is constitutional or procedural, a level in which they agree to regulate their behaviour at the coercive level.

But the coercive and the constitutional level are never entirely distinct and separate: if the constitutional protection which the parties have agreed to provide for each other reflects a degree of coercive power which one of the parties no longer enjoys, there is likely to be pressure to change the constitutional relationship, to change the rules by which the game is played. This pressure may be formally exercised or it may follow a greater degree of 'unofficial' action in which the actual behaviour of one side or another begins to show scant respect for procedural rules, although they continue to be formally acknowledged. Particular examples can be observed from time to time. In 1922 the engineering employers changed the arrangement which existed since 1898 under which they consulted before introducing changes in workshop practice; this establishment of 'managerial prerogatives' followed a real change in employers' relative power. This state of affairs survived until 1971; by then the relative distribution of power had changed again but workshop *practice* in many cases had long demanded prior consultation over changes. The change in power was formally acknowledged when the Amalgamated Union of Engineering Workers abandoned the existing procedural agreements. In 1966 the National Union of Mineworkers gave notice to the National Coal Board that it was dissatisfied with the existing procedural agreements which tied it, essentially, to the involuntary submission of issues which could not be agreed to a domestic process of arbitration which was binding upon both parties. The NUM saw that this procedure outlawed any official and constitutional strike action, perceived that it was a procedural constraint which no longer reflected its own power, and that it would become a serious impediment to its own negotiating strength in the process of centralizing the wage structure in which it and the NCB were engaged. The removal of this procedural obstacle was, from the Union's point of view, a necessary preliminary for the big disputes in which it was to engage in 1972 and 1974. In 1969 the Ford Motor Company's agreed procedural arrangements were demonstrated to be unrealistic in terms of the relative distribution of power in the Company as between the Transport and General Workers Union and the AUEW on the one hand and the other unions composing the union side of the Joint National Negotiating Committee on the other. The agreement, which had been arrived at constitutionally by the JNNC and approved by a majority of union signatories, was not acceptable, first to the TGWU and the AUEW stewards and subsequently to the two unions' executives. The two unions in question were by far the most powerful unions in the Company and their action changed not only the particular agreement but the procedural relationships within the Company.

Some of the influences at work in circumstances like these are easily recognized. Others are complex, hidden within a maze of organizational intricacy and visible only to informed insiders. These influences are brought to bear in the industrial relations field by a process of transmission and we shall try to follow, in chapter 3, the processes of internal bargaining by which influence from outside the collective bargaining context is transmitted to it and the industrial relations specialist's important role here. But other forces have to be transmitted to the negotiating table and to the parties who have to take up negotiating positions and determine their objectives. Some of these forces will closely constrain the behaviour of the parties to collective bargaining although they emanate from outside the industrial relations field. Commercial considerations, the technical nature of the production process, the state of the national and regional labour markets, the expectations of shareholders, the influence of foreign managers in multi-national companies, plans for expansion or retraction, the cost structure of the company: all these and a host of other influences can affect the conduct of industrial relations. The most dangerous circumstances are likely to arise when these and other influences do *not* exert any pressure on the conduct of industrial relations; this is because, in these circumstances, it is likely that the industrial relations function has achieved an ossified and protected position in which it is incapable of perceiving or responding to any pressures external to its own rigidly demarcated boundaries. The danger is even greater perhaps when the industrial relations function is entrenched in some other organization which is protected from any real influence from outside. It was these circumstances which led the Donovan Commission to comment on boards of directors who enjoy 'the protection provided by the existing system against their being held fully responsible for their own personnel policies'. We will suggest in chapter 3 that, for these reasons, it is important to take as much care with an internal bargaining structure as it is with the much more obvious need for adequate machinery for bargaining between management and unions.

The way in which the industrial relations function is organized and its degree of openness to pressure from other parts of the organization will both depend upon and will influence the relative strength of the roles that are to be contained within it. In most circumstances it is much too simple to speak of 'the role of the industrial relations specialist'. Managers in industrial relations are concerned with a variety of objectives (whether they can specify them or not is another question) which range between long term influence and day to day survival. We have also suggested that industrial relations is rarely an entirely specialist activity; it is open to elements in the enterprise as a whole and, in some respects, even to the wider society beyond it. Industrial relations is also an aspect of the managerial organization which overlaps with an independent and sometimes hostile external organization, the trade union. So the performance, knowledge and skills required are likely to vary as the dimensions of industrial relations change: behaviour which is appropriate at one level of activity may be damaging at another. One problem which is frequently encountered is the need to strike an effective balance between the need for expert skill and understanding and the need to attain a broader view. The immediate short term requirement of an industrial relations specialist at departmental level may be to understand, implement and control a complex agreement without permitting any serious deviation from it. This requirement may not be adequate at a higher organization level where the necessity is 'not to understand the world but to change it'. The planning and negotiation of change requires understanding of a wider environment and the parties to the negotiating process will include a variety of groups. At this level there may be risks in regarding industrial relations as an entirely specialist activity; at lower levels it might be foolhardy to regard it as anything else.

It is easy to draw up categorizations of levels in management or in personnel management and it is just as easy to imply that those levels are distinct and separate and that they represent horizontal divisions of responsibility which ought to be imitated. This is of course nonsense. But there are probably characteristic activities which may be more frequently found among managers in the upper reaches of a hierarchy, operating to longer time spans of control, and other activities which are more likely to characterize subordinate managers. At the top, managers are planners who are occasionally concerned with execution; at the bottom they are executives who may be occasionally concerned with planning.

It is also dangerous to describe the conduct of industrial relations in terms of layers, each of which demands its appropriate behaviour. Industrial relations specialists, above all, ought to be aware of the dangers inherent in rigid demarcations but it may be useful, simply as a framework, to think of different kinds of industrial relations activity even while we accept that they may occur at more than one level within a managerial hierarchy.

Planning is an essential ingredient in the management process, particularly at superordinate levels; if it is found less frequently among industrial relations specialists, this may indicate that the industrial relations function as a whole has been consigned to a subordinate position. Planning in industrial relations involves an attempt to forecast changes in the commercial, technical and social environment so as to emerge with realistic plans which will determine the management's intentions for employee conditions and relationships. Planning involves the selection of goals to be reached (it goes without saying that there are many enterprises in which the direction of industrial relations and the selection of goals to be attained appears to be in quite other hands than those of management). The goals which are determined are likely to be expressed in terms of intended changes in employee relationships concerning manpower deployment and utilization and labour costs.

In some circumstances, planning in industrial relations is a process which may take place entirely outside the industrial relations department, in which case planned objectives may be imposed upon the industrial relations specialist. But if the enterprise employs industrial relations specialists at all, it is certain to require their active responsibility for the second activity to be delineated. Achieving the organization's goals in industrial relations, however and wherever they were determined, is a job for specialists. Each party in industrial relations tries to achieve goals which it has determined. In the process, each party tries to shift the aims and expectations of the other, deploying skills to discover the true interests and position of its opponent. The most widely recognized process by which the achievement of goals is pursued is in joint negotiation or collective bargaining. Bargaining skills include the influences which one party can bring to bear upon the other. The negotiating process may move through phases which are not directly related to reaching bargaining goals but which are more concerned with attitude repair and readjustment. There are methods of achieving goals other than by negotiation and we shall look at some of these approaches in chapter 2.

Finally, when goals have been determined and achieved, they have to be administered. This third activity in industrial relations involves the application and control of agreements and the maintenance of established rules and expectations of work and remuneration. Administration involves the monitoring and control of agreements in an attempt to prevent other parties from moving away from them; it may involve a calculation of the costs involved in allowing a departure from the agreements as against the costs of its more rigid maintenance. When agreements are administered they have to be applied to particular cases and this process may further advance the extent to which agreements are defined by the continued accumulation of 'case law' and precedent. There are circumstances in which the over-rigid administration of an agreement, or of a previously established understanding, may be as dangerous or costly as sticking to a principle (which usually, upon inspection, turns out to be a slogan) at all costs.

Let us now turn to a closer examination of management's objectives in industrial relations and of the various ways in which it seeks to reach them. But let us always remember during this discussion, that management is incapable of exercising absolute control here. Management cannot do what it likes, unless it enjoys sufficient power to be able to exercise coercive, unilateral control over its workforce. Many managements do but, to the extent that they can enforce their decisions upon passive or acquiescent employees, their affairs do not belong in a discussion of industrial relations.

CHAPTER 2

Management's objectives in industrial relations

A great deal of nonsense has been talked and written about objectives in management and it is just as easy to be foolish about objectives in industrial relations. The best intentions are obvious enough and were piously stated by the Commission on Industrial Relations:

> A company's industrial relations policy should form an integral part of the total strategy with which it pursues its business objectives. In this way it will not only define the company's course of action with regard to particular industrial relations issues; it will also reflect the interaction of industrial relations with policies in other areas, such as production, marketing or finance.

The CIR continued in this high flown vein:

> a total corporate strategy needs to include a policy defining the company's industrial relations objectives and the principles which should guide management in its everday pursuit of them. The responsibilities and authority of the various parts of management for particular types of decisions within the policy framework should also be specified.[5]

Who could disagree? Well within the space of two paragraphs the CIR began to tell us that the companies which it studied, for a start, do not seem to operate by reference to quite the same criteria:

> In practice, companies differ widely both in their conceptions of the scope of industrial relations policy and in the extent to which they have actually thought out and defined their own policies . . . In some companies we studied, the main industrial relations policy decision had been to join their employers' association and observe the agreements on basic terms and conditions which it negotiates with relevant trade unions . . . on many important points company policy would often be implied in their customs and traditions which are taken as precedents for the resolution of any new problems.

Despite such instances the CIR gave some examples of companies which had explicit policies and objectives in industrial relations and, having discussed the manifest advantages of determined guidelines and objectives, the Commission recommended that industrial relations policies should be defined, integrated into the company's other objectives, written, monitored and reviewed. Policies are generally understood to be limitations or constraints which management imposes upon its own freedom of action. They are usually of two kinds: they are self-imposed in that they represent what is sometimes rather grandiloquently called the philosophy of management, by which we usually mean its particular set of values, assumptions or hunches; they can also be imposed in a recognition (real or imagined) of the limitations of the circumstances in which the enterprise finds itself. Examples of the first, self-imposed, kind of policy constraint can be found in the nationalized industries (if we see the State as a part of the management) in which managers are instructed by Act of Parliament to recognize and negotiate with unions which represent substantial numbers of employees or, in a company, referred to by the CIR, where one of the objectives is 'regarding the workforce as equal partners with the shareholders in the whole enterprise and developing methods of consultation and where possible participation with both',[6] or in a company where the policy is to refuse to recognize or negotiate with any trade union at all. Examples of the second kind might be found where a company decides to embark on a high wage policy in a necessary effort to recruit and retain labour, or where it decides to concede to union pressure because of the high costs incurred in resistance.

This last example might be thought a little odd because it represents a practice which is more usually thought to be the opposite of having a policy. One of the CIR's examples, in fact, took the view that 'management should take the initiative in industrial relations, base its position on research and avoid expedient settlement of disputes that would prejudice its long-range interests.'[7] That is a bit more like it, more like the stern and rousing stuff that we expect to see in a policy statement. But our example was deliberately chosen because continuous concession under pressure has been as characteristic of the behaviour of many managements in industrial relations, thus:

> The sellers' market conditions of the 1950s cannot be stressed enough, for they gave rise to buoyant market conditions in which the Steel Company of Wales and other companies conceded large wage claims and ignored over-manning, so that valuable orders—including many exports—could be met. During the 1950s then, there was less pressure to relate wages to productivity in a fairly precise and defined way. Bargaining strength was the key factor in wage determination: how soon would a plant close if a particular wage claim was not met?[8]

Characteristic though this sort of behaviour may have been, we do not often see a statement of industrial relations policy in which management says, 'It is management's intention to make expedient settlement of union claims in order to maintain uninterrupted production, no wage claim demand backed by sufficient force will be resisted and disciplinary decisions will never be enforced to the point of threatening conflict.' But why not? Such policy statements would meet at least two of the overall tests imposed by the CIR, they would 'clarify intentions and eliminate uncertainties',[9] and they would demonstrate that policies 'in industrial relations cannot be treated in isolation but need to be integrated with commercial and operational policies generally.'[10] Well, the Steel Company of Wales' policy was surely consistent and it was certainly integrated with commercial and operational policies generally!

The point illustrates the absurdity of expecting industrial relations policy always to be coherently determined and formally expressed. The industrial relations policy of some enterprises at some times is to survive, to do the best one can, to hang on where possible and to let go where necessary. But to say so would be the sheerest folly because it would certainly make a desperate situation worse. There are many circumstances in which management will very sensibly wish to avoid imposing constraints upon its freedom of action additional to those formidable constraints already imposed by the market and the trade unions operating so effectively together. There are even circumstances in which the merits of consistency may seem a little doubtful. Management negotiators often feel genuine admiration for the way in which a union representative can move so gracefully from one contradictory position to another, yet management often needlessly hedges itself about by a paraphernalia of policy which makes any movement difficult. Even when management has a clear and consistent idea of the direction in which it wants to travel and the position that is to be achieved, for management to express this idea may create real practical difficulties on the way.

The universal popularity of the notion of written objectives may stem from the idea of management as exercising a kind of governmental, open and democratic function in society. The idea itself is probably mistaken and our recent experience may in any case have discredited the belief that even governments are necessarily open and consistent in their processes of decision taking. The enthusiasm for policies may also be a part of the baleful influence of pedagogues and theorists in industrial relations who must systematize before they can understand.

There are no doubt some circumstances in which a written industrial relations policy might be useful to management (and many more in which it might be useful to a trade union). A written policy gives an air of dignity and gravitas to what might otherwise seem a fairly shifty operation. The CIR, at least, seems to have been impressed by companies that have policies and to be suspicious of those that have not; as most substantial companies are likely to find themselves being investigated or surveyed by a government agency these days, this might be a sufficient reason for running one up. Of the CIR's list of three advantages of written policies, by far the most substantial was the third: that written policies are easier to abandon or, as the CIR put it, 'by being written it should, in fact, be easier to change than policies which are embedded in custom and practice, tradition and precedent.'[11] This seems quite likely to be the case; if the board of directors is possessed of certain prejudices in industrial relations, such as a conviction of the absurdity of equal pay for women, their publication as a policy document may well lead to their change while being nurtured in secret might have protected them from damage for years.

Whether policies are to be formulated and written or not

it is certain that management in industrial relations has normally accrued a set of intentions which will, in part, influence its behaviour. In many cases these intentions may not be explicitly stated and they will rarely be capable of quantification but managers almost invariably know what they want to do, even if what they want to do is quite incapable of systematic expression. If this is what we mean by policy in industrial relations then most managers have one, even if they do not know it. It is impossible to achieve any sort of generalization about what these policies will be, partly because we know little about management's expectations and behaviour in industrial relations and partly because, even if we did, they would be likely to be very diverse and to be related to many different circumstances. Let us try to examine some of the possible ingredients which would influence these differences in the expectations of managers who are concerned with industrial relations.

One difference is the time-span within which the expectations are expressed. Some managers will have objectives which can only be achieved over a period of years and which will require many other subordinate or tactical positions to be previously established. Other managers may not look beyond the influence of the current wage claim or the current dispute. If we are to rely upon Professor Jaques' time-span theory, it would suggest that the longer term objectives are associated with a more senior position in the management hierarchy while the more immediate are associated with subordinate positions. But this does not seem to be so; boards of directors can be observed entirely immersed in the here-and-now while unit managers in other organizations are concerned with long term change. Yet we would be reluctant to dismiss time-span as irrelevant in the field of industrial relations. It may be that it is the relative importance of the *function* in the management hierarchy which is significant rather than the position of the particular role holders: in other words, the degree to which industrial relations affects the survival, profitability and efficiency of the organization may influence the strategic and long term or tactical and short term objectives which are determined. Where industrial relations is vitally important to the management process itself, it may be true that the time-span of industrial relations decision making is longer than in circumstances where industrial relations is a peripheral concern.

If this is so (and it is a very tentative suggestion), we should consider what it is that governs the relative importance of industrial relations to the management process. One factor is obviously the relative weight of labour costs to total. It is easy to see that the highly specialized and extensive treatment of the industrial relations function in the National Coal Board is in some way explained by the fact that wages represents about 70 per cent of total costs. But the fact that wages take up about the same proportion in the Health Service suggests that this explanation would be insufficient. Until recently no one would have said that the industrial relations function in the Health Service was either extensively or intensively organized. One factor is the importance of wages cost but, whereas in the coal-mining industry no control over wages costs is possible except as the result of negotiations with the NUM, in the health service the impact of powerful unions took longer to develop. We must then add to the relative importance of wages costs the extent and character of union organization which management faces.

In the engineering industry wages costs are important, union organization is extensive and union policies are not notably unmilitant. Yet some engineering employers are not distinguished by their reputation for managing industrial relations in the pursuit of long term objectives. In fact, some engineering employers have contributed strongly to the general reputation of management in industrial relations for fire-fighting its way from one crisis to the next. We must seek one more variable in explaining apparent differences of time-span. Here it may be the bargaining and pay structures and the way in which they have evolved which must be taken into account. In engineering in particular 'the spread of piecework in the industry involved a transfer of control over payment from the local engineering employers' associations and the district committee of the unions, which then settled time rates of pay, to managers and workers, or their shop stewards in individual firms.'[12] The result in terms of fragmented bargaining, the difficulties of exercising control over wages and costs, the development of leap-frogging, particularly in a multi-union industry, have been widely discussed. The situation contributed to a condition in which formal responsibility for industrial relations continued to lie with the employers' associations while management has seized sufficient real authority to make that degree of responsibility unreal. The result is that in the worst cases no one manages industrial relations:

> the shift from negotiated piecework lists to factory piecework systems has not necessarily been a transfer of control over pay from employers' associations to the managers of individual companies and plants. In many instances it has been a loss of control over pay which techniques of work study and personnel management have been unable to prevent.[13]

Engineering is not the only industry in which management may find it difficult to exercise long-term influences. In the British printing industry it sometimes seems as though managers find it difficult to exercise any control at all. The author of *Management in the Printing industry* was disarmingly frank: 'There are a number of reasons why this growth in the number of personnel departments has not been matched in the printing industry: (1) Entry into the industry is strictly controlled, with the trade unions exercising a large measure of control. This makes the recruitment and selection of personnel superfluous save for a few posts.'[14] Here we are back to a consideration of the organization and strength of trade unions but with the additional characteristic that in this industry management deals with a strong master-craft tradition, undiluted by the open and generalizing influences which have overtaken the 'ex-craft' unions in the engineering industry. In the printing industry the strategy of the unions may owe more to the old craftsmen's ideal of unilateral control exercised by mutual aid than they do to more contemporary notions of collective bargaining.

There are some industries, no doubt, where the difficulties were largely of managerial origin, as a description of the construction industry in 1968 suggested: 'while other industries are concentrating on bringing managerial aids, such as personnel and labour relations departments, up to a new standard of efficiency the construction industry has yet only set a hesitant foot on this path. Nor is it only the small and medium-sized firm which is at fault.'[15]

So for various reasons, only some of which have been touched upon, the range of management's objectives will differ considerably. What about the content of the objectives themselves? Is it possible to generalize about what management wishes to achieve in industrial relations? We can do so about the unions, as we shall see; why does it appear to be more difficult to arrive at a statement of what management generally wants to do?

The first difficulty is that management organizations, unlike trade unions, are discreet, even secretive organizations; they sometimes fear that if they say what they want to do it will become more difficult to do it. The second difficulty is that in British industry, within living memory, we have been engaged in an ideological conflict which has sometimes become dull and inactive and occasionally quite stimulating but, whatever its present state, has certainly made management peculiarly sensitive to certain key areas like ownership, authority and profit. This sensitivity has in turn contributed to a deal of confusion and embarrassment over the formulation of business objectives, to the extent that when they are rarely enunciated they carry the signs of unreality, even hypocricy, which we notice in statements of industrial relations policy. An additional and important complication over industrial relations objectives as opposed to management objectives are that the latter are in some sense primary objectives while the former are secondary. 'The business of business,' as Dr Michael P Fogarty once vividly reminded the IPM, 'is business.'[16] The business of the industrial relations specialist is to see to it that business can get done.

Matters get still more complicated when the managers of industrial relations realize that statements of their industrial relations objectives can have an important effect in influencing the attitudes of for example, trade unions; statements of industrial relations objectives can, quite apart from their 'reality', help in achieving the company's business objectives. The authors of policy statements therefore begin to realize that they are addressing several different audiences: they may be trying to influence their own managers by promoting conformity to agreed objectives; they may be engaged in a public relations exercise in which the audience is primarily other managers in the organization whom they are attempting to civilize by persuading them to renounce 'unfair competition' in the manpower market; and they may be addressing trade unions whom they wish to impress as to the responsibility and good will of the employer. For these reasons statements of industrial relations objectives seem more to be concerned with goodness than with efficiency.

The managers of industrial relations will at some point wish to determine what is to be done in the industrial relations field in order to enable the enterprise to achieve its business objectives. Within the given framework of the personalities of the managers who have to decide, allowing for their ethical preoccupations, their views of what is right and wrong and their prejudices, these decisions are likely to be influenced by the interplay of two factors. The first concerns the business environment itself and its predicted future. Considerations like stability or change, the rate of technical innovation, expansion or retraction, changes in competition and marketing, all determine a background which can decisively determine the probable course of industrial relations planning. When these environmental factors are taken into account, the second range of considerations becomes decisive. There are practical factors concerning the achievement of objectives once they have been determined within the industrial relations and the general personnel management field. It is these factors which are more frequently, perhaps, the responsibility of the industrial relations specialist as such. He is often the facilitator of manpower and employment objectives which are themselves related to the business environment of the enterprise as a whole. He now has to begin to make choices in a range of possibilities some of which may be closely restricted and some of which may be more open.

He is concerned not only in what is to be done but in the manner in which to do it. If he is an influential and competent manager he may have taken part in the decisions about what is to be done. In the next chapter we shall be discussing some of the pressures that the industrial relations specialist can exert in helping to determine realistic objectives, and also some of the controls that are exerted over him within the process of internal bargaining. But it is the industrial relations specialist who is almost always expected to 'fix it', to facilitate the achievement of objectives, whether or not he has contributed to their selection. And it is at this level that he is subjected to the most advice as to how it is to be done.

One of his first concerns is with the prediction of employee and trade union reaction to the plans of the enterprise. In some situations, given the composition and character of the dominant trade unions and the background out of which industrial relations has developed, it may be certain that the consequence of seeking to achieve management's objectives will be conflict and that progress will only be made by a series of tactical struggles in an effort to reach a strategic goal. It may be that this state of affairs is equally certain because of the nature of the goals that are being sought by management, because they represent a considerable change in established practice and expectations or because they seem, to the workers, to be unfair. Once again, the industrial relations specialist may seek to make his objectives more attainable by influencing the atmosphere and the relationships within which their discussion takes place.

In many circumstances the opportunities for influence are negligible. The collective bargaining relationship, although it can be extraordinarily subtle, flexible and dynamic, is constructed upon the need to deal with the division of interest between several established and powerful groups. It is not only expressive of divisions of interest: its machineries and procedures, and the postures and expectations which the parties bring to it, expect divisions of interest to exist. For this reason, managers may try to circumvent the collective bargaining relationship in order to avoid the wariness and hostility which often pervade discussions within it. Walton and McKersie distinguish attitudinal adjustment and integrative bargaining from distributive bargaining and it is one of the first two patterns of relationship which managers often try to establish. The search for alternative relationships has taken various forms. The human relations approach represented an attempt to rely heavily on techniques of effective communication allied to personal leadership and counselling with an improved understanding of the ingredients of intra-group cooperation and control. Although this approach has now come in for heavy criticism, it is important to realize that there is much that is effective in its recommendations as long as we recognize that it cannot subsume all causes of conflict under its explanations of inter-personal breakdown, and that when its remedies are applied they are part of a pattern of management control and not necessarily intended to herald the new Jerusalem. Joint consultation was a particular technique which was intended to achieve a greater degree of harmony and cooperation by emphasizing matters of common interest as distinct from the collective bargaining relationship in which conflict was likely to find expression. Again, joint consultation can be effective, particularly in its less formal aspects, as long as ambitions for its success are modest and no one expects it so totally to replace industrial conflict that the discussion of matters over which conflicting interests are to be expected is suppressed. Subtler 'strategies of cooperation' have more recently emerged which are based on the recognition that it is the nature of the production process or of the organizational structure which is the fundamental cause of alienation of the workforce, and that therefore the production process and the organization must be changed if the greater commitment of the workers to managerial intentions is to be achieved. The limits on such approaches seem to be set by the abiding fundamental purposes of the production process and the authority structure so that any remission in conflict brought about by change may tend to be temporary and to be terminated when the employees realize that change has been cosmetic rather than constitutional.

There are several more specifically industrial relations techniques aimed at inspiring a greater degree of collaboration from workers and their representatives than is normally accorded in the collective bargaining relationship. One relies upon attempts to establish lines of communication between management and the workforce independent of the control exercised by recognized trade unions. This attempt can take various forms. One version which seems to be gaining some recent approval is to capture the old union and radical vehicle of the mass meeting; it is an approach to direct open communication which has in the past been surprisingly neglected. Joint consultation was in part an approach to communicate directly with employees but it never got over the problem of bridging the gap between the workers' representatives who were members of the committees and the workers themselves. In its earlier years, the attempt by management to set joint consultation up as an obvious alternative to collective bargaining prompted an inevitable reaction from unions who determined either to boycott it or to control it. In some industries, the full orchestration of public relations techniques have been directed at improving management communication with workers. In some particular disputes, management has also resorted, usually unsuccessfully, to use the national media or their own media to attempt to wrest the union membership from commitment to the union's negotiating policy.[17] The CIR noted that 'controversy arises over the extent to which management should communicate directly with its employees over issues considered negotiable' and that 'union representatives may claim . . . that they have the sole right of communicating direct with the workforce . . . . In considering whether to challenge the claim a management has to balance the present limitations on its role in communications against the difficulties of initiating a change. It may be necessary in negotiation to convince unions that industrial and human relations will be improved by such a change in approach.'[18] The view taken by the CIR would seem to turn the control of communications to employees into a negotiable issue and, while circumstances might necessitate such a contest in some situations, in others management might be well advised to resist any challenge to its right to talk to those whom it employs simply because of the basic fundamental importance of maintaining open rights of way to its approach to other objectives. If management cannot speak there is much besides that it will be unable to do. The CIR rightly pointed out that, in some cases, these 'rights of way' have been abandoned because they have not been used, because 'management has in the past effectively abdicated from its responsibility for communicating with employees'.[19] so that the most effective defence of the right to talk is to exercise it.

Not that this will ensure management's success in reaching whatever objectives it seeks. The belief in the curative powers of communication is now limited to an awareness of the dangers of not doing it well rather than to any great confidence in its positive effects. 'Communications cannot in themselves remove conflicts of interest and values . . . Good communications are therefore best regarded as one essential component of the collective bargaining process rather than as an adequate means of solving all industrial relations problems.'[20]

Whatever approach the employer chooses to adopt, it is possible to think of his objectives as unfolding in a number of stages, the characteristics of each of which are determined, in part, by the stage that has gone before. Objectives in industrial relations are not the first of these stages. The overriding objectives are those emerging from the business strategy of the enterprise as a whole. Objectives in industrial relations begin to be determined when plans have to be made to achieve these fundamental goals. The special nature of industrial relations begins to emerge when we see that the employer is now, at this stage, embarking on an attempt to control (that is to plan, predict and adjust) a part of his environment where he has only limited power and influence. The normal situation of management is that it must attempt to achieve control in an area of affairs in which unilateral control is impossible, simply because there are other institutions involved which possess power and influence and whose perceptions are different, who do not see themselves as subsumed in the process of achieving the objectives of a business.

The inevitability of management's seeking to control and the impossibility of achieving it leads to frustration. There is always the risk that the reaction to frustration may be petulant or irrational, leading to a conclusion that it would be better to spoil the game rather than let anyone else take part in it. This is the state of affairs that is arrived at when management decides to stand out on some point of principle,[21] or determines on confrontation in order to put the unions in their place, quite regardless of the damage to the business objectives which industrial relations planning was once meant to serve and to achieve. Governments can get into this state of mind as well as employers but, fortunately, it does not last long because of the pressures within the collective bargaining relationship to seek a practical accommodation of different interests. But while these confrontations last, collective bargaining probably produces a more intense degree of hostility than its institutions and procedures are designed to accommodate and there is always the risk of permanent damage.

A more typical response to the frustration of management's drive to exercise control in industrial relations is a rational search for a means to achieve it to the maximum extent. There are, theoretically speaking, two approaches to resolving the kind of conflict or contradiction which management has to face when it tries to exercise control over independent forces with different interests. The first is to overcome the contradiction by an attempt at synthesis. The best possible training in industrial relations for managers predisposed to this approach is a lengthy course in Marxist dialectics. The aim is to arrive at a higher level of analysis in which the contradiction disappears. Despite its revolutionary character, it is an approach to which many managers are addicted. The best example is the productivity or problem-solving approach, which attempts to resolve the contradiction involved in both parties demanding bigger slices from the same cake by baking bigger cakes. The attempt at synthesis is also to be found in the widely observed tendency among managers to stress the common interest of their employees in their own intentions. This outlook has been so effectively attacked by Alan Fox that it has become a cliché among enlightened managers to dismiss it as the unitary approach to management. We should not forget the self-evident truth, however, that the unitary approach may be successful where it can work: there are some circumstances such as the existence of an outside threat (for example closure or foreign competition) or a small traditional business (based upon close and established personal ties) in which a unitary approach may be both realistic and successful. There is no inherent reason why it should not be effective beyond these limits but it probably has to be based upon a shared ideological framework and it may have to succeed in challenging the legitimacy of groups, such as trade unions, which stand aside from its own unitary claims. The whole history of modern industrialization can be seen as a search for just such an ideological foundation so perhaps we can be excused for leaving it at that.

The second response to the frustration of management's drive to control is to seek a working accommodation which recognizes that there are other institutions in command of sufficient resources and power to make management's wish to exercise absolute control unreal and unlikely to succeed, and which recognizes that these other institutions are both permanent and proper (or legitimate). This means collective bargaining which is, in one sense, the area in which management's control processes meet forces which management is incapable of controlling. There is little doubt that the uncertainty which is implicit in this situation can affect the business objectives which management sets out to achieve. Just as natural disasters or unpredictable shifts in the market can make nonsense of management's original plans, so the outcome of conflict in collective bargaining may require that business plans have to be adjusted or abandoned. In this way collective bargaining is not merely a part of the control cycle which ensures that plans are achieved: it is a part of the dynamic process of business planning itself. The fact that managers have not always been prepared to accept this, perhaps because of the formal acknowledgement of the limitations on their own power which it implies, has had the effect of relegating industrial relations to a low level of technical responsibility (such as 'fire-fighting') in which it seems to be deliberately disconnected from the business planning process. The disconnection may make it more likely that plans are unreal and will not be achieved, but at least the managers concerned have the comfort of not acknowledging that their control in industrial relations is not absolute. The divorce between boardroom and industrial relations may thus, despite its unreality and the damage that it does, enable senior managers to regret after the event that their targets have not been achieved, and to engage in formidable attacks on anarchy and subversion as an excuse for not achieving them. The disconnection between industrial relations and management planning is more a matter of comfort than common sense.

Professor Bowey has noted the 'tendency on the part of managers to separate out industrial relations from other management control activities' and commented that the 'kind of view, in which industrial relations is seen as either separate altogether from other management control activities, or else as a kind of social "oil" for greasing the bearings of those activities, is in our experience quite common amongst senior managers in industry.'[22] She suggests that 'industrial relations are inextricably bound up with all the other systems of control used in an organization'.[23] But management must first try to understand the environment within which it is seeking to achieve goals; the strength and character of union organization, the experience and expectations of employees, their cohesiveness and workplace representation; these and other factors all help to determine a rational choice of strategies for the achievement of management's objectives. In few cases, perhaps, does the choice of industrial relations practices represent an end in itself: they usually concern means to achieving what the business wants to achieve. Industrial relations strategies can begin to take on a life of their own and this can be a dangerous state of affairs. When this happens, maintaining a particular attitude towards the unions may cease to have any relationship with the objectives of the business.

The employers' objectives in industrial relations seem often to veer between two extremes, the one of relegation to low-level responsibility in which routines and procedures have to be maintained with no great relevance to business planning or to other managerial controls, the other of high-level responsibility for directing the enterprise's industrial relations by reference to broad statements of principle or to an unstated set of assumptions about what should be the purpose of industrial relations. The one state of affairs is not more likely to be related to business realities and decisions than the other. In the first condition the industrial relations function has been subordinated to a level where it cannot affect or be affected by business planning. In the second condition industrial relations has been promoted to a level of unreality.

The specific choice of controls and objectives in industrial relations are likely to concern negotiable and non-negotiable aspects of the terms and conditions of employment. British trade unions have often been criticized for the narrow limitation of their interest in collective bargaining to wages and salaries. If this criticism is still justified, it means that, despite managers' conviction that unions have severely limited management's ability to control, there must remain large areas of the employment contract in which unions have evinced little interest. Many aspects of the employment relationship, some of them of great significance in terms of their contribution to business performance are, like recruitment, training, manpower deployment, communications, production design and salary and wage structure, often virtually exempt from union influence in collective bargaining. Unfortunately (from management's point of view) that challenge has often been provoked by unilateral decisions taken by management which have had damaging and unnecessary consequences for employees. Some wage payment systems, for example, seem to be designed to do no particular service for management and to provoke a good deal of avoidable hostility among men.

One of the ingredients of management's understanding its environment might be to define those areas in which it has retained unilateral control, to use them to the maximum advantage and to protect them by seeking to avoid the generation of unnecessary conflict within them. In any one of them 'the choice of an appropriate system has to be related to the context of each organization and take account of such factors as the nature of its work and technology, its objectives, its style of management, the environment in which it operates, its career structure and its history.'[24] It is easy to say that this is what a system should do but not so easy to determine how it should do it particularly when, on examination, some of the 'factors' turn out to be both complex and to determine contradictory requirements to some of the others. In practical terms we might be better advised to follow the advice on the objectives of salary systems, that they should:

serve the aims and purposes of the undertaking as a whole
form an integral part of the manpower policies of the undertaking
allow for change and development within the organization
be flexible enough to accommodate actual changes in the relative market rates for different skills
be capable of attracting sufficient candidates for employment in sufficient numbers
facilitate the development of employees to enhance the maximum efficiency of the undertaking
help to retain people necessary to the future requirements of the undertaking
be related to the attainment and maintenance of high levels of performance by individual employees
pursue all these aims at the lowest cost.[25]

No doubt the aims set out here would be beyond the scope of many firms in helping them to determine their objectives in industrial relations. But the list may serve to help to establish some overall requirements on industrial relations objectives.

1 They cannot be determined in a vacuum: they must follow the determination of business objectives which they should be intended to facilitate. In this sense industrial relations is a subordinate function, but the recognition of this fact would certainly win for it higher status and influence than it has often been accorded in the past.
2 An Employer's practices and policies in industrial relations should not negate his intentions in other areas. Thus if a company wishes to encourage voluntary termination because of its age structure or because of contraction, its

salaries and pensions system should not encourage its employees to stay at all costs. If its training programmes encourage flexible mobility its wages system should not prevent it.

3 Management's industrial relations objectives should not provoke accidental conflict, that is, conflict which is not related to the pursuit of management's interests.

4 Management's industrial relations objectives and the strategies by which they are to be pursued should be the subject of regular critical examination by management. This should entail a survey both of what is to be done and of the environment within which it has to be achieved.

The review could usefully be conducted in three stages which roughly approximate to the way in which industrial relations is practised. The first concerns the emergence of industrial relations objectives from the general determination of business plans for the enterprise. This is the interface between board level planning and the determination of industrial relations strategies which will relate to other control systems and will, it is to be hoped, facilitate the achievement of business plans or, at least, will not contribute to their destruction. The second concerns the determination of how these industrial relations objectives might themselves be best brought about. This entails a thorough scanning of the environment and implies the application of specialist and expert knowledge to the fixing of negotiating targets, the general strategy of approaches to the unions and assessment of the extent of change to be achieved and of the most likely means for its pursuit. The third concerns the monitoring and control of performance in industrial relations, an important area because feedback from it can show whether business plans are likely to be affected by failures within the industrial relations area.

This is inevitably a hypothetical and general account. But it suggests that the conduct of industrial relations cannot be an isolated activity. It requires specialists but they cannot be protected from contacts with other inhabitants of the managerial organization. If objectives in industrial relations are to facilitate business objectives, and if there is to be a cross-current of influences within management, not only the industrial relations function but its objectives must be open to influence from elsewhere. This suggests that the process of negotiating is at least as important within the managerial organizational as it is in the much more dramatic area of negotiations between management and unions. This is why we are turning, in the next chapter, to the important area of internal (or intra-organizational) negotiations.

CHAPTER 3

Management's organization of industrial relations

It may help to divide this discussion into two sections. In the first we shall deal with the way in which management organizes its affairs to deal with an external opponent, the trade unions. This will mean discussing management's organization of collective bargaining, its determination of the levels at which bargaining will be conducted and the scope to be covered. The second section will deal with the internal affairs of management, the relationship between industrial relations specialists and other managers and the process of internal negotiation within the management organization.

1 Organization for collective bargaining

Not very much is known about managerial organization of industrial relations. There are two contradictory explanations for ignorance in a field which should have been regarded as important. To begin with, management was neglected because of an assumption that employers' organizations were the important agents and that management's influence was secondary. To end with, the discussion of management in industrial relations has been neglected because of a realization of the enormous complexity of the subject and of the difficulty of arriving at any reliable platform of generalization. The neglect of management may also have been encouraged because of the evangelistic sympathies of many students of industrial relations, who have been committed to the view that their attentions are properly confined to trade unions or workers (with 'the lads' as Beynon persists in calling them in *Working for Ford*) and that management forms no part of this preoccupation. Over-inclined to prevent access for research and too sensitive to reports which have not entirely reflected their own judgements when research has taken place, managers have done little to correct this unfortunate bias. For these and other reasons there has been little study of management activities and organization in industrial relations.

An analysis in terms of line and staff functions is of little value. In some circumstances, where personnel or industrial relations specialists are formally confined to an advisory role, the collective bargaining area is so complex and the costs of error are so high that their advice is likely to be regarded as mandatory. In other circumstances where the advisory role is highly developed, the conduct of negotiations and the responsibility for settlement may be deemed to be too important to leave to anyone other than senior line managers. In some industries the conduct of industrial relations has been subjected to continuous centralization, in others it has been decentralized so as to give managers at the periphery greater autonomy. Instances can be found in which centralization and decentralization follow each other in regular succession; there are others in which both policies seem to be followed at the same time.

Such distressing contradictions are not necessarily evidence of ineptitude, although they may be. They suggest, rather, that generalization about industrial relations organization is impossible because of the great diversity of circumstances which have to be met. One variable which is instantly visible is unit size. The management of ice-cream stalls is not likely to demand that industrial relations becomes a highly organized and discreet function because ice-cream stalls are scattered, small and employ few workers in each unit. Another variable is the history and extent of labour organization. Industrial relations in the coal industry is highly developed not only because of the industry's size (as we noted earlier, it is smaller than the Health Service) but because the ground has long been occupied by a large and powerful trade union. We cannot talk simply about management organization of industrial relations because management faces a vast range of different circumstances. In the retail trade, 17.8 per cent of employees are covered by company level negotiations, 9.2 per cent by nationally negotiated agreements, and 10.4 per cent by both. It is not altogether surprising, therefore, that only 2 per cent of all retail establishments employ someone to handle personnel matters at establishment level and that 'as few as 10 per cent of retail employees may be members of a trade union'.[26] In more general terms, 'union membership is low in small firms and even in those few industries where it is relatively high the amount of collective bargaining that take place is often very limited.'[27] In these circumstances, the conduct of industrial relations, in so far as there is any, is likely to be the responsibility of the owner, unaided and unconstrained by expert assistance.

At the other extreme is the large corporation employing thousands of workers in different countries, different occupations and different industries, facing many different and effective trade unions. If we could generalize on the basis of a simple variable of size and unionization we would say that, while small non-unionized companies show little evidence of industrial relations organization, large unionized companies have developed the industrial relations function to a high degree. But it is not so simple.

The CIR's study *Industrial Relations in Multi-Plant Undertakings*[28] helped us to understand some of the further complexities which must be taken into account. The report suggested that the company structure and the way in which it developed was of great importance in influencing the organization of industrial relations. Companies which developed as the result of linear growth, by means of extending production of the same commodity in new and distinct plants, were likely to be faced with problems different from those of companies which grew by lateral development into a number of different product fields.[29] The difference emerged over the extent to which industrial relations was centralized or decentralized in the firm. Lateral development of the company 'presents obstacles to a centrally determined industrial relations policy in that newly-acquired organizations often have industrial relations systems which differ from those of an acquiring company.'[30] The managerial requirements in a wide product range pointed to the delegation of authority to specialized managers and this, in itself, created some pressure for the decentralization of industrial relations. A wide product range will also involve different worker groups, with different patterns of union organization, different bargaining traditions and expectations.

A greater degree of product uniformity may make centralization seem a more rational approach to industrial relations. The relationship between product and industrial relations response may have encouraged some multi-plant organizations to organize themselves on a product division basis; it may have been a significant consideration in the British Steel Corporation's reorganization of 1972 but such an attempt to impose a degree of national uniformity can be troublesome because the product and the technology involved is not the only basis of comparison of earnings. The CIR explained that 'for industrial relations purposes geographical or market considerations may often be more relevant', particularly where plants from various divisions may exist in the same locality or on the same site.

Technical complexity and diversity, the greater competence of local management in terms of the production process and its close relationship with industrial relations all combine to push responsibility for industrial relations out from the centre to the periphery. The high cost of labour, narrow profit margins, the dangers of precedent and the prevailing social system by which relative deprivations are measured by employees all tend to pull responsibility of industrial relations back to the centre. It is a matter of measuring a delicate balance of advantages as to which view prevails at a particular time and, as the CIR said, a company 'may move in one direction to achieve one purpose and move back again to achieve another';[31] plant bargaining may be encouraged to achieve gains in productivity followed by tighter group control to achieve gains by removing discrepancies.

A shift from peripheral to central responsibility or back again may be a strategy aimed at changing the character of industrial relations in an industry. Until 1966 the wages of face workers in the coalmining industry were determined by piece work price lists in which the level of collective bargaining was the colliery. The industry was characterized by a high level of disputes almost entirely concerned with unofficial actions taken at local level. In an effort to bring about greater control and more central regulation the power loading agreements of 1966 introduced a much more centralized collective bargaining process. The attempt was successful, the level of disputes dropped and the incidence of isolated and unofficial action was considerably reduced but the change, in part, made it possible for the NUM to engage in the massive national industrial action of 1972 and 1974. The lengthy discussions of 1974 between the NCB and the NUM and the internal arguments within the NUM about a proposed 'national productivity scheme', although directly concerned with the re-introduction of incentive payments for face workers, have been interpreted in some union quarters as an attempt to break the solidarity of the union and to re-establish a low level of bargaining which will make a general dispute impossible. The level at which bargaining is conducted in the industry certainly seems to be related to the pattern of industrial conflict and to the general characteristics of its industrial relations. These changes may also suggest that management can be successful in promoting changes in industrial relations while subsequently deciding that the changes were not for the best.

Decisions about whether to centralize or to decentralize industrial relations may also depend upon the perceptual horizons of workers in an industry as to what relativities are appropriate to their own circumstances. In the airlines, pilots are apparently given to compare their terms and conditions on an international basis and similar suggestions are made concerning feelings of relative deprivation among British doctors. It is more usual, among less informed and less mobile groups, for comparisons to be made on an industrial basis but these comparisons can be confused by references to what workers doing similar work receive within a region. Members of a particular trade or craft can also use rates common to the craft to cut across company, industrial or regional comparisons. Comparison between plants within the same region and the same industry can also provide a point of reference. The steel industry has from time to time been the subject of disputes based upon several different bases of comparison when claims have been founded upon rates established in neighbouring plants, upon rates within the same plant for a group against which some relative advantage is claimed or upon rates for a craft group enjoyed in another region.

Management may succeed in promoting or in protecting

itself against some of these comparisons by the sense of identity which it seeks to impose upon its employees:

> Where identification with the company is strongly-based, a work group can be less concerned to claim separate treatment from other workers and can be more easily assimulated into the larger unit. But where identification is low the strategically-placed workers may be reluctant to participate in any broader bargaining arrangements preferring to maximize their bargaining position or to insist on maintaining a differential in their favour on pay and conditions over all other groups.[32]

The CIR went on to point out that a strong feeling of identity with the company could give rise to problems, identification with the company:

> manifests itself in matters related to pay . . . . The existence of pay differences between similar work groups in different plants of the same company can lead to parity claims and can lead to considerable problems for both unions and managements.[33]

The company may not provide a natural basis of comparison, particularly where it is engaged in different industries facing different unions and concerned with different products. The company in these circumstances is more of a financial arrangement than a preconceived corporate entity as far as its employees are concerned. To foster consciousness of company identity, to establish a strong central personnel management function and to centralize collective bargaining may all create unnecessary and costly hazards for management in industrial relations. In other circumstances the projection of a special identity for the company may have to come to terms with an equally strong perception of the special character of the industry within which the company is operating. Ford Motors has always enjoyed and encouraged a sense of its uniqueness; it established its collective bargaining procedures independently of employers' associations and it conducts its employee relations affairs with considerable professionalism and with a high degree of centralization in collective bargaining. Yet Ford is not immune from earnings comparisons based upon norms claimed to have been established by the British motor industry in the Midlands.

Large organizations also have the problem of dealing with outposts, that is, groups of workers who are almost totally isolated from the company's main business and who link in comparative terms to another industry in which they have established status and earnings. Every large employer has to come to terms with the problem of determining the earnings of some relatively small group, such as electricians in the Health Service, who enjoy bargaining advantages elsewhere and hence look elsewhere for their comparisons. The employer's response may be to meet the rate for the trade, often established by national negotiations with an employers' association. This can lead to pressures on the organization's wage structure from an imported level of earnings for a particular group which, because they were independently determined, do not relate easily to the earnings of other employees.

As the result of such complexities and comparisons and because of the problems posed by the recognition of many unions, large employers find themselves operating within several 'systems' of industrial relations at the same time. Even a multi-plant company which has grown by a process of linear development within one industry can find itself engaged in layers of different bargaining processes. A study of a well-known company in the engineering industry, with a reputation for established procedures and advanced personnel management, reported modifications and additions to the national engineering agreements on the following matters: status distinction for skilled men; lieu bonuses; incremental payment schemes; differential shift allowances; merit rating; company job grading for administrative and technical staff; plant salary scales for administrative and technical staff; service increments; sick pay schemes; pension schemes and guaranteed overtime payment for drivers.

Further than these acknowledged additions which the company had arrived at, the report added that sectional bargaining had flourished and 'recently shows issues involved to include manning, promotion, bonus payments, overtime working and dilutee labour. These settlements are not normally made the subject of formal agreements.'[34]

Even in a comparatively straightforward instance of a company, we can find an extremely complex structure of bargaining. At the 'formal level' a company's industrial relations affairs can be variously determined by employers' federation agreements, local employers' association arrangements, company agreements, plant bargaining, formally acknowledged sectional agreements and informal sectional arrangements. Some large organizations show signs of adding one more level of influence. However well regularized the machinery for determing terms of employment, some groups of employees are likely to find themselves unrepresented by unions and not to be the subject of negotiation. These groups typically involve white-collar workers over whose conditions the employer is likely to enjoy greater unilateral control. The employer's freedom of action can be an embarrassment because it can lead to precisely the kind of competitive scramble which the employers' association were first designed to control. In some regions, large companies have arranged to meet on a regular monthly or quarterly basis in order to exchange information about rates and conditions for staff, the extent of union pressure and the companies' response to it. These arrangements, frequently conducted over dinner, are an interesting and contemporary example of a nascent employer-organization response, and one intended to meet the challenge of slowly developing pressure in a field of employment which reflects manual labour organization and response a century ago.

The complexity of industrial relations organization in which management is engaged suggests the unreality of describing it in terms of a system, or even of 'two systems', of collective bargaining. It may seem that we have lost track of our purpose in discussing management organization for collective bargaining. The digression, if so it was, was intended to serve two purposes: to establish the relationship between management's industrial relations structure and the complex organizational situation of the company and, secondly, to suggest that decisions about centralization of collective bargaining, the level at which it is to be conducted and the relative authority to be given to the specialist are likely to be neither uniform nor to be the result of policy decisions.

Whether they are consciously taken or determined by circumstances, management's decisions are likely to be influenced by many considerations, some of which have no direct and immediate relationship to industrial relations. Some of the more important of them could be summarized as follows:

1 *Group ownership*	international, national, private, public
2 *Financial organization*	linear development, lateral development, financial (holding) control, direct (technical) control
3 *Cost structure*	ratio of wages costs, profit margins

4 *Technical organization*	product range, product homogeneity, product disparity, the number and importance of technical 'outpost' operations, production systems
5 *Company ideology or 'philosophy'*	avowed company identity or company anonymity, benign attitude to unions, hostile attitudes
6 *Imposed organizational patterns*	membership of employers' associations, residual freedom from association arrangement, legal constraints
7 *Imposed union patterns*	single industry or multi-industry structure, complexity of union recognition, inter-union communication and cooperation, character of unions recognized, their centrality or devolution of authority
8 *Perceptual horizon of workers*	reference group structure in determining relativities
9 *Managerial organization*	line managers' control of production process, their authority, development of bureaucratic structure, development of specialist support groups including personnel management.

It may by now be apparent that it would not be very helpful to provide a series of charts to suggest various formulations of industrial relations organization. It is not that there is no best pattern of organization, it is that it is extremely difficult to suggest what is even an appropriate form of organization. The CIR concluded, 'there is a certain simplicity in a centralized system of industrial relations',[35] particularly where the company is engaged in the same product market, or where the employees exhibit some degree of homogeneity, but centralization can become cumbersome, slow and runs the risk of decisions at the centre taken in ignorance of the real situation in the plant. Centralization probably leads to more equitable treatment, it may reduce the risk of mistakes by ill-informed managers, it may exert some control over wage creep which follows from reducing bargaining to the level of invisibility. But it depends upon good managerial communications and it may contribute to fewer, bigger and better organized strikes.

Plant bargaining may have absolute advantages for holding companies operating in many different product fields where 'the idea of such companies having consistent industrial relations policies except in the broadest terms does not seem to be realistic'.[36] In other circumstances plant bargaining can promote costly confusion, allowing for a great deal of union manoeuvre on grounds of relativities against any one of a variety of chosen reference points. Devolution of bargaining may also require a high level of managerial skill and knowledge in industrial relations.

In order to provide that skill and knowledge, management organization frequently tries to achieve the advantages of both centralization and devolution. The attempt is made in one of two ways (and sometimes both). One method is to allow peripheral managers considerable autonomy in industrial relations within a centrally established framework of decisions. The central decisions may be laid down in cost bands, in negotiating limits, in fixed ceilings on bonus proportions or by a framework of policy decisions concerning union recognition, disciplinary rules. At this point, policy statements in industrial relations begin to take on some real meaning because they are intended to be constraints upon decision-making freedom rather than vague statements of company philosophy and intentions. A second method is to scatter personnel specialists throughout the lower levels of the organization with the intention that they will have an educational and advisory relationship with the managers who are to exercise authority. This can be, at best, a vague and inconclusive role and the unhappiness which it can create in the incumbent may drive him into acting as a secret agent in which he reports managerial indiscretions to his functional masters in headquarters. This reaction in turn threatens the effectiveness of his advisory and educational role.

There is no evidence, as far as I know, that these arrangements are effective but then there is little evidence about anything in this particular field. The best course would seem to be to pursue the organizational pattern (or patterns) that seem most appropriate to the affairs of the enterprise and, until it is proved wrong, to pursue it consistently. Consistency over time would seem to be most important. Consistency in the approaches to different employee groups (staff and manual workers, for example) might not be so important; as long as the groups concerned do not regard themselves as comparable it may be quite sensible to centralize for the one and to decentralize for the other. Inconsistency towards the same group may be disastrous. The British Steel Corporation has shown some sign, over the years, of promoting the development of a national wage structure which diminishes the importance of plant-based bonus earnings while at the same time encouraging plant productivity schemes. Such a course is likely to provide several different hostages to fortune.

The discussion has now begun to involve relationships between specialists and managers and the roles which they are required to fill in different organizational arrangements. It is time therefore to move on to the second part of our description of management's organization of industrial relations.

2 Internal negotiation

We are here concerned with relationships within the managerial organization and between different managers as they are concerned with industrial relations. The term 'internal negotiations' refer to an aspect of industrial relations and collective bargaining which has been widely neglected but which has received attention in Walton and McKersie's wide ranging discussion of collective bargaining.[37]

It is a commonly held fallacy that negotiations take place across a frontier between two organizations, union and employer. The view is understandable because this is where negotiations visibly occur in dramatic form but it is mistaken because it simplifies a complex, subtle process of adjustment which takes place over a range incorporating both organizations. The positions which each organization brings to the negotiating table have been formulated and changed by a process of internal adjustment which is necessary before each organization can meet the other in effective external negotiation. Neither union nor management is a simple, monolithic structure with clear and distinct objectives which it wishes to impose upon the other. We are concerned here with the adjustment which take place within the managerial organization; the adjustments within the union organization will be reserved for the next chapter.

Managers have learnt, by diligent attention to Alan Fox, that industrial organizations are pluralistic coalitions, composed of many different interest groups with aims and frames of reference which overlap only in part. We are still too prone to conclude that the managerial organization, at least, is unitary, composed of members sharing a common concern for the efficiency or survival of the enterprise. Any inhabitant of a large organization who is capable of introspection and common sense analysis of his surroundings will know that this is not so. Managers, like other men, are prone to identify and defend their own interest and their perception of what is best for the organization is likely to differ from that of other managers. Management is itself a coalition of interests. Not only do managers have to balance the claims of competing groups (customers, workers, shareholders, the community) but, as functional specialism is typical of large organizations, they come to represent special interests. Accountants become especially concerned with cost control, production engineers with maintaining a steady output, sales managers with satisfying market demands and personnel managers with good labour relations, sound procedures and avoiding the dreadful disturbance of precedent. Managers, in short, are role holders.

In the context of industrial relations we can also distinguish separate managerial roles. There is likely to be a strategic role concerned with the determination of long-term objectives in industrial relations; it has often been illustrated in productivity bargaining (classically, in the Fawley agreements[38]). There may be a political role in which an attempt has to be made to strike a balance between various disparate managerial objectives in order to emerge with a 'realistic' position in industrial relations: it may be that this role is often not assigned to a particular personnel manager but that it is dispersed between many senior managers or directors. There is certainly a tactical role in industrial relations in which the specialist is required favourably to influence behaviour during negotiations so as to reach immediate, short-term objectives at least cost to the organization: this role is consigned to the negotiator. There may be a frontier-guard role[39] where a specialist is expected to police the agreements, to patrol the frontier already established in collective bargaining, to exhibit expert knowledge of the local terrain, to observe any sign of movement on the other side and to report it, or shoot.

These differences of outlook in industrial relations are

likely to exist even where the managerial organization of the function is primitive; where it is advanced they are more likely to be sharply differentiated as the result of being assigned to specialist personnel.

Managers are distinguished by their roles, which influence the perceptions which they bring to industrial relations. They are also distinguished by the distance which separates them from the front line and from the union on the other side of it. There is some evidence and a great deal more common observation to suggest that senior managers and directors, who are not in frequent contact with union representatives and members, develop unreal and even self-contradictory images of reality. Winkler reports that 'most directors had no significant contact with any manual or clerical staff other than their secretaries . . . Non-contact was also just as much the norm for production directors and for those normally responsible for personnel matters.'[40] Their separation from workers and from the conduct of industrial relations affairs is no accident, 'the separation is purposively constructed'.[41] 'Directors literally do not want to know about industrial relations.'[42] Their withdrawal, says Winkler, is a coping device which enables low-level compromises with unions to take place on a pragmatic basis which do not threaten any fundamental principles, it is an attempt to preserve the power and autonomy of a sub-unit (the board) of the managerial organization and, psychologically, it is a defence mechanism which allows directors to blame workers or subordinate managers for failures, 'isolation and ignorance have their uses'.[43]

It is to be observed with equal justice that union members, whose work and lives hardly bring them into day to day contact with executives at board room level, are also likely to possess peculiar stereotypes. The perceptions of each other at the base of each organization, managerial and trade union, are likely to be distorted, to the extent that, as Winkler suggests, it is 'functional' (that is important for its survival) for an organization's directors to maintain a deliberate and decent distance from the everyday conduct of industrial relations affairs. If so, this suggests a real illustration of the 'principle of cumulation' or vicious circle, in which unreal perceptions caused by distance require the distance to be maintained, which guarantees the unreality of the perceptions, which . . .

It means that personnel occupying the most distant extremes of each organization must be kept well away from each other. Collective bargaining is concerned with reaching temporary and acceptable accommodation between organizations with different interests but it would not work if the accommodations had to be reached between shareholders and Clydeside boilermakers or blast furnacemen from South Wales.

The distance is filled by a machinery of transmission. This represents an unformalized negotiating process within each organization. It is more visible in unions than in management where it occurs with such discretion and, sometimes, in such a confused and non-conscious manner that it may seem not to occur at all. The least that can be claimed is that to think of a process of internal adjustment taking place within management presents a rational explanation of the various disparate managerial perceptions of what might be attained and what is to be avoided in collective bargaining and of the way in which these perceptions are given some sort of coherent formulation when management meets the union at the bargaining table. Directors cannot be without influence although their expectations may be unreal. The control exercised by management negotiations cannot be absolute although their influence may be considerable. Within the managerial organization there are extreme views of what is an acceptable outcome, the process of internal transmission is concerned with the control exercised over each other by sub-groups within management.

We have described these extreme differences as aspirational optimism at the position in the managerial organization which is furthest removed from contact with unions and their members, and aspirational rigidity at the position where management representations are occupied in the negotiating process.[44] Managers remote from negotiation develop unreal expectations of what can be achieved. Managers involved in negotiations develop expectations, the reality of which is conditioned by what is acceptable to the other side. The process of internal adjustment is concerned with exchange between these groups, with preventing negotiations reaching accommodations which are determined by the opponent and which are not, in turn, threatened by remote expectations, totally unacceptable to him.

This process of exchange is more confused and less visible in management organizations than it is in unions for several reasons. Managerial organizations are not open or representative organizations, they are not responsible to popular support and they are less likely to become the scene of active lobbying, pressure group activity or opposition movements. Winkler examined the sources of information by which directors are made aware of what goes on in industrial relations. He summarizes them as:

1 the normal management hierarchy
2 crisis revelations
3 consultation and bargaining—in which most directors are not involved
4 one man chains—the existence of a director tuned into the grape vine
5 personal service personnel, secretaries or chauffeurs, regarded, wrongly, as voicing typical worker views
6 past experience
7 the mass media

We are largely concerned here with internal adjustment and exchange within the managerial hierarchy. Winkler points out that 'subordinate managers have a strong incentive *not* to communicate upwards information on emergent disorder. They are under pressure to hide problems, in the hope that they can reach covert accommodations with workers before the director finds out . . . Normal management reporting systems are, in the industrial relations context, systems of concealment.'[45]

Censorship imposed by the subordinate manager is, in part, a defensive strategy against control by his seniors: 'The personnel specialist, if he is the management negotiator, is a member of a group whose behaviour is bound to be subject to certain controls.'[46] The controls exercised over him by management are, once again, likely to be less visible than they are within the trade union but they may be more effective. The management negotiator is often not the chief executive (for reasons that Winkler discusses), he is subject to direct command, to precise instruction, he is told what to do. Control may be exercised by a quite contrary strategy in which the negotiator is given imprecise instructions. The deliberate arrangement of 'calculated incompetence' is intended to make sure that the negotiators 'themselves do not have significant knowledge of their party's resistance points'.[47] In these circumstances negotiation can be seen to take place in two stages, the negotiator behaves like a delegate carrying back messages to his own organization which are the subject of negotiation, the outcome of which has to be communicated to the union for external negotiation to continue. Union leaders, Clive Jenkins in particular, have often been heard to complain about the ineptitude of management in sending representatives to bargain with unions when the representatives have no authority to settle.

It is no accident, and Clive Jenkins should not be surprised by it. In public service negotiations, the same strategy, intended to create an internal control zone, explains why the Treasury is often described as 'the ghost at the bargaining table'.[48] Managerial control over the negotiator may also serve to strengthen his bargaining position, it may provide a commitment by way of open and explicit instructions from which it is apparent to his opponent that he cannot deviate; the negotiator may be grateful for restriction of his freedom to manoeuvre which is obvious to everyone: it serves as an obstacle which the union must strive to overcome by getting through to those in control.

This means that, to some extent, the extent to which the negotiating specialist is involved or by-passed in a stampede to reach the boardroom is itself subject to the negotiating process. It may be a deliberate policy to set up the personnel department as an intermediary defence which can suffer the tragic fate of an outpost isolated beyond the enemy lines when its work has been done. Michael Poole, reporting on the comparative isolation of personnel departments in two Sheffield factories noted 'the inevitable sociological consequences which result from personnel departments having no real executive responsibilities' and that 'the personnel officer employed in a purely advisory capacity is placed in the almost intolerable position of having to take responsibility for labour relations problems and conflicts while having no executive authority.'[49] But it is not a simple question of the allocation of executive responsibility and of the precise definition of managerial functions. The personnel department's position in industrial relations may be intended to be intolerable.[50] Its occupation of the negotiating role cannot be seen as its entire manning or location in which it wins or loses, is responsible or not, has authority or is denied it. The personnel department's function is to be explained not simply in terms of its formal responsibility for negotiation with the unions but in terms of its position within the process of internal adjustment.

The balance of control in this process may appear to be weighted against the negotiators but there are powerful counter-controls available to him. Gottschalk summarizes these as:

1 norms which deny the competence of outsiders
2 protective myths
3 norms of secrecy and
4 protection of their knowledge through controls on entry.[51]

These characteristics are similar to those defining professionalism and the negotiators have been compared to a professional group. Much of his claim for influence will rest upon competence and upon the necessity of a 'professional' trust which he must maintain with his opponent. A negotiator has to retain the confidence of the other side and his own side knows it so that his claim to have entered into an understanding which his own side must honour is often forceful, it takes on the character of a commitment to the environment beyond management's control and, on some occasions, the commitment may be deliberately entered in order to shift management's position. Negotiators develop a close relationship with their opponents: on both sides they are sometimes suspected of co-operating too closely with the enemy, to the extent of entering into secret deals. The suspicion is not entirely groundless; negotiators have to understand each other and the techniques for achieving understanding are not always publicly displayed. The management negotiator is expected to understand his opponent partly so that he can make better or more expert predictions about his behaviour. His predictive ability and his knowledge of his opponent's behaviour are both formidable assets in the influence he uses to counter management's control over his own.

The tension that exists between senior management and its

negotiators is probably necessary to the success of the bargaining process with unions. Negotiators must be influenced by what the union will accept without being allowed to do the union's job for it; they must be controlled while remaining influential. The process can be illustrated in an elementary fashion if we visualize management and union organizations meeting at a point where the external bargaining process takes place between them.

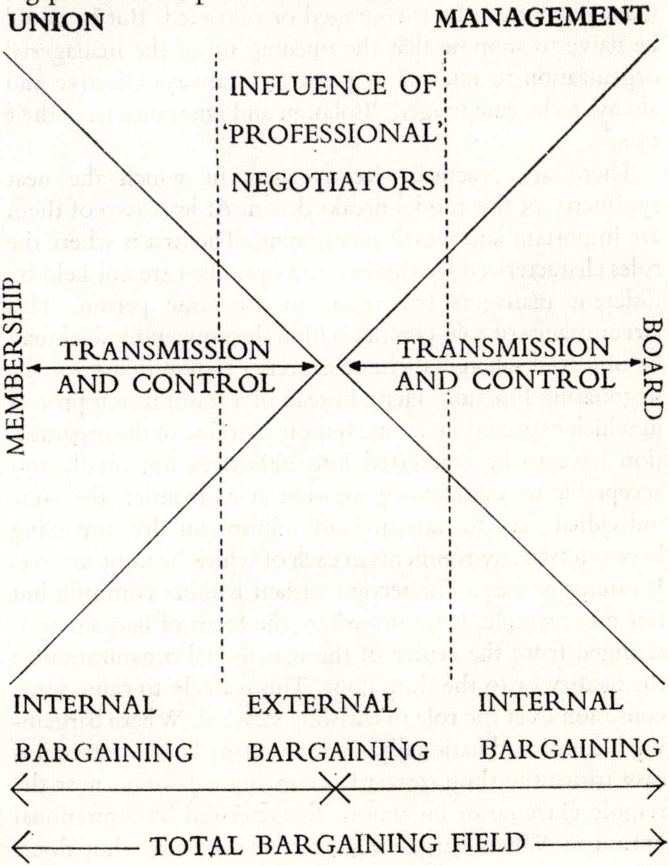

The negotiating process is just as real across the whole range separating the extremes of both organizations. Without the internal transmission process, bargaining between the extremes would be impossible. This has implications for the construction of the managerial organization, which is the point at which this chapter began. Managerial organization can be constructed so as to facilitate the process of internal adjustment, that is, the internal negotiating process within management can be encouraged or restricted. But it would be naive to suppose that the opening up of the managerial organization to internal negotiation is always effective and always to be encouraged. 'Isolation and ignorance have their uses.'

There are practical circumstances in which the neat symmetry of this model breaks down. At least two of them are important and worth mentioning. The first is where the roles characterized by rigidity and optimism are not held by different managers but reside in the same person. This circumstance of role-conflict within the same individual may be observed where a director exercises responsibility for the negotiating function. Here, instead of a transmission process in which expectations at one remote extreme of the organization have to be converted into objectives not totally unacceptable to another organization at its frontier, the same individual has to attempt an adjustment by travelling between two environments in each of which he must survive. It cannot be easy. The second variant is more common but not more simple. It occurs where the focus of bargaining is changed from the centre of the managerial organization to the factory or to the shop floor. This is likely to cause some confusion over the role of the shop steward. Where bargaining is conducted nationally, or at company headquarters, it is easy to see the shop steward occupying a position near the remote extreme of his union, characterized by aspirational optimism. Where bargaining is carried out on the shop floor, however, the relative position of the shop steward moves to the front line, emphasizing the importance of his seeking an accommodation with management, of his understanding management's expectations and outlook. But what is his situation when bargaining takes place at different levels for different parts of the effort bargain? It is probably not simply analagous to that of our fleet-footed director who has to move easily, or at least quickly, between boardroom and negotiating table. These are complications, however, that more properly belong in a discussion of trade union organization.

CHAPTER 4

Trade unions and employees

Work is a cooperative activity. In large scale industrial, commercial or service organizations, the form which cooperation takes is rarely voluntary, it cannot depend upon individual and transitory acts of will in order to bring about complex processes dependent upon co-ordinated tasks and skills contributed by many different people. The characteristic of work in an industrialized society is that it takes place within 'organizations'; that is, within situations in which cooperation is organized. This state of affairs produces a paradox: cooperation necessarily depends upon a voluntary foundation; if it is removed both cooperation and work are impossible. But the cooperation of industrial enterprise is achieved by a measure of coercion without which the enterprise cannot function because purposeful work cannot be done. This paradox explains a great deal of the ambiguity that characterizes work and industrial relations; workers display voluntary cooperation in tasks which they believe it is appropriate for them to do, but they are subjected to controls in the performance of these tasks which they are driven to resist. Work is a cooperative activity even when it seems to resemble nothing more than a bloody battlefield. Beynon's description of *Working for Ford* in which the general view of industrial relations is of total war, acknowledges that 'It isn't an either-or question of being like a football team *or* being like two opposing camps. Factory production involves *both*. Because production has a social basis the factory can obviously be seen, at some level, as a collectivity with management operating in a co-ordinating role.'[52]

There is an assumption in closely co-ordinated work situations that voluntary cooperation is not enough, it will not produce sufficient effort in the right kinds of tasks at appropriate times to satisfy the purpose of the employer. The worker must be controlled.[53] 'The incumbents of certain positions are endowed with the right to make decisions as to who does what, when and how; the incumbents of other positions have to submit to these decisions . . . For the industrial worker, the labor contract implies acceptance of a role which is, *inter alia*, defined by the obligation to comply with the commands of given persons.'[54] The first element in control is supervision, first the employer and then his agent, the supervisor, subjects the worker's activity to surveillance.

Supervision is an inadequate method of control, however. It is not constant. It engages the supervisor in close personal relationships with the worker so that by a process of socialization, the employers' standards which the supervisor is expected to impose are themselves subverted and, to the extent that they are not subverted, they provoke hostile responses from the worker. Close supervision involves management 'in a vicious cycle: the supervisor perceived the worker as unmotivated; he then carefully watched and directed him; this aroused the worker's ire and accentuated his apathy, and now the supervisor was back where he began.'[55] Gouldner goes on to argue that the construction of bureaucratic rules may help to reduce some of these tensions by introducing precise and unchanging instructions, by depersonalizing the process of command or by screening the supervisor, by legitimating punishment, by providing some leeway in which the application of rules is negotiable and by enabling the worker to remain apathetic, so that he can 'take any attitude toward his work that he wished, so long as he conformed to the rules'. The rules, says Gouldner, make supervision feasible rather than replacing it and while they reduce many of the tensions which derive from close supervision, they do nothing to reduce the tensions which create it.

Supervision is constantly likely to provoke opposition from those who are supervised. Supervision is therefore supported by bureaucracy. Bureaucracy simply organizes the opposition. But this is no mere downward flight into incompetence. Bureaucracy, the specification of tasks, the nomination of authority and its prescription by acknowledged rules is not produced simply as a response to the problem of controlling labour. It is an accompaniment to the process of dividing, sub-dividing and co-ordinating work. In terms of the discipline and control which this process inevitably requires, bureaucracy has the function of providing some comfort and protection both to those who receive orders and to those who give them.

Work and its control produces tension. The machinery of control gives rise to the development of strategies of independence. The practical operation of these strategies has been noticed at least since the bank wiring room observations in the Hawthorn experiments. The general verdict upon those studies was that the reaction of workers to the final system of control which was imposed upon them was of an emotional or non-rational kind and that it succeeded in establishing norms and standards within the group which were more firmly enforced than the official expectations of management.

Many other researchers have discovered evidence of an alternative system of control to that formally imposed by management. Roy noticed not only subversive activity but a network of supportive alliances which could include line foremen and specialist support groups and which 'effectively modified certain formally established shop routines'.[56] Roy reported 'that operators and their allies joined forces in certain situations in a manner not only unmistakably at variance with the carefully prepared designs of staff experts but even in flagrant violation of strongly held managerial "moral principles" of shop floor behaviour. In short, machine operators resorted to "cheating" to obtain their quotas.'

A significant difference of interpretation emerged between these later studies and those at Hawthorn. Roy expressed doubt as to whether the resistance to control manifested on the shop floor was purely emotional, whether it could be seen as conflict between an economically rational management and a non-rational work group. From the perspective of the shop-floor it often seemed that the work group's deviousness was believed to be essential in getting the work out in spite of the obstacle of an obdurate, distant and ill-informed management which insists upon imposing unrealistic controls. In these circumstances it is the worker (and his foreman) who knows what has to be done; the manager is a very uncertain ally.

This is a response which may relate to the nature of bureaucratic control. Gouldner distinguishes between three important forms: mock-bureaucracy, which is deemed to be irrelevant and inappropriate, often emanating from an external agency (or from a level of senior management so distant from the work-place that it is perceived as though it were external, as 'them'); representative bureaucracy, characterized by some day to day participation of workers in its administration; punishment-centred bureaucracy, in which deviation is followed by punishment. The purposive alliances which Roy described are sometimes a response to mock-bureaucracy as in the American aircraft factory in which the tapping of mis-aligned drill holes in wing assemblies was regarded as an offence so serious as to justify instant dismissal, 'the use of the tap is the most serious crime in the plant. A worker can be summarily fired for merely possessing a tap. Nevertheless, at least one half of the work force in a position to use a tap owns at least one. Every well-equipped senior mechanic owns four or five of different sizes.' The observers point out that this inconsistency between the rules and general standards of behaviour would not be possible without the connivance of foremen and inspectors; both depend upon workmen's cooperation and the penalties which follow reporting an offence are too severe for the inspector's comfort. The potential conflict is diminished by subterfuge; there is a convention that tapping does not take place in the presence of the inspector. The observers of this particular scene concluded that:

> the use of the tap is literally a major crime which is intrinsic to the system . . . The tolerance of the tap is a means by which workers, inspectors and production supervisors attempt to achieve their respective ends in mutually tolerable manner in a situation where they are forced to work together according to directives which, if closely followed, would result in mutual frustration.[57]

Other observers have described the necessity or rationality of defensive strategies among workers which might wrongly be dismissed as the result of an emotional reaction to control.[58]

At some point (and it is likely to be different in different places or at different times) resistance to control goes too far to carry with it the overt approval of immediate supervision. The circumstance is often associated with some change in previously acknowledged norms of behaviour; higher management institutes a purge, there is a change of personnel, foremen become subject to stricter control, workmen demand formal and explicit recognition of standards which have been implicitly accepted: there is, in short, some disturbance of the indulgency pattern. The reaction is likely to take the form of some sort of withdrawal on the part of individuals or groups. It may mean a literal but unco-ordinated withdrawal from work in the form of absence or termination. It may mean the manifestation of negative responses to the requirements of the work situation. In some circumstances the reaction will be organized and planned, the response to the application of power through greater bureaucratic control will be to counter it with power which is also controlled and co-ordinated. Gouldner concluded that the extent to which bureaucratic routines and rules is resisted by those subject to them is a function of:

1 their adherence to belief systems which are violated by bureaucratic measures
2 conditions legitimating active resistance
3 conditions making the resistance expedient
4 the degree to which their status is injured or impaired by increased bureaucratization
5 the strength of informal solidarity among the resistors.[59]

All this is to suggest that resistance which management is likely to meet in work is not simply a question to be determined by negotiations with trade unions. Conflict is generated in work: it is the form of its expression which is determined by the interaction of managers and trade unions. To regard industrial relations as concerned only with formal relationships between management and unions is to confine it to consequences rather than causes and to leave its practitioners without influence or understanding.[60]

The conflicts which are produced in work take on a different form when they are subjected to organization. The bureaucracy of management produces defensive responses from workers but the responses take on new forms when they are formalized and expressed by trade unions. One bureaucracy is now faced by another.

All unions are bureaucracies but the characteristic features of their rules and constitutions are influenced by many factors. Professor Turner makes a most important distinction between open and closed trade unions, a distinction which, he says, explains not only 'the general pattern of British trade union organization' but 'some important differences in the normal behaviour and preoccupations of various unions'.[61] Trade unions are open 'in the sense that they are able to impose no restrictions on entry into many of the occupations that they organize, but are content to recruit all workers in those occupations whom the employers themselves engage.'[62] Closed unions, on the other hand, are restrictionist, 'not merely in the sense that they base themselves on a capacity to control the supply of labour to particular occupations and maintain an exclusive claim to employment within those occupations, but also in the sense that they have little intrinsic interest in increasing their merely numerical strength . . . the shape of British trade unionism in general might be described as one in which open, expansionist unions have spread around islands of stable closed unionism.'[63] The bigger unions are open and expansionist, relying for bargaining power on size and strength of members, preoccupied with wage questions and tending to take the lead in general wage movements. Closed unions are smaller, not primarily concerned with numerical expansion and defensive of the relative status of their members within wage structures rather than with general levels of wages. Closed unions are more likely to insist upon the pre-entry closed shop and to rely upon techniques of autonomous job regulation involving the maintenance of trade rules and customary practices. Open unions are much more dependent upon the establishment of effective collective bargaining relationships with employers.

These differences are associated with others concerning the

centralization of authority within the union and its relationship with its members. 'Mass bargaining power, as in general unions like the NUGMW, is likely to produce a strong executive, workshop bargaining as in the AEU, a weak executive.'[64] Professor Turner distinguishes between three characteristic forms of trade union government:

> 'exclusive democracies', usually closed and homogenous unions in which officers share an understanding of the trade with the membership which engages in a high level of participation; 'aristocracies', in which a particular occupational group plays a key role in the union's affairs; 'popular bossdoms', often open unions with a low level of participation in which expertise and initiative is concentrated in the hands of officials because their experience is much wider than that of the membership, scattered as it is between a wide variety of occupations.[65]

Martin suggests that:

> the impact of membership spread upon bureaucratization similarly varies between different types of unions. Bureaucratization is most highly developed in general unions with a diverse semi-skilled and unskilled membership, like the National Union of General and Municipal Workers. In unions like the NUGMW the lack of common interest between different groups of members and the unsuitability of settling particular industrial problems at annual representative conferences increases the power of the full-time officials as the only unifying element.[66]

The influences which determine the relative distribution of power between the union hierarchy and the membership emerge from the union's growth path and strategy (whether it is open or closed), its constitution and its environment. A union's constitution and rules will define its electorate, the method of voting, the importance of ballots and referenda and the issues over which the electorate is likely to have influence. The constitution will determine the relationship between the union's administration and the organizational level at which the membership is allowed to participate in its operation. The branch (or the lodge in mining, the chapel in newspapers and printing) is the grass roots level of union organization. It may be based upon the place of work or it may be geographically constructed; the distinction is often a practical one but it can have considerable influence on membership participation in the union's affairs: geographically based branches can be difficult to get to and be predisposed to the discussion of business which is not a reality for some of those who attend.

The trade union official who is nearest to the membership is normally the branch secretary or chairman. For this reason, the branch used to be regarded as of fundamental importance in union structure, particularly in terms of the maintenance of democratic control. This emphasis has been reversed in recent years. Professor Clegg pronounced that: 'There exists a formidable body of evidence that the union branch is a body of relatively small and declining importance . . . They remain administrative units, and most branch secretaries are burdened with a heavy weight of routine clerical business.'[67] Branch officers may be elected by the membership of the branch or they may be appointed, they may be full-time or part-time officers and they may sit as members of district or regional committees. Where the branch is based upon the place of work they are likely to have important functions in negotiation with the employer. Although the branch has tended to be discredited as a level of great significance and although the branch officer has been outshone by the growing attention given to the shop steward, the branch is probably still important as the point at which union structure is articulated to union membership.

It continues to be important in the apparatus of union representation because the branch still has some hope of influencing union policy as it is expressed in the resolutions of annual conference; shop stewards may have come to be regarded as more influential in bargaining terms but unions are not entirely bargaining organizations.

Professor Clegg puts forward a 'simple theory' of trade union government before proceeding to qualify it beyond recall. The theory is:

> that an elected conference decides the constitution and policy of the union on behalf of the members; an elected executive has responsibility for administering the union's affairs between conferences in accordance with the constitution and policies laid down by conference, and for giving directions to the general secretary; and he, in most unions also an elected representative of the members, is responsible to the executive for the day to day running of business and supervising the work of the other full-time officers.[68]

The theory, Clegg continues, is too simple and the qualifications of it are important and numerous because trade unions are subject to Michell's iron law of oligarchy. Their electoral processes of control over the administration are weak and often subject to central influence, the influence of annual conferences is tenuous and temporary and is also subject to manipulation by experts and the influence of full-time officers and specialists in the administration of trade union affairs is considerable and is probably increasing. Even where the constitution and rules are explicit in the formal checks on central sovereignty which are provided for the membership to exercise, these checks are still open to interpretation and sometimes to wayward application. As the checks become more complex so they become more open to abuse or more subject to expert manipulation. The problem, as Hughes says, is to achieve a balance between a degree of precision such as to ensure fairness with reaching a degree of complexity which make the rules themselves the subject of tactical skill and deployment. The NUM is often regarded as a model of democratic control because major decisions have to be submitted to ballot of the membership and the votes are counted by an independent body, the Electoral Reform Society. But the Society only counts the votes; in the ballot over the productivity proposals of October 1974 the vote itself must have been heavily influenced by the Executive's recommendation to vote 'no' printed on every ballot paper.

Trade unions are social and political organizations as well as economic institutions and, because of their history and their ideological commitment, attacks on them arouse strong emotions and defensive reactions. British trade unions, in particular, may have insulated themselves from criticism by characterizing it as hostile. Criticisms of their bureaucratic character, or their centralist tendencies are, therefore, likely to be rejected out of hand and to be described as prejudiced. This reaction has been so frequent and so marked that we run the risk of appearing to be prejudiced simply by being critical. One safeguard against this charge is to suggest that attacks on the centralist nature of the unions and the weakness of the control exercised by the membership through constitutional channels come not only from the right but the left. Here are Lane and Roberts describing the NUGMW, for example:

> In giving evidence to the Donovan Commission on Trade Unions, the GMWU claimed to be democratic—a claim since contested by the Pilkington strikers. If democracy means rule by the people then clearly the GMWU and every other British trade union are undemocratic for patently the union members do not rule their unions. But most people's conception of democracy seems to

> mean the election of people to represent them, the right to remove their representatives if they prove inadequate and the toleration of opposition. Even on this conception of democracy it is clear that the GMWU, in company with most other unions, is not democratic. The officials, once elected, stay elected, and can only be dismissed by the National Executive Committee, itself half composed of 'elected' officials.[69]

The authors go on to point out that candidates for election are screened for suitability by the Executive under Rule 19 (no member is eligible for nomination or election unless 'his or her qualifications are in keeping with the standard required by the Union' (such standards to be determined by the National Executive Committee in its absolute discretion) and that effective criticism from within the Union by any-one 'who acts singly or in conjunction with any other member or persons in opposition to the policy of the Union' renders the critic liable to expulsion under Rule 43.

The debate about the representativeness of trade unions has considerable significance for management (and even greater significance for society at large and for workpeople) because the issues it embraces influence the kind of response which unions make to managerial initiatives. They concern what managers sometimes like to call the union's degree of responsibility. Managers usually mean by this that unions are responsible to the extent that they can carry the membership along with the union's decisions and with agreements into which the union has entered. In this context 'responsible' unions are said to be capable of exercising leadership while 'irresponsible' trade unions are swayed by vagaries of rank and file opinion or by the demagogic influence of militants. Now one set of factors which influence a union's behaviour and which lead to such judgements being passed is the union's constitution and rule-book. In some unions, officials are appointed rather than elected, ballots are unknown, conferences infrequent or unrepresentative, branches badly attended and communication is scant. In circumstances like these what the leadership says goes and management may find itself dealing with an admirably 'responsible' trade union. In other circumstances the opportunity for rank and file pressure to be exerted upon the leadership is much more considerable and the union's leadership may be much more sensitive to the opinion of its members. One American analysis suggests that union democracy depends upon the maintenance of a two-party system within the union. This is probably too formalized a requirement (and there are suspicions within the political environment that the existence of two parties hardly in itself guarantees democracy). Any electoral process is open to abuse or to the expert manipulation of the permanent officials. Martin takes a more sensible view, that 'union democracy exists when union executives are unable to prevent opposition factions distributing propaganda and mobilizing electoral support.'[70] Martin recognises the necessity of constraints upon union leadership, his framework 'assumes that union leaders will not tolerate faction unless constrained to do so . . . most union leaders regard opposition as an aid to the economic enemy.'[71] He classifies these constraints as the political culture, government attitudes, pattern of membership distribution, industrial setting (ownership concentration and the collective bargaining system), economic environment, technology, union bargaining power, membership characteristics, membership beliefs, opposition expertise, leadership beliefs and union structure. Clegg doubts whether organized opposition is, by itself, a satisfactory guarantee of union democracy and he adds a number of other factors to be considered, decentralization to separate constituent institutions, regional or trade group decentralization, decentralization to the branch, decentralization to the workshop, the pressure group activity of trade union officers.

Management may be prone to welcome strong central leadership within a trade union but an over-strong centralist character may become an embarrassment. The membership is always exerting a pull in the opposite direction. Unions not only have to contain tension between the need for efficient administration (tending to turn them into pure bureaucracies) and the need for representativeness, they also have to resolve a need for reaching an accommodation with management (that is, with an entirely different organization in pursuit of different objectives) with the perpetual suspicion that the accommodation is too close. This suspicion, although it has been given recent and lengthy expression, has never been put better than it was 60 years ago:

> What really is blameworthy, is the conciliation policy which demands leaders of this description. First, they are 'trade unionists by trade' and their profession demands certain privileges . . . The leader, then, has an interest—a vested influence—in stopping progress. They have, therefore, in some things an antagonism of interest with the rank and file. The conditions of things in South Wales has reached the point when this difference of interest, this antagonism, has become manifest. Hence the men criticize and are discontented with their leaders. But remedy is not new leaders.[27]

If the 'professional leader's' interest in accommodating with the employer is too marked and if he presses it by a too zealous control over the union's machinery of administration then the reaction of the rank and file, though long delayed, is likely to be very damaging. Every aspect of Dahrendorf's analysis of conflict regulation, every pronouncement about the necessity of understanding the reality of conflict so that means for its expression (and, so, its regulation) can be constructed, applies with as much force to relationships within the union as to relationships between the union and management. In a trade union in which the leadership shows a 'cavalier' disregard for the expression of rank and file interest, in which the leadership is such a model of responsibility as to give management no great trouble, there is always the risk of a disturbance which, although delayed, may damage the union when it occurs. The danger of constitutional checks and balances, of access to the conference floor or to the means of publicity and lobbying is that it prevents a delay in manifesting discontent while pressure has to mount to a dangerous degree before it is noticed. The analogy with the mechanism of the safety-valve is obvious and the danger of the comparison is that it can be extended to the extent of admiration for a union apparatus which merely allows the membership to let off steam so that it can the more easily be manipulated by the leadership.

This hazard reminds us that it may, in the long-run, be unwise to rely upon purely constitutional correctives. The final safeguard against centralism in trade unions must be the threat of counteraction by members who have become so aggrieved that they act in the various ways described by Professor Clegg or in some other manifestation of concern. The link between constitutional quietism and open revolt or anarchy is probably provided by the shop steward.

The general view of the shop steward has been totally transformed in recent years. Suspected both by trade unions and employers, regarded as revolutionaries and anarchists by more distant observers of industry, shop stewards now seem to appear in a much more moderate, not to say heroic, role. There are three aspects of this transformation. The first was summed up by Donovan and has been repeated without qualification since: 'the shop steward is more of a lubricant than an irritant'. The evidence for this judgement is based upon the views of those who work with stewards, union officials and managers. The evidence is also remarkably consistent (confirmed in several independent studies of shop steward activities) in suggesting that managers believe stewards to be important, comparatively moderate and often to be preferred to full-time officials in handling issues.[73] The earlier stereotype of the steward as agitator can hardly survive, although we should observe, in passing, that evidence of the attitudes of inhabitants of an institution can simply support conclusions about their judgements, not about the 'fact' of whether stewards are moderate or immoderate. If managers believe stewards are moderate the only conclusion we can reach is tautologous (as in so much of social science), that managers believe stewards are moderate. Lawyers, bank managers or politicians acquainted with the same behaviour might form a very different judgement. The point is made, not simply as a quibble about research methods but because it is now widely reported that the steward *is* moderate, *is* a lubricant.[74] The judgement depends upon the viewpoint of the judge and we should remember that there is an inevitable tendency for inhabitants of institutions to regard their environment as 'normal'. The tendency emerges in shop stewards' views about managers. Goodman and Whittingham report that 38 per cent of stewards in their survey got on very well with the departmental manager, 31 per cent got on well, and 62 per cent thought that industrial relations in their place of work was either satisfactory or very satisfactory. Those figures tell us something about the outlook of stewards, nothing about the state of industrial relations. In fact the consistency of the evidence and the mutual support which it reveals might justify the suspicion that insiders who have to rely upon each others' help might not be the best judges of a situation which they may have constructed for their mutual comfort.

There is no doubt that this first change in the perception

of the shop steward's role is related to a proper understanding of his great importance in bargaining relationships at shop-floor level. In some cases shop steward bargaining and bargaining organization has developed to an advanced degree to the point at which 'a state of parallel unionism' has developed in which the formal unions are simply 'a means of obtaining occasional general wage increases and for demonstrating class and occupational solidarity'. Unofficial strikes are not 'against the union' 'they are simply conflicts to which the union's existence has become largely irrelevant . . . The Shop Stewards' organization has become the real union.'[75]

The reasons for the development of the steward's bargaining role have been widely discussed. They concern a confluence of influences which have had the effect of emphasizing the importance of the place of work and, therefore, of the only bargaining agent of the union available at the place of work, the steward. The fragmentation of bargaining, the relative decline in the influence of employers' organizations, the inappropriateness and confusion of union structure in terms of workplace problems, the incidence of payment by result systems, high levels of demand for labour and the practice of bidding up plant earnings, all these factors have helped in the development of the steward's importance in bargaining. Managers have, consciously or unconsciously, assisted this development:

> Some management policies, and the absence of policy add to the power of stewards. Decentralized supervision of payment schemes, procrastination in dealing with problems, inconsistencies of treatment by different managers and arbitrary actions all facilitate the development of strong workplace representatives, all afford opportunities for militant activities. Management has quite widely fostered the growth of shop stewards, and

promoted their wider areas of responsibility.[76]

The general encouragement of plant and company level bargaining makes this emphasis of the importance of the steward in bargaining relationships more marked and more deliberate.

The belated acknowledgement of his role and its deliberate emphasis leads to some paradoxical results. Some of the explanations for his emergence reside in the informality of his background. He became an effective negotiator with managers because he emerged from a work situation with which he had close contacts and which he thoroughly understood. Agreements which he made were likely to be honoured because he might be more truly representative of worker aspirations and understandings than the more distant full-time union officials; his bargaining posture might be more extreme but it might also be more realistic and representative of workers' feelings. The steward filled 'the gap in the union structure' partly because he operated at the place of work, where the gap was most serious; his evolution was an almost natural development to meet needs which the union structure could not meet and his advantage was that he existed outside the formal framework of union rules. He was produced by formal deficiencies which he was able to meet by a spontaneous response.

We have now reached the position in which his importance is acknowledged and the usual prescription is that the steward's representative and bargaining functions should be formally recognized. His exclusion from trade union rule books and from procedure agreements are said to be matters of regret which should be corrected. The CIR recommended that steward facilities and functions should be formally acknowledged and that such matters should be the subject of written agreements with management.[77] The danger is, of course, that this tardy bestowal of legitimacy may destroy the lustiness of the child.

The point is clearly implied by Turner, Clack and Roberts who, observing that, as far as detailed employment conditions and labour relations are concerned, 'the shop stewards' organization has become the real union', go on to say that the organization is:

> one with an almost similar degree of elaboration and complexity. And because this organization is now the main agency for the bargaining of actual working conditions—with what amounts to its own full-time negotiators—it has assumed, in relation to management on the one hand and the rank-and-file of operatives on the other, many of the characteristics that the official unions once displayed under the earlier development of national or industry-wide collective bargaining. The senior stewards, like the full-time union officials before them, are forced to assume something of the role of buffer between the employer and the operatives . . . in general, the stewards' organization is under pressures that compel it towards certain responsible patterns of institutional behaviour—'responsible' at least in the sense that its leaders are obliged to balance a variety of group interests against the particular sectional claims with which they are confronted, and to bear in mind the long-term desirability of maintaining good negotiating relations with managements.[78]

We began to discuss this problem at the end of the last chapter when we were examining the controls and tensions within the internal bargaining process. We saw that it was necessary for the 'professional' bargainer to achieve some sympathetic understanding with the position and perspective of his opponents and that it was necessary for him to communicate this understanding to his own controllers or managers. We saw also that it might be necessary for those managers, while open to influence by this communication, to remain suspicious of its intentions and to seek to exercise over the professional negotiator a counter influence compounded of considerations of the wider interest of the organization and independent of its opponent's objectives. These internal controls and influences are as characteristic of union organizations as they are of management, they may indeed be more visible. The discussion in chapter 3 was broken off when we had noticed two special cases in which this description of the bargaining process as covering a total field within two polar extremes and a middle ground occupied by the negotiators of each organization. There seemed to be a special problem of explaining the position of the shop steward.

The problem arises because of differences in the level of bargaining. In 'traditonal', centralized bargaining at national level, the negotiating bodies are formally constituted and, although they may include 'lay' members of the union they are often not shop stewards. The tensions between the official negotiators, remote in time and place from the membership, are perfectly illustrated and it is the shop stewards who are likely to represent rank and file opposition to policies and agreements arrived at by their negotiators. This distance is a necessary characteristic of the organization and location of the bargaining process; it is illustrated in this comment on Ford stewards:

> They knew better than ever before that they couldn't trust the national officers of the union. They couldn't trust them, but on occasions they needed them. They had to try to use them. More importantly they learned something else that they already knew (*sic*). Their strength lay with the membership.[79]

This is the reason why, in the literature of the new left the shop steward appears as the new hero, as the courageous, self-sacrificing,[80] defender of 'the lads' against not only the employer but, when necessary, the union too. But the situation of the steward can appear to be more equivocal than this simple horse-opera characterization. If bargaining is mainly conducted at plant level and the steward is the principle bargainer then it is he whom the bargaining role thrusts into a relationship of partial dependence upon management. The hero may then begin to appear as villain because, in changing the negotiating context, we have entirely changed the relative position of the actors: in the national context the steward's position was removed from the central position, isolated from close contact with managerial negotiating perspectives, close to rank and file opinions, whereas now in the context of plant bargaining it is he who must accommodate to management and accept responsibility for the accommodation. Turner's phenomenon of the 'unofficial—unofficial strike' can mean that there are many disputes in which 'the shop steward committee had lost control'[81] and in which 'by accepting the new agreement, the method of job evaluation and the grievance procedure the stewards increasingly came to be seen as responsible not to their members but "the computer at Worley". The new wages structure was effectively isolating the shop steward from the men on his section . . . Even a guarded acceptance of a managerial rationality had created considerable problems for the stewards' committee and the individual steward.'[82]

This should serve to remind us of the essential relativism of the negotiating process. It is not always helpful to discuss the role of the steward, or the manager or the foreman, because the role is not entirely conveyed by the title: it depends largely upon its position in relationship to other actors upon the stage.

We suggested that there were three respects in which understanding of the shop stewards' importance had been transformed. The first concerns their relationship to collective bargaining. The second concerns union organization. A great deal of concern used to be expressed about the difficulties of branch organization: low attendance meant that unions found it difficult to communicate with their members or keep in touch with their opinion. In some unions (like the AUEW), the organization of branch activities on a district basis meant that there was no effective union organization at the place of work. Concern about the inadequacies of branch organization has recently diminished. In terms of communications, McCarthy and Parker established that 41 per cent of the union information received by members was conveyed by means of the journal, 54 per cent of this was delivered by stewards and that 40 per cent of union information was delivered by shop stewards themselves.

Concern about union organization at the place of work has been diminished because of a recognition of the extent to which the need for it has been met by joint shop steward cooperative activities not only within the union but between different unions. Goodman and Whittingham distinguish between different levels of shop steward committees.

1 Single union, single department or plant committees which are used to exchange information and co-ordinate action.
2 Multi-union, single department committees, characteristic of very large plants in which there is a particular need to co-ordinate action in order to face management with a unified strategy.
3 Multi-union, whole plant committees, the most usual form of organization and normally called joint shop stewards committees. They are composed of stewards from all unions represented in the plant. Goodman and Whittingham comment of this level of organization that,

'though performing a useful function, formal recognition by union and management is minimal'.

4 Company-wide combine committees made up of stewards representing different establishments in a multi-plant firm. The authors point out that this is the level at which approval and recognition tend to break down because steward organization may cut across the district or regional basis of trade union formal organization, the boundaries between different industries in multi-product firms and the boundaries between different collective bargaining procedural machinery. For these and other reasons the background of some of these combine committees has sometimes been secretive but they have acquired, in recent years, greater recognition of their general utility.

5 Industry-wide committees established in particular industries from time to time. This is the level at which attitudes to shop steward cooperation continue to be hostile. 'Most committees lead a shadowy existence, spasmodically emerging during crises ... Most cannot be regarded as permanent, national bodies. More accurately they are groups of militants, frequently dominated by members and sympathisers of extremist political bodies ... Officially, most unions dislike or prohibit participation in them.'[83]

6 National or regional committees, organized irrespective of industry. These are said to be the least significant form of organization, concerned with occasional conferences or for specific purposes of protest or challenge.

At factory and company level, shop steward organization has come to be seen as important to both the unions and employers. The CIR found that 'the growth of Joint Shop Steward Committees is an important factor in industrial relations ... They can encourage unified bargaining.' The

CIR added that 'unions also could provide encouragement for such co-ordination at workplace level. If they do not do so, this is likely to arise spontaneously and be more difficult for the union's institutional framework to accommodate.'[84]

We see here two aspects which characterize current discussions of the shop steward in industrial relations. The first is that he appears as a sort of saviour of the trade union movement. Whatever criticisms have been levelled at trade union organization, communication, representativeness, all tend now to be dismissed as irrelevant because the shop steward has met the need, whatever it was. In several different ways we have concluded that 'the shop steward is the union'. For that reason, agitation about union health has now diminished. In some ways this is an unreliable conclusion. It can promote a degree of smugness; it does not matter what ills are manifested by the trade union organization, the shop stewards will compensate for them or cure them. This is a dangerous conclusion because there are certain kinds of activities which the shop steward is not likely to develop effectively. Turner says that 'the shop steward organization . . . has developed mainly to fill in the inadequacies of current union structure' but he warns us that:

> at the same time, the shop steward system is itself inadequate to meet all the requirements of the situation. It does not always provide full co-ordination between the different working groups in bargaining activities and grievance settlement at the workplace level. It is particularly weak in achieving co-ordination in this respect between the different plants of the same firm. And it is almost totally ineffective in achieving co-ordination at the level of the motor industry as a whole.[85]

The second aspect of much of the current discussion of shop stewards is that, because they are seen so often to make up for union deficiencies, they have come to be seen as substituting for the unions and as justifying the belief that the unions no longer matter. There are several sides to this argument. One suggests that trade unions are such diverse organizations, each contending with so many internal tensions, that it is absurd to continue to talk of a trade union movement. This ignores the political and representative nature of trade unions but even on this ground, as we shall see, the trade unions are believed in some quarters to have become moribund and redundant. Another argument suggests that, with the decline of industry-wide collective bargaining, the unions have experienced diminished authority and influence; as one writer put it, in absurdly exaggerated terms, 'the existing official structures would continue as an organizational rump, exercising general co-ordination of social and economic policy and acting as an important political pressure group. The negotiating structure would be the result of further developing the emerging network of joint plant and industrial committees.'[86]

The most serious criticism of the relevance of the trade unions suggests that they have become so embedded in the administrative apparatus, so responsible in their attitude to government and so occupied with the problems of operating large scale organizations, that they have ceased to represent rank and file opinion or working class interests. The most severe of these criticisms is that this is no accidental characteristic of particular rule books and particular union leaders but an inevitable consequence of the nature of unionism:

> Trade unionism was a standing and continuing assertion of a fundamental cleavage of interest, yet simultaneously, because of its insistence on the regulation of that conflict, it could not be the vehicle of its abolition... The trade unions could not transform society because their very nature... required them to work within it, to take it for granted.[87]

Lane takes these criticisms still further:

as long as trade unionism was about remedying the present, so long was it inevitable that the union leader was abstracted from his roots, forced into the patterns and practices of 'secret diplomacy', the 'shabby compromises', that so aroused the anger of the rank and file from time to time . . . the possibility of corruption was inherent in trade unionism unsupported by a vigorous socialist movement.[88]

These quotations serve two purposes. They first demonstrate that trade unions are seen in some quarters in a very different light from that in which they are frequently presented by employers. Secondly, they show that the very same qualities of flexibility and accommodation to tensions and strains which we have argued is a characteristic of the internal aspects of collective bargaining can be interpreted as total subservience to the collective bargaining relationship. Within the field of bargaining (in which we are here primarily interested) the distances separating or relating the actors, the differences between the perceptions and perspectives which they carry, the force with which they can exercise or resist control, all seem to be essential features of the process of achieving accommodation between two essentially different interests. But if a purely political outlook is brought to bear on this same field, the achievement of that same accommodation may begin to look like a squalid compromise. Unions are both economic and political institutions but the goals which they seek in these respective spheres may not be mutually compatible unless they become more compatible as the result of the triumph of the one over the other. The point of left wing criticisms of the unions is that this is precisely what has happened, that unions are market institutions which have superimposed upon the Labour Party the politics of the market place.

Amongst the many unchallenged assumptions in all this is that the unions are, or ought to be, representative of a working class, socialist outlook. If they are they have not always been so. The identification, or otherwise, of unions with the labour movement is a lively contemporary question because it becomes a matter of some importance in determining whether white collar unions are properly to be regarded as trade unions at all.

It is widely known, since the evidence published by Bain, that the growth of white collar union membership is not as rapid as it was once believed to be and that it is of the greatest importance to the trade union movement in this country.[89] Subsequent investigation by Bain and Price showed that, although white collar union growth remains important, the trade unions as a whole are no longer quite so dependent upon white collar expansion. The growth in union density in 1969 and 1970:

> was due to the unusual conjunction of strong growth in both white collar and manual unionism. In two years the union movement gained almost one million members, at a time when the labour force was declining. Thus, although the rapid increase in density of organization among white collar workers has been the basis of the new dynamism of the union movement, it was the halting and reversing of the downward trend in manual union density that permitted the striking upturn of 1969–70.[90]

An immediate impression of the importance of the white-collar union and of the public sector is given by a brief examination of the identity and membership of the five biggest British unions:[91]

TGWU	1,857,308
AUEW	1,427,839
NUGMW	883,810
NALGO	541,918
NUPE	507,826
EET &PU	414,189

Almost one-third of the membership of unions affiliated to the TUC are in unions in the civil service and post office, public employees, professional and clerical and technical engineering and scientific sections. The TUC's 'public employees' trade group is, numerically, its second largest after transport.

Apart from their numerical significance, white collar unions could have a marked effect upon the outlook of British trade unions and upon the TUC. On the one hand there is a good case for denying that they are in any sense a special case, so that any account of trade unions should apply to them too. This view is supported by the very real difficulty in arriving at a definition which establishes a satisfactory principle of division between white collar unions and the rest. Thus Bain and Price look at various attempts at distinguishing between white collar employees and the rest and reject them all as inadequate.[92] They acknowledge, however, that the notion that white collar workers (and hence white collar unions) are different persists in spite of these difficulties and, in order to account for it, they finally accept Runciman's association 'with that part of the productive process where authority is exercised and decisions taken'. White collar workers are, in this view, a group which has become assimilated by association because of a symbolic association with the possession of or proximity to authority. This 'symbolic association' suggests that what distinguishes white collar workers is more a matter of subjective outlook than objective fact and this, in turn, suggests that what makes them different is the way they look at the world rather than the way the world regards them. This very disparity is what has prompted Marxists to regard them as the victims of false consciousness and to hail their increasing unionization as evidence of a more realistic conclusion, on their part, that they belong to the proletariat and must share its struggles and its tactics.

This was something like the view taken by Lockwood:

> In the case of black-coated workers, class consciousness may be said to emerge when the members of a clerical association realize, first, that their common interests are engendered by the conflict of interest between employer and employee, and secondly, that their common interests are not fundamentally dissimilar in type from those underlying the concerted actions of manual workers. The trade union movement is a working class movement and to the extent that clerical workers become involved in trade unionism they have to come to terms with its wider class character.[93]

But if trade unions and trade unionists have to come to terms with the labour movement then this may be a sufficient reason for having to distinguish, once again, white collar unions from the others, simply because so many clerks are conservative and, if anything, hostile to the labour movement. If identification with the labour movement is to become a matter of definition of trade unions, then many white collar unions must be something else.

We should hasten to add that a personnel manager, confronted with a hostile white collar union, may be forgiven for not noticing the difference.

Operationally, white collar unions are capable of considerable militancy. In fact, it has been suggested that the very concern of traditional unions for the wider social and political interests implied by association with the labour movement may prevent them from pursuing the narrow, sectional interests of their members with quite the same energy as can be shown by a white collar union. White collar unions, because they are confined more exclusively to a bargaining role, can pursue it more energetically. The whole discussion becomes more confused when we are told that the traditional trade unions, against whose zeal for the labour movement white collar unions were unfavourably compared, are themselves losing their more idealistic associations. It was Lockwood who pronounced that white collar workers must realize that trade unions are part of a working class movement. It was Lockwood who later came to say that, for the majority of 'affluent workers':

> neither as a way to greater worker participation in the affairs of the enterprise nor as a political force is unionism greatly valued. Rather, one could say, the significance which unionism has for these workers is very largely confined to issues arising in their employment which are *economic* in nature and which are *local* in their origins and scope . . . the unionism of the workers we studied is distinctive in its instrumental and 'self-interested' emphasis.[94]

The affluent workers are apparently creating a 'new type of unionism consistent with the wants and expectations which they bring to their work'. Their outlook is likely to result in both militant collective action and a decline in the traditional 'commitment to trade unionism, understood as a social movement or as an expression of class or occupational solidarity'.[95] This may suggest that some sort of convergence is taking place between the essentially economic, new, white collar unions which never have been concerned with social goals and the older manual unions who are becoming less attached to their ideological foundations.

This would be a dangerous over-simplification. Unions are not only differentiated vertically by type and by organization, they are stratified horizontally. The responses, noted by Goldthorpe, Lockwood *et al* were responses in work to a work situation, very much a product of the relationship between the job and the attitude which the worker brings to it. The flexibility of union structure in the workplace, the effectiveness of shop steward representation and the irrelevance of union organization above the work-place have all been noted before. Shop-floor organization has come to be seen as so important, and often so efficient, that there is a current tendancy to regard it as having replaced the formal structures of trade unionism in relevance and importance. It has also, however, been described as showing an essentially economic concern for the interests of workers. If trade unions are concerned with both economic and social objectives it is the economic which are emphasized at the place of work. But few would deny that the wider social concerns of trade unionism are important; they are the concern of the national organizations and of the Trades Union Congress. It may be that this separation of functions has great utility because it enables trade unions to avoid, without too great a display of hypocricy, a contradiction between wider social objectives (like concern for the low paid or for women) and the immediate economic interests of the members.

The separation of functions certainly seems to involve some critics of trade unions in quite extraordinary paradoxes. When trade unions became big institutions, says Lane, they began to exhibit sectionalism, 'a word designed to express the failure of the unions to control and direct the source of their inspiration. The failure was endemic and ineradicable.'[96] 'Sectionalism was at the root of many a conflict between trade union leaders and was the characteristic basis of rank and file rebellions . . . as soon as unions started to operate on a national scale sectionalism became a major problem.'[97] Now Lane sees the problem largely in terms of keeping 'a close eye on the secretary', of controlling the bureaucracy and here, rank and file action and shop steward vigilance are essential qualities. But at times Lane seems to acknowledge that it is the rank and file and the shop steward who *contribute* sectionalism to the trade union movement while it is the central union leadership which fails to convert this fragmented energy into a unified political movement. The paradox is that it is the union bureaucracies which are most concerned with political activities (albeit of a character which Lane dislikes) while the heroes of the shop floor usually have other fish to fry (however divided or competitive their interest in the catch). The fact is that the tensions between bureaucratic leadership and rank and file opinion may not coincide with divisions between appeasement and militancy or economic interest and political concern. Unions are not simply bargaining organizations but they are often more concerned with bargaining at the periphery and less so at the centre. This distinction may help to explain the often misleading impression that they are more militant at the periphery and more conservative at the centre. The impression can lead to grave misunderstanding. We have seen that white collar unions are capable of great militancy in the bargaining relationship but their political objectives are hardly revolutionary. Lockwood *et al* demonstrate that manual unions, too, can combine economic activism and political quietism. It may even have occurred to Lane, in a nightmare insight which led to the pessimism of his conclusion, that the perpetual and noble struggle of the rank and file to control its leaders has made them more conservative than they would have been had they been able to persist in bureaucratic and political isolation from the sectional interests of their members.

We should take one more example to illustrate the complexity of attitudes and organizations present among trade unions. In many fields of study, the clearest expression of form is observed in a structure which is evolving rather than in one which has achieved its final form. Similarly, associations which are developing towards trade unionism can reveal interesting characteristics more readily than more mature institutions.

Some managerial and professional groups are interesting

for this reason. In the first place, managerial associations like the British Association of Colliery Managers, the Steel Industry Management Association, the United Kingdom Association of Professional Engineers, suggest the absurdity of concluding that the 'white-collar' use of trade union methods of defence proves that white collar workers have at last made common cause with the proletariat. This is particularly unlikely in the case of managers and professionals who may see themselves as using union methods of defence against attacks on their relative living standards, which are launched by the unions themselves. In this case the imitation of methods cannot suggest fraternal association so much as rivalry.

The willingness to engage in militant action has often been an obstacle for the professionals but it is an obstacle that has often been overcome. Dickens' study of UKAPE is a fascinating account of a professional association baulking at the obstacle.[98] 'Militant action is not part of UKAPE's professional image.' Dickens points out that the refusal to engage in strike action 'may be the result of a realistic appraisal of the situation rather than the restraining influence of the code of ethics to which its members subscribe' but she adds that, in other countries, professionals have been ready to take strike action and that, 'to be effective, UKAPE will have to modify its professional image and become in effect a craft union for professional engineers'.

Her discussion suggests that purely professional control of entry, standards and fees payable by clients may be a perfectly appropriate response in a given 'market' situation. Professionalism may still be appropriate for lawyers but when the members of a profession find themselves employed by the State or by very large organizations, when the individual's competence and relationship with his client is no longer rewarded, when his job is graded and his skills are collectively remunerated, purely professional control becomes irrelevant. In these circumstances, pressures are applied to turn a professional association into something more like a craft union:

> mounting demands for more militant action have forced professional bodies to set up complementary bargaining organizations, some of which have been registered as trade unions under the Industrial Relations Act (1971). In adopting a collective bargaining strategy they have followed a precedent set up in the first established profession to be submitted to the process of bureaucratization, the BMA.[99]

This is a situation in which an established professional body responds to a change in market and employment conditions by turning itself into a union or by learning to co-exist with a parallel union body. There is an alternative situation in which an ill-co-ordinated, ill-defined group of employees, often commanding newly developed and scarce technical skills, first forms a professional association partly in order to announce its identity as a group. Professor Loveridge suggests that new expertise is increasingly acquired within large corporations and through bureaucratic channels. 'If levels of technical complexity and occupational identity are high, then a high level of professional or craft control is to be expected', the unavoidable exchange of information between groups sharing the same work-based problems in other organizations sets off a demand that 'employers recognize and pay salaries that relate to a professional qualification'. In this way 'the desire for professional membership can be a symptom of a growing separation and conflict between management and the professionally aspiring group.'

What we see here is two processes of unionization which can be observed, in the Health Service, for example, going on at the same time. The first is the erosion of established professional organizations like the British Medical Association, or their conversion by a managerial environment into a union organization (this is an over-simplification of a complex process but it will have to do for the moment). This involves the dismantling of a professional structure and the construction of a union which can engage in collective bargaining. The second process appears to be running in the opposite direction. An unorganized group of employees processing some new skill begins by attempting to establish a professional organization. Hence we have the paradox of new groups, like hospital radiographers, hastily assembling a framework of professionalism which is being as hastily destroyed by its original designers. The new groups, on the face of it, seems to be imitating methods of defence which they perceive to have been effective for the established professions; they are simply imitating their betters (in the status hierarchy, that is). This simple explanation rests upon a fallacy because, while the established professions are adapting to a changed environment, their imitators are engaging in an out-moded response.

A more realistic explanation might suggest that the two processes of professionalization and de-professionalization are not necessarily opposed to each other. The attempt to establish a professional association by the new groups of employees is in the first place unreal. The newer professional groups are pseudo-professional associations in that they fail to achieve the distinguishing characteristics which have been noted of the established professions. The attempt at pseudo-professionalization may simply be an attempt to form a power-base independent of the employer's control, at the very least intended to maintain and publicize the distinctive identity of the new group and at most to set up an alternative source of control and of power. This explanation would see the new-professional associations not as contradictions to developments which have overtaken the established professions but as embryonic trade union organizations and as occupying an intermediary stage in a development which it has taken the established professions much longer to achieve. Their tardiness must not be put down to incompetence, false-consciousness or an unrealistic view of the world. Professional association has proved to be a most powerful form of defence; it has simply been superseded by the vast extension of bureaucratic control to which professional people have been subjected. An association like UKAPE, perhaps, occupies the middle ground. If Dickens' analysis is correct, new professional associations like it will either disappear or become trade unions.

What we have had to say about trade unions suggests their bewildering complexity. In terms of their internal structure and constitutions, the tensions between representatives and members, the differences between various occupational groups and the marked contrast in character between craft, manual, white-collar and professional organizations, the most tempting conclusion is that there is no such thing as a trade union. That summary of our discussion is useful as a reminder of the many differences which exist, but it is untrue. Trade unions have much in common although they may not share each characteristic to the same extent. Those that have the most in common justify the reality of the phrase 'the trade union movement'; others which in some respects seem to be trade unions seem also to be only marginally attached to the movement, or even to be outside it.

Dr Blackburn attempts to measure these variations by assessing the character or 'unionateness' of trade unions.[100] An organization, he says, is 'more or less *unionate* according to the extent to which it is a whole-hearted trade union, identifying with the labour movement and willing to use all the powers of the movement'.[101] He proposes seven key characteristics: an emphasis on collective bargaining, independence from employers, militancy, declaration as a union, registration, affiliation to the TUC and affiliation to the Labour Party. The danger of this approach is that it is both inflexible and unreal. It is inflexible because after the Act of 1971 and before 1974 Dr Blackburn would presumably say that *de*-registration was an essential characteristic of a true union. It is unreal because it makes accidental characteristics a matter of definition; within these terms many white-collar trade unions cannot be true trade unions because they are not associated with the labour movement or the Labour Party. A Conservative or a Communist union becomes, by definition, a contradiction in terms. The definition means that organizations which are unions cannot be acknowledged to be unions.

No doubt in order to avoid these difficulties the TUC contents itself with the Webbs' broad definition of a 'continuous association of wage-earners for the purpose of maintaining or improving the conditions of their working lives'[102] and quickly moves on to a more practical discussion of the objectives of trade unions. It lists 10 objectives:

1 improved terms of employment
2 improved physical environment at work
3 full employment and national prosperity
4 security of employment and income
5 improved social security
6 fair shares in national income and wealth
7 industrial democracy
8 a voice in government
9 improved public and social services
10 public control and planning of industry.[103]

These objectives seem to form themselves into three broad groups: economic objectives, social or political objectives and representative objectives—those concerned with challenging the authority and control of the employer over the employee. These are very different concerns and the TUC went on to describe the appropriate and different means by which they were pursued. Economic objectives have been associated with collective bargaining which has been more frequently conducted at company, plant or shop-floor level in recent years. This tendency has detracted from the importance of national union structures and has emphasized the independent and sometimes rivalrous activities of shop stewards. But the representative and, most certainly the social and political objectives of trade unions, cannot adequately be pursued by isolated shop floor representatives. It is in the areas of pressure group activity, Parliamentary representation, education and international affairs that it makes sense to talk of a trade union movement. Flanders stressed the diversity of trade unionism in another way when he said that, although their constant purpose was participation in job regulation, they were:

> a mixture of movement and organization . . . Movement, in the words of G D H Cole, implies a common end or at least a community of purpose which is real and influences men's thoughts and actions, even if it is imperfectly apprehended and largely unconscious. The members of a movement combine because sharing in some measure the same sentiments and ideas they want to achieve the same things. The bonds of organization are different. An organization must have effective means for ensuring that its members comply with its decisions. These means are its sanctions; the rewards it can offer and the penalties it can impose to uphold its internal discipline.[104]

Trade unions have much in common and it does make sense to talk of a trade union movement. But the manager in industrial relations will do well to recognize the diversity of structure and outlook with which he may be faced. They are different in size, density and in ideology. The number of trade unions affiliated to the TUC has fallen from 232 in

1942 to 109 in 1974 while the number of members has risen from 5½ to over 10 millions. There is still considerable variation in the size of trade unions and in the number of trade unions established or competing in particular industrial sectors.

Some idea of the spread of trade unions is conveyed by the distribution of unions within each of the TUC's 18 sectors or trade groups. The number of unions, the total membership and the membership of the biggest single union in each sector is given in table 1 opposite (the figures are taken from the *Report of 107th Annual Trades Union Congress*, 1975 and are for the year 1974):

The dismay often expressed about the bewildering number of British trade unions is more properly confined to particular sectors. In five of the TUC's groups representing a total membership of 5,350,529 (well over half the total) one big union represents 60 per cent of the membership in railways, 90 per cent in mining, in transport and in engineering, and 100 per cent in electricity, in agriculture and in the general sector. The greatest complexity arises in textiles (the smallest group apart from agriculture), and in the civil service and post office. There are 17 unions in the former and 11 in the latter. Some of the textile unions are very small and their number is diminishing. The number of unions in the civil service suggest that similarity of employment, a common employer and a reputation for intelligence are not enough to provide a drive to single unionism. Amalgamation and the reduction in the number of trade unions has probably proceeded faster in the older manual and craft union sectors than elsewhere.

The TUC's categories are to some extent artificial, a matter of administrative convenience rather than real distinction. The situation is not so tidy in the place of work where one steel plant may recognize and bargain with 10 unions, a motor manufacturer with 20. It is these situations

Table 1

Group	No of unions	Total membership	Biggest union	Membership of biggest union
1 Mining & quarrying	2	276,636	NUM	255,296
2 Railways	3	272,762	NUR	172,558
3 Transport	6	1,966,303	TGWU	1,857,308
4 Shipbuilding	1	129,598	ASBSBSW	129,598
5 Engineering, founding & vehicle building	10	1,449,511	AUEW (including Construction & Founding sections)	1,300,477
6 Technical, engineering & scientific	5	523,242	ASTMS	351,000
7 Electricity	1	414,189	EET & PU	414,189
8 Iron & steel	10	1,444,730	ISTC	106,048
9 Building, woodworking & furnishing	5	346,830	UCATT	257,796
10 Printing & paper	6	306,582	SOGAT	193,804
11 Textiles	17	130,092	NUDBTW	55,324
12 Clothing, leather, boot & shoe	6	262,553	NUTGW	116,121
13 Glass, ceramics, food, drink, tobacco & distribution	9	495,506	USDAW	352,610
14 Agriculture	1	90,000	NUA & AW	90,000
15 Public employees	9	1,615,452	NALGO	541,918
16 Civil service	10	785,696	CPSA	215,144
17 Professional, clerical & entertainment	9	270,489	APECCS	137,716
18 General	1	883,810	NUGMW	883,810

of multi-unionism and union overlapping which are often the cause of concern. It has prompted some commentators, some as expert as Will Paynter,[105] to stress the advantages of industrial unionism. Most seem, however, to be impressed more by the problems than the advantages of progress towards industrial unionism. The first is that it is difficult to define an industry. Trade unions have histories, loyalties and mythologies, they are not simple economic constructions. Their members may share a quite rational view that their union provides them with special and precise representation which no bigger or more general union could replace. The officers and staff of unions may have an understandable reluctance to see the administrative advantages of amalgamation demonstrated in their own redundancy. Finally, when all other explanations have been exhausted there is the abiding influence of practical inertia.

There has been a tendency in recent years to play down the problems of multi-unionism, partly because of a realization, as Hughes pointed out, that amalgamation does not in itself cure union overlapping in the plant, that in some circumstances it can make it worse. There has also been a more practical tendency to look to arrangements which managers can influence rather than to wait for a distant solution when union structure will somehow become simplified. These practical arrangements include the kind of inter-union joint negotiation structure represented in the staff side of the Whitley Councils. Outside the public sector, joint industrial councils have provided an effective framework within which unions can cooperate for bargaining purposes. The process of co-ordination was extended in productivity bargaining and we have seen that shop steward organization has shown great flexibility in crossing the barriers of union boundaries.

CHAPTER 5

Constraints upon management: the State

Until recently it seemed that the great superiority of British industrial relations was that the British, unlike lesser breeds, were without the law. This was believed to be an advantage. Freedom from legal regulation meant that the parties, employers and unions, were able to regulate their affairs to their mutual advantage and only to the extent that they believed to be desirable. The excessive intervention of the law was believed to have great disadvantages. It was thought that it conceded control to outsiders who did not or even, because of their professional conditioning, *could* not understand the subtleties and realities of the industrial environment. The law, it was said, allowed the crude regulation by statute or court interpretation of an employment relationship which should be cooperative rather than combative, which required voluntary effort rather than minimal performance of obligations in return for carefully measured rights. The view rested upon a belief that the coercive force of the law could not be sufficient to control the immensely powerful organizations representing different interests in continuous conflict.

In the context of British industrial relations, managers were taught not to look to the law and unions' representatives were encouraged to believe that legal regulation and protection was an acknowledgement of union weakness, a confession of failure and a second best to the sturdy independence of collective bargaining. The 'attitude of abstention was the outstanding virtue of British law. It allowed the two sides of industry, by their own creative action, to develop an impressive body of rules and sanctions which safeguarded an equilibrium of power and thus a reasonably well functioning system of industrial relations.'[106] Legal regulation was not as effective as collective bargaining and was tolerated only to the extent that it enabled collective bargaining to be properly conducted; 'the first task in the reform of British industrial relations is to bring order into collective bargaining in the company and plant, the second is to extend the coverage of collective bargaining and the organization of workers on which it depends.'[107]

To the extent that these statements are an expression of the belief in the voluntary system of British industrial relations they reveal that it was always an exaggerated view. British industrial relations never did without the law. Collective bargaining was never a sufficiently extensive method of determining conditions of employment to obviate the legal protection of minimum standards. Collective bargaining, apart from protecting insufficient numbers of employees, protected an insufficient range of conditions of employment. Even when they were members of powerful trade unions, workmen were glad of the protection of the law in terms of health and safety. At the height of voluntarism, women and juveniles in employment may have had more reason for gratitude for citizenship than for union membership.[108] The State has not only protected the rights of workers, it has limited the power of employers and it has frequently intervened in the relationship between employers and trade unions. National emergencies, both in war and in peace, have excused the legal restriction of the right to strike. Until

1971, when they were freed by the Industrial Relations Act, workers in gas, water and electricity undertakings were prevented by law from engaging in industrial disputes which would predictably interrupt the supply or service in the provision of which they were engaged. Section 5 of the Conspiracy and Protection of Property Act 1875 made a worker who broke his contract so as to threaten life or injure property criminally liable.

The most controversial aspect of the Industrial Relations Act 1971 was that it supposedly marked the end of voluntarism in this country. It certainly enlarged the role of the State and diminished the freedom of action of unions and employers (or it sought to) but it is worth a passing comment that its intended effects were to be brought about in defence of 'the principle of collective bargaining freely conducted on behalf of workers and employers'.[109] The principle of free collective bargaining was to be defended by major innovations. They included the illegality of the pre-entry closed shop, the presumption of the legal enforceability of collective agreements which did not contain specific disclaimers, the imposition of compulsory ballots and waiting periods in certain industrial disputes, the provision for the establishment of agency shop agreements and of sole bargaining agencies, the enforcement of a procedure upon unwilling parties 'as a legally enforceable contract, as if a contract consisting of those provisions had been made between those parties'[110] and the reinforcement of trade union registration and the introduction of penalties and disadvantages for unregistered unions. The Act also introduced, and was generally welcomed for introducing, the concept of unfair dismissal and the legal protection of the individual against unfair dismissal by his employer.

It was the common belief that a voluntary system of industrial relations had existed, that it was destroyed by the Industrial Relations Act of 1971 and that it was restored by the Trade Union and Labour Relations Act 1974, and by the Employment Protection Act 1975. That this view is too simple is suggested by a characteristic that we have noticed; change in British industrial relations, whatever its intention, is likely to be presented as a defence of free collective bargaining. The voluntary nature of industrial relations is now in danger of becoming a myth, commanding the greatest respect as its real manifestations become more rare.

Law is likely to construct an environment which constrains the behaviour of the parties with differing degrees of severity.

Much that is sensible in the defence of voluntarism rests upon the belief that it is dangerous for the law to attempt to constrain the behaviour of large and powerful groups unless the law can rely upon social approval for the recruitment of sufficient force to overcome the groups' resistance. For this reason alone, this kind of law is best left out of industrial relations; its intervention is likely to convert industrial disputes (which the collective bargaining machinery has been designed to contain) into political conflicts over the scope and nature of law. For this reason, many of the critics of the 1971 Act were more concerned with its effect on law than on industrial relations. Coercive legislation is always present and it is always necessary but it may require to be justified by the importance of the issues with which it is concerned and by a general agreement throughout society that the issues are sufficiently serious to warrant legislation of this kind. Coercive legislation 'might be reserved to prevent or mitigate circumstances which are a threat to human safety . . . freedom or dignity. There will rarely be consensus about the means to be adopted but perhaps a fair test for the necessity of such legislation is that there should be consensus about the existence of circumstances which need to be corrected.'[111]

The most considerable change in legislation in British

industrial relations has been in the very considerable increase in protective legislation. We shall see that the Employment Protection Act 1975 also extends the influential range by way of making adjustments in the environment which are certain to influence the behaviour of the parties.

Professor Kahn-Freund distinguishes between the intentions rather than the means of legislation in employment:

Regulatory legislation, he says, is 'legislation directly laying down rules of employment' and he points out that, until recently, 'the policy of the law has always been not to regulate the employment relation by statute where this could effectively be done through collective bargaining.'[112]

Auxiliary legislation which seeks to regulate the making of rules of employment by the parties and the ways in which they are enforced, 'those branches of labour law which are designed to promote collective bargaining as well as the making and observance of collective agreements.'[113]

It would seem to be most helpful to examine the principal legal constraints and influences on the behaviour of the parties under these two headings.

Regulatory legislation

(a) *Hours of work*

The first important acts designed to protect individuals from the power of employers or from their own careless or over-zealous application to their work were introduced in the nineteenth century. The first act limiting the hours of work of apprentices was introduced in 1802 and, after years of agitation and argument, the 10 hours act was introduced in 1848. Professor Wedderburn suggests that 'the most important innovation in British labour legislation'[114] was the appointment of four inspectors under an Act of 1833 to limit employment of juveniles in the textile industry. Legislative limitation of hours of work has been confined to women and young persons and 'the exceptional areas in which the hours of employment for all workers including adult men receive statutory control today reflect, in the main, occupations where overwork brings special dangers to the men, the public, or both.'[115] Elsewhere, adult males' hours of work have been deemed to be suitable for the joint control of collective bargaining although the result has more often been the adjustment of earnings rather than the limitation of hours.

(b) *Wages*

Since the nineteenth century controls have been imposed on the method of wages payment and, since 1909, on the minimum amount of wages to be paid to particular groups of employees. The Truck Acts required that workers be paid in coin and the Payment of Wages Act 1960 recognized the legality of payment by cheque. Payments in kind are prohibited and deductions from wages at source require the authorization of the employee before they can be made by the employer. Concern about conditions in the sweated trades led to the first Trade Boards Act in 1909. Subsequently, wages councils were established by orders made under the Wages Councils Acts in a variety of trades and occupations where there was little or no prospect of employers and workers organizations establishing effective collective bargaining relationships. Wages Councils, where they were established, were meant to imitate the results of collective bargaining and they were intended to encourage the development of the real thing. The structure of the Councils themselves was intended to be representative of workers' and employers' interests, presided over by a neutral chairman. The deliberation of the Councils led to recommenations which, if approved by the Secretary of State, established minimum wages for the industry or trade by statutory order. The Donovan Commission reported that there were 57 Councils covering some 3½ million employees. Although they succeeded in providing minimal standards for many employees who would not be covered by collective bargaining, they disappointed expectations that they would encourage the extension of collective bargaining. As a result the CIR recommended the abolition or the amalgamation of many Wages Councils. The Employment Protection Act 1975 extended the power of Wages Councils to fix other terms and conditions of employment as well as pay and holidays. The Act gave the Secretary of State powers to convert a Wages Council into a Statutory Joint Industrial Council; in these cases the new SJICs would have no independent members.

The Equal Pay Act 1970 set out to secure 'that employers give equal treatment as regards terms and conditions of employment to men and to women' and came into full effect at the end of December 1975. Claims of failure to comply with the Act are heard before industrial tribunals.

The Employment Protection Act entitles employees to guaranteed payments (normal daily earnings up to a maximum of £6 per day and for a maximum of five days in a quarter) if they are not provided with work on a normal working day other than as a result of a trade dispute involving other employees.

(c) *Terms of employment*

The Contracts of Employment Act 1972 required employers to give employees written particulars of terms of the contract on pay, hours, holidays, periods of notice, pensions and sick pay. Employers may avoid giving a complete statement of all the terms under these headings by giving to each employee a statement telling them where, in a readily accessible place, a description of these terms can be seen. The Act also required that minimum periods of notice should be given, rising in proportion to length of service. As a result of an amendment introduced in the Employment Protection Act of 1975, the minimum periods of notice are now not less than one week for each year of continuous employment for those with two or more years of continuous employment but less than 12 years, and not less than 12 weeks notice for those with 12 or more years continuous employment.

The Employment Protection Act (Section 81) gives employees the right to be given itemized pay statements by their employers which show the gross wage or salary, the amounts of variable and fixed deductions and the purposes for which they are made, the net amount of wages or salary and, where different parts of the net amount are paid in different ways, the amount and method of each part-payment.

The same Act also replaces Section 8 of the Terms and Conditions of Employment Act 1959. Under the new arrangements a claim can be made to the Advisory, Conciliation and Arbitration Service that an employer's terms and conditions of service are less favourable than the recognized terms and conditions of the industry or, if there are no recognized terms, that the general level of terms and conditions in comparable employment are better than those observed by the employer. If there is no settlement of the claim it is referred to the Central Arbitration Committee, which may make an award of terms and conditions which the employer is required to observe.

(d) *Dismissal*

Until the Industrial Relations Act 1971 the only legal defence of the employee against dismissal was a civil action for breach of contract and, for the most part, a successful case depended upon inadequate notice. The employer could summarily dismiss the employee for serious misconduct, that is, for some deficiency by which the employee had himself broken the contract of employment. Apart from misconduct, which may be a matter for the courts to decide, 'each party can normally end the contract, where no ground exists for summary dismissal, only by giving notice to terminate it'.[116] This continues to be so: the employer can still summarily dismiss an employee for serious misconduct and he can still terminate an employee's contract by giving him due notice. Since 1971, there are certain defined circumstances in which he cannot 'fairly' dismiss him. The Industrial Relations Act introduced these circumstances under the description of unfair dismissal and it laid down that an employee dismissed unfairly had recourse to an Industrial Tribunal which, if it found his case sound under the Act, could award him compensation for the loss of his job.

The Employment Protection Act and the Trade Union and Labour Relations Acts 1974 and 1976 have broadly speaking retained the same safeguards for the employee and have extended them. Section 70 says that a dismissed employee is entitled to be given, on request, a written statement giving reasons for the dismissal.

The Trade Union and Labour Relations Act, 1974 (Schedule 1) re-enacts sections of the Industrial Relations Act which gave the employee the right not to be unfairly dismissed by the employer and which provided the right of complaint to industrial tribunal. It maintains that it is for the employer to show what was the reason for dismissal and that it was a reason which:

(a) related to the capability or qualifications of the employee for performing work of the kind which he was employed by the employer to do, or
(b) related to the conduct of the employee, or
(c) was that the employee was redundant, or
(d) was that the employee could not continue to work in the position which he held without contravention (either on his part or on that of his employer) of a duty

or restriction imposed by or under an enactment,[117] or that there was some other substantial reason to justify the dismissal of an employee holding the position which he did. The Act says that it is unfair to dismiss an employee for joining or taking part in the activities of an independent trade union or for refusing to join a trade union which was not independent. (In the Industrial Relations Act this provision was for joining a registered rather than an independent union, and the Act also gave an employee the right *not* to be a member of a trade union, registered or otherwise). The Trade Union and Labour Relations Act specifically states that the dismissal of an employee shall be regarded as fair if there is a union membership agreement which makes it the practice for all employees, or for all employees of that kind, to belong to a specified and independent trade union or to one of a number of specified independent trade unions, and if the reason for the employee's dismissal was that he was not a member or that he refused to join. The only qualification which the Act accepts on fair dismissal of an employee who refuses to join a closed shop is where an 'employee genuinely objects on grounds of religious belief to being a member of any trade union whatever'. The alternative provision which added 'or on any reasonable grounds to being a member of a particular trade union' was removed by the Trade Union and Labour Relations Act 1976. The paradoxical result, as some sceptics might see it, is that dismissal for refusing to join a union is allowed, except for the least rational of reasons.

The Act says that dismissal is unfair as a result of redundancy if the employee has been improperly selected for dismissal or was selected for dismissal in contravention of a customary arrangement or agreed procedure. Dismissal in a strike or lock-out is not to be regarded as unfair if the person dismissed is offered re-engagement on the resumption of work. Dismissal of an employee who is taking part in a strike is not unfair unless it is shown that others taking part were not dismissed for taking part in it.

The remedies for unfair dismissal, which must be decided by an Industrial Tribunal, are set out in the Employment Protection Act. If a dismissal is found to be unfair, the Tribunal must first look at the practicability of reinstatement or re-engagement. If it is practicable and is what the complainant wants, the Tribunal may order the terms of reinstatement or re-engagement. If the order is not complied with, the Tribunal may award additional further compensation. Awards of compensation are composed of a basic award and a compensatory award, the former related to period of service and the latter to compensation for loss sustained as the result of dismissal.

The Employment Protection Act makes the dismissal of a woman employee because of pregnancy unfair. Women are entitled to maternity pay for the first six weeks of absence if this begins after the eleventh week before the baby is due. Women who have worked for the employer for at least two years are entitled to return to work, to the same or a similar job, for up to 29 weeks after the birth of the baby. Complaints about the non-payment of maternity pay or about a refusal to re-engage are heard before an Industrial Tribunal.

(e) *Suspension*

Employees suspended on medical grounds in consequence of any legal requirement or any regulation under the Health and Safety at Work Act 1974 are entitled to be paid for a period not exceeding 26 weeks.

(f) *Redundancy*

The Redundancy Payments Act 1965 helped to provide 'the first faint beginnings of a law of job security'.[118]

The Employment Protection Act requires employers who propose to dismiss an employee as the result of redundancy to consult with recognized trade unions. Consultation is to begin at the earliest opportunity and at least 90 days before the first dismissal where the employer is proposing to make redundant 100 or more employees or at least 10 days where 10 or more employees are to be dismissed. The Act specifies what it means by consultation (possibly the first time this has been done in law): disclosure in writing to the unions of the reasons for the proposal, the number and description of employees to be dismissed, the total number employed at the establishment, the proposed method of selection. Consultation means that the employer shall consider any representations made by the union, shall reply to them and, if any of these representations are to be rejected, shall give the reasons for rejection. An appropriate trade union may complain (if it believes the requirements for notice and consultation have not been met) to an Industrial Tribunal and if the complaint is well-founded, the Tribunal may make a declaration and a protective award. The award will instruct the employer to pay remuneration for a protected period. The Act also requires employers to give notice of redundancies to the Secretary of State. The sections of the Act dealing with redundancy were implemented on 8 March 1976.

(g) *Safety and health*

Acts for the protection of employees against industrial injury have been passed since the first half of the nineteenth century. The protection of the employee against hazards in his working environment is probably the aspect of employment in which law has consistently been regarded as a better defence than collective association. A succession of factories acts and mines and quarries acts were added to by the Shops Act 1950 and the Offices, Shops and Railway Premises Act, 1963 and were intended to prevent accidents and protect against hazards in the environment. Most of the existing legislation was superseded by the Health and Safety at Work Act 1974, which covers all people at work except domestic workers in private employment. It imposes obligations on employers, the self-employed, employees and on the manufacturers and suppliers of machinery and substances to be used in work. Employers are required to ensure, as far as is reasonably practicable, the health, safety and welfare of their employees at work, and employees are required to take reasonable care for the health and safety of themselves and of other people who may be affected. The Act set up a Health and Safety Commission which is to be advised by expert committees on conditions in particular industries. A Health and Safety Executive is responsible for carrying into effect the directions of the Commission and the Executive is responsible for the enforcement of provisions, the appointment of inspectors and the conduct of research.

(h) *Rights against discrimination*

The Race Relations Act 1968 makes it illegal to discriminate against employees on the ground of race. A new Race Relations Bill, introduced in the Commons in February 1976, proposes to extend protection against racial discrimination. The Sex Discrimination Act 1975 makes sex discrimination in employment unlawful. The Act extends the effect of the Equal Pay Act 1970 by dealing with non-contractual aspects of employment. It distinguishes between two kinds of discrimination, direct discrimination involving an intention to treat a person less favourably on the ground of sex and indirect discrimination which involves practices discriminating in their effect, whether intentionally or not. The Act makes it unlawful to discriminate in the recruitment, promotion, training, transfer or dismissal of employees. An Equal Opportunities Commission is established to help to eliminate discrimination, to promote equal opportunities, to investigate unlawful practices and to enforce in cases of general contraventions (such as advertising). The complaints of individuals in the area of employment will be heard by Industrial Tribunals.

Auxiliary legislation

This is legislation which is designed to influence the way in which the parties make the rules of employment and the manner in which they are enforced. It is the increase of law of this description, apart from the increase in the scale of regulatory legislation, which makes the most significant recent change in the character of British industrial relations.

The Industrial Relations Act was a departure from the principle by which the law, although related to collective bargaining, maintained a discreet distance from it or kept itself at arm's length. It introduced, in effect, a measure of approval for some kinds of trade unions, those which were registered and of disapproval for others, those which were not. It introduced an element which, if not unprecedented, was a fairly original departure from the principle that only the parties to a contract could determine the terms which it contained and which bound them. The Trade Union and Labour Relations Act and the Employment Protection Act repealed much that was controversial in the Act of 1971, and all of it that was not acceptable to the trade unions. They did not entirely remove the law to the position of distant respect which it had previously held.

Part 1 of the Employment Protection Act is concerned with machinery for promoting the improvement of industrial relations. It establishes the Advisory, Conciliation and Arbitration Service on a statutory basis in which it continues to offer the services of conciliation and of independent arbitration and is charged with the responsibility for giving advice to employers and unions, inquiring into industrial relations questions and issuing codes of practice on general and on specific industrial relations matters.

(a) *Certification of unions*

The functions which used to be discharged by the Chief Registrar of Friendly Societies are taken over by the Certification Officer who maintains a list of trade unions and employers' associations. In addition, the Certification Officer makes enquiries following an application by a trade union for a certificate of independence and, if he is satisfied, he will issue a certificate. He may withdraw it if he believes that a union is no longer independent. 'Independence' to a large extent takes the place of 'registration' in the 1971 Act in that the advantages conferred on unions in terms of recognition and enforceable membership, and on employees in terms of protection against victimization, are confined to independent or certificated trade unions. Applications from unions whose names are not entered on the list of trade unions maintained under Section 8 of the 1974 Act are to be refused certificates of independence. Section 8 of the Act states that the Registrar (as he was then described) shall enter into the list those unions which were registered under the Trade Union Acts 1871 to 1964 (before the Industrial Relations Act) or have since been amalgamated or were affiliated to the TUC immediately before the 1974 Act.

Up to 10 August 1976, certificates of independence had been issued to 155 trade unions, of which 113 were affiliated to the TUC or were constituents of affiliated trade unions.[119] Applications from 55 trade unions (six of them affiliated to the TUC) were under consideration. The Certification Officer was reported as having referred to a number of tests of independence which included:

evidence of involvement by management in the union's affairs
evidence of undue reliance by the union on an employer
evidence of rules providing for the determination of union policy and of industrial action

evidence of procedure agreements and the light they throw on the union's status as an independent body
the union's involvement in genuine collective bargaining
the main sources of the union's income
whether members' subscriptions represented a real level of income
whether the union had full-time officials and the arrangements for their payment
whether the accounts suggested that the union might be receiving financial support from the employer.[120]

Having rejected registration, the trade unions find certification by an independent officer unsatisfactory. Addressing the TUC Conference on 6 September 1976, Clive Jenkins accused the Certification Officer of 'eccentricity, lack of sensitivity and inadequate competence'. Jenkins believed that only genuine or 'classic' trade unions should be given certificates and that 'non-independent or competitive organizations should be denied a negotiating role in fields where legitimate trade unionism is established.'[121] Successfully proposing a resolution to deny such organizations' survival, Jenkins implied that recognition and certification should be confined to TUC affiliated unions.

The unions' criticism of certification is made to appear to rest upon the advantages of orderliness in collective bargaining; the certification process, they say, ought to have regard to the consequences of recognition as well as to independence. The suspicion emerges that some trade unions mean more by 'independence' than common usage implies and that the law's recognition of trade unions should depend not only upon respect for their strength and importance but upon approval of their character. If it is true that the Employment Secretary 'was quite willing to do what was necessary to resolve the question sensibly',[122] certification of independence may come to require some of the characteristics of what Blackburn calls 'unionateness', affiliation to the TUC and association with the objectives of the Labour movement. This is a state of affairs taken in conjunction with the provisions for the establishment of closed shops which some employees, particularly white-collar and managerial, might find irksome. The desire on the part of the affiliated unions to fend off competition from staff associations (regardless of whether they meet the Certifying Officer's tests of independence from the employer or not) is rather ironic. What makes their competition more serious is the provision for the establishment of closed shops which the unions demanded. Now that such provision has been made, its relationship with certification could be used to keep out the very unions which expected to be its beneficiaries. The unions then turn against not the closed shop but certification, which admits rivals of whom they disapprove. In order to distinguish their enemies they have to attack their ideological purity, a quality rare among many British trade unions. But some might regard purity of character as a dangerous test; they might come to include trade unionists if times and the political climate were ever to change.[123]

The 1974 Act says that the purposes of a trade union shall not, because they are in restraint of trade, be unlawful so as to make any member liable to criminal proceedings for conspiracy or to make any agreement or trust void or voidable. The Amendment Act 1976 broadens protection to all forms of contract which has the practical effect of protecting secondary boycotts.

(b) *Picketing*

The Act provides the right to engage in peaceful picketing, at or near the place of work or anywhere else other than a person's home, 'for the purpose only of peacefully obtaining or communicating information, or peacefully persuading any person to work or abstain from working.'

(c) *Collective agreements*

The Act reverses the innovation of the Industrial Relations Act 1971 in presuming collective agreements to be legally enforceable; Section 18 says that any collective agreement shall be presumed not to have been intended by the parties to be a legally enforceable contract unless the agreement is in writing and states that it shall be a legally enforceable contract.

(d) *Recognition*

One of the most controversial aspects of recent legislation concerns the provisions for trade union recognition. Under Section 11 of the Employment Protection Act, an independent union can refer a recognition issue to the Advisory, Arbitration and Conciliation Service. The Service will then examine the issue, consult all the parties likely to be affected by it and set out its findings and recommendations including the extent and levels at which recognition is proposed. A recommendation for unconditional recognition shall become operative within 14 days of the employer receiving it from ACAS. After an interval of two months, a union may make a complaint to ACAS that the employer is not complying with a recognition recommendation. ACAS is first required to achieve a settlement by conciliation but, if this fails, the union may apply to the Central Arbitration Committee. If the CAC finds the complaint well-founded it shall specify the employees concerned in the recommendation and the matters in which the employer has failed to comply with it; the CAC may make an award that the employer shall observe terms and conditions specified in the claim by the union or other terms considered appropriate. Terms and conditions in an award requiring an employer to observe them 'shall have effect as part of the contract of employment'. Thus the innovation of the 1971 Act that terms can be treated as though they had been agreed by the parties is continued in the Act of 1975. There may even be something of a paradox in that terms not agreed but presumed to be part of a contract are regarded as legally enforceable in a way in which *agreed* terms cannot be regarded (under Section 18 of the Trade Union and Labour Relations Act of 1974).

In its passage through the House of Commons, the Trade Union and Labour Relations Act came to incorporate several changes concerning the provision of trade union rules. The most important of these provisions were that the rules were to state the purpose for which funds were to be applied or invested, to specify the regulations for elections and ballots, the offences under which the union is entitled to expel members, the penalties applicable to offences and the procedure for appeals against decisions. The Act said that the union's rules should set out procedures for settling disputes between members and the union and that they should be 'so framed as not to depart from, or permit any departures from, the rules of natural law'. The Act gave these provisions force by specifying that the Registrar of Friendly Societies (who became the Certification Officer in the Employment Protection Act) should maintain a list of unions and that a union's name should be removed from this list if 'its rules do not comply with the provisions of this Act'. The entire section of the Act concerning the union rules and the reference to removal from the Registrar's list was taken out of the Act by the Amendment Act of 1976. The Employment Protection Act, as we have seen, confers important benefits on trade unions deemed to be 'independent'. The provisions in the 1974 Act about rules meant that there was a powerful mechanism for controlling both the rules and the relationship between unions and their members. That control was abandoned in the Amendment Act of 1976 so that the benefits of 'independence' are achieved with no cost to the unions in terms of the public scrutiny of their rules.

The protection of the unions against the defence of the individual member's interest has been taken a step further. The 1974 Act gave union members the right not to be excluded or expelled from membership by way of arbitrary or unreasonable discrimination and it gave members who were aggrieved by exclusion the right of appeal to an Industrial Tribunal. These rights were removed by the 1976 Amendment Act. A union member continues to have access to the courts under common law to claim a right not to be expelled; but one of the important tests will be whether the expulsion was in accordance with the union rules and there is now no method of controlling the union rules. There is also no common law right which provides access to union membership. In return for the abandonment of the regulation of the law in an area in which hardship can be caused to individuals by powerful institutions, the TUC has undertaken to set up its own review procedure to hear complaints from workers about their exclusion or expulsion. The TUC's procedure will, of course, have no legal authority. One commentator has pointed out that:

> from an employer's point of view, the repeal of S5 of the 1975 Act does have important implications. If a union membership agreement is conceded, employees who are not admitted to unions or who are expelled from unions will have to be dismissed. This transfer of power to the union is the inevitable price of a closed shop but there may be a powerful case for including a provision in the union membership agreement to the effect that an employee will not be dismissed whilst he is pursuing the union's internal appeals machinery or has a claim before the TUC independent body and that if the TUC body rules in the employee's favour he will not be dismissed.[124]

For the moment perhaps this is the most that can be done, apart from informing all employees of their 'right' of access to the TUC procedure.

This brings us back to the question of the closed shop. We have seen that the Trade Union and Labour Relations Act says that the dismissal of an employee is fair if he is not a union member where a closed shop agreement exists. The practical circumstances are that, faced with a closed shop agreement, an employer is likely to be required to dismiss a non-member of the specified trade union[125] and is protected from legal constraint in dismissing him. It has been strongly argued that the Trade Union and Labour Relations Acts 1974 and 1976 do nothing other than restore the situation as it stood before the Industrial Relations Act 1971, as far as the closed shop is concerned, that 'the Bill (the 1976 Amendment) neither requires any employer to have a closed shop nor does it provide any statutory mechanism whatsoever for a union to secure a closed shop' that 'the only way in which a union can obtain a closed shop is through agreement by the employer and this is not in the slightest altered by the Bill.'[126]

There are, however, some differences between the situation as it existed before 1971 and as it exists now, both in terms of the law and of the industrial environment within which the law operates. Although the recognition of a trade union is not the same as an agreement conferring closed shop status upon it, recognition may be synonymous with a closed shop or it may lead to the subsequent establishment of a closed shop. The important change, made first by the Industrial Relations Act 1971, is that a process is introduced which can lead to union recognition whether the employer wishes to confer recognition or not. This process is now outlined in Sections 11 to 16 of the Employment Protection Act under which an independent union can refer a recognition issue to ACAS, can become the beneficiary of a favourable report recommending its recognition, can complain to ACAS if recognition is not afforded by the employer, can have its case pursued by 'conciliation' carried on by ACAS with the employer and, if still unsuccessful, can complain to the Central Arbitration Committee which may make an award of terms and conditions. These are powerful additions to the unions' case for recognition and they are bound to have the effect they were designed to achieve—of extending the number of unions recognized by employers. Before 1971, the principle means outside the public sector by which unions could achieve recognition was by the application of their own industrial power. Now there is a legally recognized process of appeal which will, in some circumstances, provide recognition when the union is supported by a lower level of power and commitment on the part of its members than would have been required to win it against employer opposition. Recognition, no doubt quite properly, is going to be easier to achieve. In these circumstances, and particularly in the highly competitive area of white-collar unionism where the great prizes of recognition remain to be won, once employers have conceded the principle of recognition, they are likely to prefer the order and simplicity of the closed shop. If employers see themselves threatened by a competitive scramble for recognition in circumstances where recognition cannot be resisted, they are likely to see the closed shop as offering protective advantages. For practical reasons, it is reasonable to assume that closed shop agreements will proliferate, particularly in white-collar areas.

It was this extension that led to the greatest argument over the 1974 Act. Unfortunately, the argument became entirely concerned with the issue of press freedom which, important enough in itself, served to obscure some equally serious industrial relations issues. Union recognition, when it was achieved by power, had often been resisted by management and was not likely to encompass managers in membership of the union. The growth of white-collar unionism, the hostility (now legally reinforced) to non-independent, professional or managerial unions which might once have challenged the extension of unionism to the managerial sector, and the strength of what might be called the new industrial white-collar unions (like NALGO), all promise or threaten to extend union membership to managerial levels. This means that there is at least a potential for the union to submit managers' decisions to the authority of the unions' own rules and policies. Concern about this in relationship to the control of the press finally achieved the insertion of a section on 'Charter on freedom of the press' in the 1976 Amendment. It seems likely that the same ingredients of extension of unionism to management, the greater probability of the establishment of closed shop agreements and the legitimacy of dismissal for non-union membership are likely to have just as worrying consequences in, for example, local government or the universities. It is to be hoped, if these problems develop, that the only solution to them will not be by way of a proliferation of charters for managerial freedom.

The extension of closed shops and the associated dismissal of employees who do not join or are prevented from joining or are expelled from trade unions may not be a matter, as it has so far been discussed here, of hypothetical development. The Trade Unions and Labour Relations Acts of 1974 and 1976 say that a membership agreement is one which requires employees of the description to which it relates to be members of the union party to the agreement or of another specified union, that is, a union which is specified in the agreement 'or is accepted by the parties to the agreement as being the equivalent of a union so specified'. But the Employment Protection Act (Schedule 16, Part III, section 12) adds to the 1974 Act that 'a union shall be treated as specified for the purposes of or in relation to a union membership agreement (in a case where it would not otherwise be so treated) if the ACAS has made a recommendation for recognition or if the union has referred a recognition issue to the ACAS.' Now this amendment would seem to have the effect of extending the effect of a closed shop beyond the circumstances in which a closed shop agreement has been made. If this interpretation is correct, the establishment of a closed shop may not depend entirely upon an agreement to do so.

(e) *Information*

The collective bargaining relationship is likely to be affected by the requirement that the employer should disclose information. The Industry Act, the Health and Safety at Work Act and the Employment Protection Act all require information to be made available but it is the last piece of legislation which specifically relates to collective bargaining. Section 17 says that it is the employer's duty to disclose, on request, all information in his possession about his undertaking if it is information without which the union would be impeded in carrying on collective bargaining, and if it is information which it would be good industrial relations practice to disclose for the purpose of collective bargaining. The more precise requirements of 'good industrial relations practice' were to be determined by a code of practice and a draft code was issued by ACAS in July 1976. The draft suggests that it is impossible to present a list of items of information which could be relevant to collective bargaining but it gives examples under the headings of pay, conditions of service, employment, productivity and financial matters. If the examples are to be followed it seems that the code will impose further demands upon the record keeping and analysis of many small and medium sized firms. The draft suggests that employers and unions should consider entering agreements for the disclosure of information and that both management and unions should formulate policies on disclosure. Management's policies should be 'as open and helpful as possible in meeting trade union requirements unless there are genuine considered reasons for refusal' and such reasons should be explained where they exist. Agreements should cover the information required and available, the form and manner of information disclosed, the regularity and frequency of disclosure, arrangements and criteria for judging confidentiality and procedures for clarifying information and for resolving disputes about disclosure.

There are some qualifications on the employer's legal duty to provide information. An employer need not disclose information which it would be against the interests of national security to disclose, or information given to him relating to an individual or given to him in confidence. The employer need not disclose information which would cause him substantial injury—as long as the injury was not brought about by collective bargaining. There are also qualifications on the duty to disclose concerned with the trouble and cost in discovering or presenting the information.

(f) *The control of incomes*

The direct intervention of the State in industrial relations has been pressed further since the end of the second world war by attempts to control incomes, sanctions by law and sanctions related to the control of prices. The first such attempt was in 1948 with the publication of a White Paper, *Statement on Personal Incomes, Costs and Prices*. The control which was proposed was by voluntary means and the proposals were generally supported by the unions and the TUC. Fels concluded:

> There is wide agreement that the policy restricted the growth of wage rates and earnings: in the two and a half years from February 1948, despite the fact that prices rose at 8 per cent, nationally negotiated wage rates increased by only 5 per cent.[127]

In 1956 a Conservative Government appealed for wage restraint, with no great success. In 1957 the Council on Prices, Productivity and Incomes was set up. The Council was reconstituted in 1960 and dismantled in 1961. In the same year the Government introduced a pay pause which it applied with particular severity in the public employment sector. The White Paper of 1962, *Incomes Policy: the Next Step* introduced an attempt at restraint which sought to keep income increases within a guiding light of 2 to 2½ per cent and allowed for a degree of flexibility by accepting exceptional increases in return for increases in productivity or reductions in restrictive practices. In order to support this policy the National Incomes Commission was established in 1962 to give advice, to announce a norm for wage increases and to give its judgements on particular pay settlements after they had been arrived at.

In 1964 a Labour Government arrived at a 'joint statement of intent on productivity, prices and incomes' and the National Board for Prices and Incomes was set up in 1965. A norm of increase in incomes was announced which was intended to relate incomes to increases in national productivity. A reasonably clear relationship was established between income growth and increase in productivity and allowed for exceptional settlements, which were excused by reference to socially desirable criteria (low pay, wage or salary reconstruction and equal pay for women). Fels suggests there were five phases of prices and incomes policy between 1965 and 1970:

a voluntary phase from 1965 to 1966
a compulsory standstill following the Prices and Incomes Act of 1966
a mainly voluntary pursuit of a 'zero norm' with enforceable delays on settlements from 1967 to 1968
an extension of the Government's power to delay settle-

ments, following the Prices and Incomes Act of 1968

a relaxed and voluntary policy in which the power to delay was reduced and pay settlements were recommended to fall within a range of increase from 2½ to 4½ per cent.

The Conservative Government which took office in 1970 began with a commitment to its election manifesto: 'We utterly reject the philosophy of compulsory wage control' and a general conclusion 'that incomes policy had been tried and failed.'[128] Its commitment to free collective bargaining was signalled by the dismantling of the National Board for Prices and Incomes in 1971. By the end of 1972, the Counter Inflation (Temporary Provisions) Act had reversed this policy and introduced the first stage of the Government's policy for incomes control which carried a standstill in wage increases. The second stage, in January 1973, extended the standstill and established two agencies, a Price Commission and a Pay Board. Pay increases were limited to £1 per week plus 4 per cent of the pay bill for the group. In stage three, introduced in November 1973, some flexibility was introduced for the correction of anomalies created in earlier stages. Both this version of incomes control and the Government that had introduced it ended with the national strike of the NUM in 1974.

The succeeding Labour Government introduced its White Paper, *The Attack on Inflation* in July 1975. It announced its determination to reduce the rate of inflation to 10 per cent by the third quarter of 1976 and, with this end in view, it announced an agreement with the TUC that there should be a limit of £6 per week on pay increases of up to £8,500 per year. The White Paper stressed that it was 'opposed to criminal sanctions on work people' and that the Government did not favour detailed intervention in collective bargaining; it emphasized that the limits had been voluntarily agreed with the TUC within the framework of the social contract. Some force was reserved for use against employers since the Government would not 'allow firms which make excessive pay settlements to reflect these settlements in higher prices to the consumer.' The policy was attended by an unusual degree of success which was explained by its simplicity, by its voluntary character, by the special relationship which had developed between the TUC and the Government and by the fact that incomes policies seem to be attended by the greatest success in the initial periods of their operation, before the problems which they have themselves initiated have accummulated. By the spring of 1976 the strains on differentials imposed by a flat rate policy were beginning to be visible.

In the spring of 1976, after an unusual introductory offer in the Chancellor's budget speech, incomes policy returned to a percentage basis. In return for substantial tax relief, the TUC and the Government agreed to a limit on pay increases of 4½ per cent on average wages and salaries with limits on increases to £2.50 for those earning up to £50 per week, to 5 per cent between £50 and £80 and to a maximum of £4 at higher levels.

In a White Paper, *The Attack on Inflation, The Second Year*, the Government announced its proposals for pay policy for the year beginning 1 August 1976.[129] It incorporated pay guidelines agreed between the TUC and the Government for a limit of 5 per cent 'on total earnings for all hours worked with a cash minimum of £2.50 and an upper cash maximum of £4 per week', payable as an earnings supplement. The figures apply to all full-time adults with pro rata payments for part-timers and juveniles.

It is not our business to assess the effectiveness of incomes policy as economic policy. In terms of its impact on industrial relations it seems to be certain that incomes policy, however temporary the current version may be, has become a permanent feature of British industrial relations. It has also, at least in the period 1964 to 1970, had a considerable impact on the character of collective bargaining in that it contributed to the proliferation of productivity agreements. An attempt was made by the NBPI to control wage increases by reference to guidelines establishing true or 'copper-bottomed' productivity bargains.[130] One of the most unusual criteria was that, in proposing effective controls to ensure that increases in efficiency were actually achieved, the Board said that 'Particular care also needs to be taken to distinguish the contribution of workers from other sources of more efficient working.' General application of the notion that increases in wages should be financed by contributions to productivity made only by workers would have truly revolutionary implications but fortunately this idea escaped general attention and general application. More seriously, incomes control has been said to construct a 'dam' which builds up pressure for wage adjustment which, when finally released, contributes greatly to higher wage demands and to inflation. This was precisely the reason given by the Conservative Government in 1970 for avoiding incomes control. Incomes control also alters the character of collective bargaining (to the extent that some say they are incompatible) by changing the relationship between unions and employers and of each with the Government. It also seems to raise a question of social control in alternative forms; either incomes control strains the relationship of Government and unions, raising questions of ultimate political authority (the problem of Edward Heath and the miners) or, if that problem is solved by the acquiescence of unions in Government policy, incomes control strains the authority of unions over their members (the problem of the 1950s and, possibly, the problem yet to emerge in 1977). This is an aspect of industrial relations to which we will return in the final chapter.

The State's influence on industrial relations

The State, apart from direct intervention by statute and by statutory or 'voluntary' control of incomes, exercises a considerable and continuing influence by the creation of State agencies.

The most obvious example is when the State becomes an employer. The Government directly employs some 2 million people in the civil service, the National Health Service and the forces. If employment in 'independent' public institutions (like the postal services and the nationalized industries) is included, then from one-fifth to one-quarter of the British work force is employed by the State. There are several consequences for industrial relations. There is a public commitment to collective bargaining; the management of the nationalized industries is under a statutory constraint to recognize, bargain and consult with unions' representative of employees. Two practical consequences are a considerable extension of union organization in the white-collar sector of public employment and a unique (for the present) extension of managerial or professional unionism in the public sector. Public employers also have a more vague but real responsibility for developing 'good' personnel and industrial relations policies. For this reason, disciplinary and dismissal procedures in the public sector have been generally in advance of those of private industry.

Government influence on industrial relations exercised through the ownership or partial ownership of enterprises has been extended by way of the investment of public funds in enterprises to avoid bankruptcy and closure or in order to provide capital for necessary investment. A controversial and unsubstantiated aspect of this policy is that the Government's commitment to the survival of the enterprise is so visible and so costly that the balance of power in the collective bargaining relationship is altered in favour of the unions, or of work groups who wish to assert pressure to their own advantage. The bargainers, it is sometimes suggested, have the advantage of being able to continually press the employer in the knowledge that the State, if its investment and its public commitment is sufficiently large, will never allow the enterprise to close. It is also argued, conversely, that the State exercises more absolute control over collective bargaining than it has ever done before because it controls investment. Workers at Chrysler and at British Leyland plants are frequently reminded that continued capital investment depends upon their good behaviour in industrial relations.

The Government also influences the conduct and character of industrial relations through the work of various State agencies which are intended to influence the performance of the parties, by providing advice or information, by establishing standards of performance, by providing incentives to change or by engaging in processes of planning. The ACAS, apart from the particular functions which it is required to carry out under the law, has inherited from the old Commission on Industrial Relations responsibility for carrying out general investigations and the additional task of producing codes of practice. This is an important and probably a permanent feature of industrial relations: 'a key question in the achievement of reform . . . concerns the adequacy of external inducements to change.'[131] The agency given the responsibility for setting standards and influencing performance in industrial relations must, to be effective, be expert and authoritative, it needs to conduct its investigations and provide its advice with some discretion and it needs to be independent, not only of both employers and unions, but of any executive responsibility for the enforcement of government legislation.

CHAPTER 6

Constraints upon management: ethics and standards

There is a close relationship between constraints on management behaviour imposed by the law and those concerned with ethics and social standards. The law positively influences our standards and our notions of what is right and wrong; the rationale of the Industrial Relations Act was that it would not have to be applied but that it would mould our standards of behaviour by its existence: it would be a normative force. One of the ways in which the law influences our behaviour is by bringing about a voluntary change so as to avoid its painful coercion. Business standards not only conform to what the law requires, they are also adjusted from time to time in order to pre-empt a change in the law, 'the cultivation of social responsibility by American managers represents their conservative response to a changing business environment in which threats of greater public and governmental pressures are being felt'.[132]

Industrial relations is an area of management in which ethical concerns are particularly relevant because the interests of people are directly involved and because there is often a publicly visible division of opinion as to what these interests are and how they are best served. Employment has also been notable for a great deal of confusion amongst the various protagonists as to what their own interests are and whose good they purport to represent. These confusions are more easily recognized in nineteenth century debates about employment than in the contemporary scene. Andrew Ure said of the Factories Regulation Act of 1833, which proposed to prohibit the employment in mills of children under nine and to limit the hours of older children, that it was 'an act of despotism towards the trade and of mock philanthropy towards the work-people who depend on trade for support', children would be dismissed and are thrown out of the warm spinning rooms upon the cold world, to exist by beggary and plunder—in idleness and vice'.[133] Such extravagant distortions are now as rare as the extreme conditions of brutalized employment which required their expression, but they remind us perhaps that we should always be sceptical of a representative who claims to forward someone else's interest as surrogate for his own.

Employment continues to encourage statements of this kind although they are now expressed in much more muted tones. There may be a particular and fundamental reason; one of the most widely acknowledged statements of a universal ethical imperative that has ever been made is Kant's dictum that men should be treated as ends, never as means. Now the employment relationship requires men to be treated as means. A definition of management is that it involves the co-ordination of material and human resources in the pursuit of managerial objectives; the objectives are those of managers, the means are subordinate workers. In this sense, mass, specialized and controlled employment may be a fundamentally unethical process.

This statement is not the vast exaggeration that it may appear to be. There is a great deal of evidence to suggest that mass employment in industrial conditions has attracted continual criticisms from successive generations of observers. The ancient Greeks regarded subordinated work with contempt not because of the degraded nature of the tasks involved (a view with which we might sympathize) but simply because it was controlled by someone else and therefore entailed a loss of freedom bordering on slavery. It was perfectly alright for an Athenian citizen to toil in his own field: it was despicable for him to toil for someone else.

A tradition of criticism of organized work has continued, countered by a radical view which, because it venerates the worker, has valued his work. We recognize these confused and complicated notions currently in concepts like anomy and alienation, the meaning of which is often vague, but which clearly convey a deep and abiding concern about the moral implications and effects of industrial work. The supposed alienation of the industrial worker has become a major preoccupation of industrial society and a great deal of political and managerial attention has been devoted to overcoming the problems which it seems to pose. Work has important ethical implications. Marxist theory holds that the worker is exploited and that his reaction to his exploitation is fundamental to an explanation of social change. Whether he is exploited in capitalist society or not, the worker's subordination to the authority of management carries ethical implications for the relationship between them. The way in which the authority is exercised and the way in which it is resisted by organized workers entail problems concerned with justice and equity for society as a whole, problems which are partly the concern of law and social administration. The exercise of authority by managers means that they are not only constrained by laws but that they are concerned directly with the ethical implications of managing men.

In some ways this has become more of a problem for managers than for the employer. The distinction between manager and employer has become important. In their analysis of business ideology, Sutton, Harries *et al* made a distinction between two versions of the American business creed. The classical version was based on private ownership and operations within a free market, 'a decentralized, private competitive capitalism, in which the forces of supply and demand, operating through the price mechanism, regulate the economy in detail and in aggregate'.[134] The managerial version does not stress competition or the legal rights of owners to dispose of their property and to maximize their profit; it emphasizes, alternatively, the importance of the professional manager exercising authority for the common good. This division has become associated with a well-known argument concerning the split between ownership and control. Berle and Means argued that ownership of corporate enterprises had become so diffuse as to be irrelevant and that the real source of authority rested with managers.[135] The argument was presented in an extreme form by Burnham, who said that managers were emerging internationally as a class in their own right and that wide political changes were likely as the result of their exercise of power in their own interests.[136] Whether a divorce between ownership and management has taken place is a matter of continuing debate but there is little doubt that:

> during the course of this century, a managerial ideology stressing the responsible social role of managers towards groups within and outside the enterprise has been much in evidence and that this ideology has often been explicitly linked to the idea of a divorce from ownership.[137]

This suggests the much greater convenience, in exercising legitimate authority over subordinates, of a view which stresses the importance of managers rather than owners. Capitalism, or private enterprise, has evolved a rich framework of economic theory but it has never worked out an effective ideological basis from which statements could be derived explaining why employees *should* do what their employers want or tell them to do. It has had to fall back at worst upon coercive law or upon statements of self-interest, but it has been singularly weak on ethics, on producing any moral compulsion. The failure has not been for want of trying. The employment relationship in the nineteenth century can be seen as a continuing attempt to substitute the employers' ethical framework for the workers:

> The worker's own ethics were such that he was not normally susceptible to the kind of inducements which his employer could provide within the new working conditions. Ambitions to rise above his own idea of a 'subsistence' income by dint of hard work were foreign to him. He had to be made ambitious and 'respectable', either by costly provisions of material goods . . . or by the cheaper means of changing his attitude, often falsely called his 'character'. For unless the workman wished to become 'respectable' in the current sense, none of the incentives would bite.[138]

The two most consistent ethical appeals, within a business framework, derive from the notion of self-help in the first place and from the service ideal in the second. *Self-Help* was the name of an enormously successful book published by Samuel Smiles in 1859. Smiles and self-help are now something of a joke but they still provide the basis of an appeal for hard work. Smiles discounted the advantages of birth and privilege; indeed, he developed a radical contempt for them because he believed that rich men began life with a serious disadvantage from which the poor were free. Everything which we enjoy, individually or in our social environment, is the result of hard work. Talent was unnecessary in this most egalitarian view:

> the greatest results in life are usually attained by simple means and the exercise of ordinary qualities . . . The

road of human welfare lies along the old highway of steadfast well-doing, and they who are the most persistent, and work in the truest spirit, will usually be the most successful.[139]

The succession of biographical sketches of the great and the successful which Smiles presents demonstrates that they have one attribute in common: they worked hard.

This appeal had three advantages. It provided common ground between master and man establishing values which they could both share. It provided hope and the prospect of material reward for the poor, it removed all insuperable barriers to success. It had the greatest utility for the employer and for an industrial society because it encouraged the development of labour self-discipline. It could not survive the onslaught of radical criticism of capitalist society and it could not be squared with the facts of industrial life. The moral justification of success, that it followed effort, could not survive comparison with the readily observable instances of effort which did not produce success and of success which was not produced by effort.

The service ideal has been a more continuing thread in the moral appeal of business enterprise. It was expressed clearly by Henry Ford:

> money comes naturally as the result of service. And it is absolutely necessary to have money. But we do not want to forget that the end of money is not ease but the opportunity to perform some service.[140]

Service meant two things: it meant producing what people wanted and what they would pay for; service meant business which meant profit. Service also meant a sense of social responsibility, it meant that the business institution was a source of good in the community. 'Everyone', said Ford, 'who is connected with us, either as a manager, worker or purchaser—is the better for our existence. The institution that we have erected is performing a service'.[141] Ford went on to make it perfectly clear that this sense of service did not involved any charitable obligations: that would be poor business, service depended upon and flowed from good business. Ford was also notoriously capable of demanding not only hard work but impeccable morals from his managers and men.

The service ideal has survived almost without amendment to this day. Ford would probably not have disagreed with one word of this statement:

> Since business is the wealth-producing institution of our society *it must be profitable*. The greatest social irresponsibility would be to so manage business that wealth was not produced for the community's fabric of schools, homes, roads, and so on. This is recognized even in countries where the word 'profit' is not acceptable. . . . Responsibility and profitability are inseparable.[142]

The service ideal also seems to underline Copeman's recent work.[143]

The association between business and service to society has been heavily criticized.[144] It is not our business to examine this argument other than in its application to the ethical responsibilities of business for its employees. The problem in launching an ethical appeal to employees from the basis of private ownership has always lain in establishing a coincidence of interest in the face of what are sometimes intransigent facts like unemployment, redundancy, strikes and lock-outs. Robert Owen was among the first to maintain that good employment policies were good business and his *Report to the County of Lanark* (1821), was intended to persuade his fellow manufacturers that sound personnel policies were a matter of self interest. Precisely the same injunctions can be found in Roman views of the treatment of slaves; in Cato's opinion 'the best principle of management is to treat both slaves and animals well enough to give them the strength to work hard'.[145] That is an extreme view from a remote age but it serves to illustrate by caricature an abiding characteristic in the employer's attitude to his workers, that his ethical concern for their well-being is limited by the extent that it serves his own interest and that where the interests are incompatible the one will be subordinated or sacrificed to the other.

This suspicion not only derives from actual accounts of the employment relationship; it is, much more seriously, logically entailed in the nature of the appeals which are made for employers to treat their workers well and is a strand which is unbroken from Robert Owen to Doulgas McGregor. Humble acknowledges the suspicion when he says that a business which improves its safety provisions could be motivated by moral obligations to its employees, by enlightened self interest in the pursuit of higher productivity, by a concern with corporate image, by a wish to avoid conflict or by anticipation of the law. 'How does one distinguish which was the dominant concern'? asks Humble and he replies 'Personally, I am grateful for the improvement and content to leave spiritual and moral values for every person to settle with his conscience and his maker!'[146] Now that is a strange confession for someone whose avowed concern is with the social responsibility of business.

It is strange because it reinforces the suspicion that the expressions of concern about ethical responsibility are essentially in the interest of business, are a defence against independent challenge and cannot be seen to represent the exercise of reponsible concern about other groups unless the interests of the business are challenged. It is certainly likely to remind employees that the employer's concern for them is secondary and subservient to his own objectives. As a practical man, Humble is satisfied when interests coincide and when what he judges to be improvement is the result. But what about circumstances in which there is no coincidence and when there are different views about what constitutes improvement? It is these circumstances which lead us into the field of collective bargaining, when the employer's view of what is in the best interest of workers is challenged by the workers themselves.

Conflict may seem less likely to take place when the more obvious distinctions of interest between owner and employee are removed. A significant part of current approaches to the employment relationship is directed at achieving this end. It may be pursued by one or more techniques of participation in which workers or their representatives are persuaded of a common interest. An alternative approach is to argue that:

> the only lasting way to reduce the level of conflict between capital and labour is to abolish the basic difference between employers and employees. This is essentially a difference of ownership. Turn the employees into owners and the distinction goes.[147]

Copeman therefore concludes that it is advantageous to distribute a company's shares amongst its employees, up to a limit of 25 percent, that is. A third and perhaps a more subtle approach is to suggest that the owner is dead, that he has been replaced by the manager who is not divided by interest from the worker because he too is an employee. The end of ownership, whether it has occurred or not, provides an excellent slogan because it not only erodes the more obvious distinctions of interest, it provides the manager with a much more legitimate base from which to issue commands or appeals to his subordinates. The owner's authority was legal, founded in property or inheritance; the manager's authority is his expertise, so much the better if it can be illuminated by diplomas, degrees and appointment by competitive selection.

The licence of expert authority does not free the manager from responsibility, in fact it increases it. The owner, resting upon property rights, can be wayward, doing what he likes with what is his. The manager must consistently justify his claim to know what is best. He must also maintain his claim to possess a kind of neutrality between the contending factions in the employment relationship. His managerial role gives him some advantage over the employer, he is advanced as the representative of no single faction but as the expert, impartial co-ordinator or judge of the demands made by shareholders, customers, society and employees, 'one of the critical and difficult management tasks is *balancing* these objectives at any time, taking into consideration the changing requirements of stockholders, employees, customers and society generally.'[148] Notice that ownership has now been reduced to one contending interest among many.

If the claim for the manager was that he is an impartial judge, that he is in the position of a disinterested and benevolent administrator (and the claim is often advanced in these terms) then it would have to be rejected as spurious. The manager is not impartial. In the first place the close association between management and ownership has not been severed, many observers have denied anything resembling a divorce between ownership and control, and one has said that, rather than a divorce between the two, it makes more sense to talk of a 'marriage of convenience',[149] The distinction of interest between owners and managers is problematical and from the perspective of the shop-floor it may be invisible. In the second place managers, like everyone else, have their own interest, their own axe to grind. The claim to be disinterested is also a useful tactic, and therefore to be suspected, in advancing a case and in overcoming opposition to it; like the unitary view which Fox has made so unpopular with managers, it works until it is challenged and when it is challenged it disintegrates. The managerial claim to impartiality is challenged every day in every workplace. It has disintegrated.

The manager is not impartial and he is not a reliable representative of the interests of other parties to the employment relationship. But he has to respond to them. Even on the most cynical account of his pursuit of his own objectives, he must be able to judge what he can get away with. This purely practical and self-interested concern does make him responsive; just as in the collective bargaining relationship, although no one would accuse the industrial relations specialist of representing the unions, he must be capable of a sympathetic understanding of their intentions. This is a part of his claim to expertise. His 'professional' ability, which is an important part of the whole managerial claim to exercise legitimate authority, demands that he understands the aspirations of other groups and can assess the power and skill with which they can advance them.

This necessary understanding has led to a great deal of confusion in which the personnel manager is still seen as some sort of middle man, occupying the ground between conflicting factions, owing absolute allegiance to neither. Many students aspiring to careers in personnel management see their role in these terms; one suspects that, for some of them, the attraction of personnel management lies in its equivocal attachment to the managerial cause. Their misapprehension of reality is excused by the welfare origins of personnel management, when welfare officers were genuinely ambivalent in their attachments and when they may have occupied a more truly professional realtionship with their clients, the workers, whose interest they honestly believed they were to serve. Those days are gone. Confusion continues, however, because the expert's need to understand employees becomes translated into a belief that he must represent them. There are moral overtones in the personnel management role which continue to haunt it; personnel managers continue to perceive a shadowy responsibility to the employees which comes nearest to a clear expression in the commitment to 'good', 'sound' or 'responsible' personnel policies.

These vague perceptions could easily be expressed as constraints upon the specialist's performance in industrial relations, as a set of moral parameters beyond which the industrial relations manager must not go. In the sense of moral responsibility to workers it is doubtful if such constraints exist or, if they do, if they could ever be operationally described or defined with any clarity. Personnel managers may be as moral as the next man, they are as likely as our neighbours to believe that they should not lie (although the collective bargaining process may submit personnel managers to unusual temptations in this respect) but it is doubtful if their role now imposes any especial moral constraint upon their behaviour in terms of their responsibility to workers.

They are constrained but not necessarily out of consideration for employees. Their effectiveness demands that they recognize ethical limits but it is the claim to exercise managerial authority that imposes these limits, not a moral responsibility to employees. Professor Child has suggested that management thought has two functions, the first legitimatory and the second technical. The first was directed at securing:

> social recognition and approval for managerial authority and the way in which it was used, while the technical function was primarily linked to the search for practical means of rendering that authority maximally effective.[150]

Recognition and approval, the managerial posture of licensed authority, demands restraint in the way managers exercise their functions. The technical aspects of management also requires restraint. The history of employment has been until recently the history of appeals and exhortations directed at the work force with the intention of making it work harder. The opposition to this process of persuasion has been considerable. It has encountered the haggling of the bargaining process, some counter-propaganda on an organised basis and considerable obduracy on the shop-floor. The utility of this direct appeal for cooperation has recently been overtaken by a more roundabout approach in which management attempts to elicit the cooperation of workers by bringing about a change in their environment so that a cooperative attitude is produced almost unconsciously. Ever since Hawthorn we have seen a series of variations on this theme, sometimes suggesting that a change in their physical environment, or the communication system or the style of supervision currently arguing that a new approach to organizational design, to the process of objective-setting or the more satisfying construction of tasks will, of themselves, produce a more favourable response. In one form or another this theme is the preoccupation of contemporary management writers like Argyris, Blake, McGregor, Tannenbaum or Herzberg. Without pausing to debate the validity of the claims they make, one feature is common to all: they demand no conscious action on the part of the worker, they demand action on the part of the manager in changing the worker's environment. Management is the agent of change so that managers become the target of appeal; as they must act in order to bring about a suitable environment at work, so it is they who must be addressed, not workers.

In this process of appealing to managers to do the right thing, that is, to make the correct (social or psychological) adjustments in the working environment, it is easy to confuse the old moral responsibility for the worker with the new technical responsibility for his environment. Whether we are aware of the confusion or not, and in practical terms whether it matters or not, the result is that the manager of the employment relationship is considerably constrained by the need to behave properly, not to the worker but to management. He has new and complex responsibilities which arise because he is seen as influencing the worker's response which was once believed to be amenable to direct appeal. He is now responsible for the worker's effective effort although he is no longer required to appeal for it. The position of the manager could now be compared with that of the enlightened parent who believes that the development of his children depends no longer upon Victorian morality judiciously mixed with coercion, but upon his own construction of a suitable environment and the application of the findings of child psychology. The responsibility in this situation is the parent's, not the child's. Professor Anne Crichton contended that:

> the choice for the development of personnel management in the future lies between the clerical or the medical pattern—well-codified doctrines about a faith or scientific knowledge backed by rigorous training . . . academics are suggesting that the time for science is here. Not only must the personnel specialist learn about technology, the general manager is being told that he must begin to understand behavioural science concepts and the way in which they can be applied.[151]

This all adds up to the pursuit of professionalization and personnel managers have shown some attachment to the need for rigorous training, even if there has been some disagreement about either the job that is to be done or about the existence of a precise body of scientific knowledge which enables people to do it. These uncertainties have not been entirely resolved although continuing uncertainty did not prevent the IPM from insisting that from 1975 entrance to its corporate grades of membership would henceforth be open only to those who have passed a qualifying examination. A cynic might conclude that, while there were still doubts about what a personnel manager had to do and what he needed to know in order to do it, the IPM had insisted upon his passing an examination first. But Wilensky pointed out that the final stage in professionalization is the establishment of a training institution to set standards for entry. The IPM has not gone quite that far but in the supervision of courses and syllabus content which is now exercised by its Examinations Committee it does not need to do so. Whether the body of knowledge is relevant to whatever it is that personnel managers have to do is not the important question. After 1974, all entrants to personnel management must acquire some proficiency in a body of knowledge (heavily influenced by a substantial 'behavioural science' content). This fact must in itself have some influence upon the way in which personnel managers see their role and concern themselves with its performance.[152]

In these general senses, by a belief in the importance of the environment of work in affecting the behaviour of its inhabitants, by a belief that the environment can be planned so as to induce planned changes in behaviour, both beliefs strongly reinforced by a compulsory educational process, the performance of personnel specialists is influenced by what we may loosely call ethical constraints. We have specifically suggested that ethical concern for the interests of workers as clients has been reduced since the days when personnel management was conceived to mean welfare work. But there are influences which make a respect for other men's feelings a continuing concern for the manager in the field of industrial relations.

The first we have already mentioned but, to avoid the impression of a cynical disregard for other men's interests as being characteristic of management in industrial relations, it is worth repeating that managers, simply as men or women, are capable of exercising moral judgement. Perhaps, as men or women who exercise an unusual degree of responsibility for other people, they *should* be influenced by moral judgements, quite independently from considerations of what is good for their business.

The second is that, in industrial relations, there is a particular and practical need to judge the nature of other people's moral judgements. This is not a question of sharing an ethical concern with the interests of employees, it is a purely practical requirement to estimate the moral feelings with which they have invested the representation of their interests. This means that the industrial relations specialist may have to arrive at a 'professional' and detached judgement in which he can separate out his own enterprise's view of what is the 'right' view upon a particular issue (a view which organizational pressures will normally expect him to share) from his judgement about the feeling of rightness which unions or their members have about a totally different view.

The third concerns the area of social influences and expectations which the industrial relations specialist inhabits, sometimes in relative isolation from other managers. The influences here are diffuse. They can include a working knowledge of the current version of Marxist ideology for the very practical reason that that particular view of the world might explain the perspective upon affairs which is taken by men with whom the industrial relations specialist has to negotiate. I once had occasion to remark to a group of managers that productivity bargaining was seen in some quarters as 'part of a major offensive by the employing class of this country to shift the balance of forces in industry permanently in their direction'.[153] The managers responded with incredulous amusement. In some industries it would be a serious deficiency in industrial relations specialists to be so protected from such a view as to find it funny, particularly as it has probably gained wider allegiance since it was expressed in 1970.[154]

Industrial relations is the area of management which, more than any other, has to encounter opposing ideologies, different views of right and wrong, different versions of the truth. Areas of management more remote and more sheltered from ideological conflict may preserve an innocent confidence in the ideas their inhabitants share. From the boardroom, it may be quite clear the Marxists are both mistaken and a serious threat to the economy. Industrial relations specialists are likely to know that both views are not entirely right. It would be an exaggeration to describe any part of a managerial organization (science and technology excepted) as a hive of intellectual activity, but at least in industrial relations ideas are encountered which the managerial organization cannot control or censor. In this sense, an industrial relations department is like a frontier post through which news and, sometimes, stimulating ideas can be transmitted. But it sometimes serves quite the opposite function when it becomes the place at which all intellectual baggage must be jettisoned before journeying to the interior of the organization.

This is to suggest, once again, that the industrial relations negotiators have an internal bargaining role in terms of ideas and of different views of justice. I know of no evidence to suggest what view the industrial relations specialist takes of these matters or of his views about the legitimacy of private ownership but I suspect that he tends to take a purely market-place view, that his version of what is 'right' is confined to going rates and a pragmatic application of the rule book, that justice is a compound of job evaluation and what the union will tolerate. If this view is correct then the industrial relations specialist is likely to resist new ideas and different ethical values. If he shares this ethical conservatism with his union counterparts then the whole area of industrial relations and collective bargaining becomes a layer of insulation impenetrable to the exchange of different norms, protecting both managerial and workers' organisations from the transmission of unwelcome shocks. This could help to explain the widely acknowledged conservatism of the collective bargaining process.

The personal relationships of the bargainers probably strengthen this conservatism. Effective negotiation is probably impossible between negotiators who do not trust each other, who do not acknowledge, like opposing prop-forwards who respect each other's strength and guile, that they share respect for their own rules and for each other.

Social influence and expectations bring a wider adjustment to bear. When we speak of ground-rules in industrial relations we often mean the procedural rules governing the relations between unions and managers. Marsh pointed out there was a wide range of general understandings about the conduct of collective bargaining. These were, he said, that procedure should be exhausted before either of the parties took unilateral action, that genuine attempts should be made by the parties to apply agreements which they have arrived at, that issues should be settled at as low a level as possible and that general, flexible, all-purpose agreements were preferred.[155] Since then, it seems likely that some of these expectations have changed but research has recently indicated the existence of a much more specific (but unformulated) set of practical understandings and expectations. Gennard and Lasko, in a study of the strike of the Union of Post Office Workers in 1971 and of maintenance electricians at Chrysler (UK) Coventry in 1973, reported that in both instances there was evidence of management going beyond what was absolutely necessary for it to do in order to give strikers pay in hand, tax rebates, and other payments, amounting to an income which management influenced of up to 45 per cent of total strike income. In the electricians' strike, the Electrical Electronic Telecommunications and Plumbing Union said that strike pay was conditional upon production of a paid up union card. When management was told that many of the electricians had left their cards in their toolboxes, management allowed the electricians on to the premises to get their cards. Gennard and Lasko suggest that one reason for such benevolent attitudes was that:

> when management and workers are in dispute there is an informal acceptance that there are rules to this 'game'. It was clear that in both disputes company and union considered that certain types of behaviour were acceptable and others not. Pay in hand, tax rebates and holiday pay were therefore paid out by Chrysler and the Post Office because it was viewed as the 'proper' way to behave towards one's striking workers. The strikers also shared this view and if one party breaches the 'rules of the game' it produces moral resentment.[156]

There has long been a convention in coal-mining that disputes do not affect pumping and safety work in the maintenance of the mine so that a breach of the convention is usually an indication of bitterness in the dispute.

Conventions of this kind may serve several purposes. They demonstrate that the process of conflict regulation is not simply a matter of formalization and procedural rules. There are expectations about behaviour and about the 'rules of the game' which reduce conflict to a level which does not impose unacceptable damage. An acknowledgement of the importance of observing these unwritten rules also represents a realisation that the employment relationship is a continuing one and that cooperation is necessary to it, despite temporary interruptions caused by a dispute. There is every reason, therefore, to limit conflict in order to prevent it threatening long-term cooperation. Finally, there is no doubt a reciprocal element of respect for the rules.

They can be seen as an extension of the bargaining relationship even into the area in which bargaining has been replaced by dispute. The rules create a kind of indulgency pattern in which one side or the other can continue to withdraw cooperation or apply sanctions.

All this suggests that moral obligation in industrial relations takes the form of conventions intended to limit and control conflict in circumstances in which conflict between the parties is inevitable. The conventions are shared between the players but respect for the conventions may require that collective bargaining is an inappropriate activity for exchanging different views of justice. The success of collective bargaining as a control process may require that it never has to come to terms with real differences of values. Observers of the negotiating process may have noticed that negotiation stops when one party launches an ideological attack upon the other. The attack tends to be treated as ritual and the opponent waits for it to subside before 'getting back to business'.

This is not to say that ethics have no part in industrial relations. It is obvious that the parties often have quite different values and ideological concerns but they are usually persuaded by their mutual respect for negotiating rules and conventions to exclude them from the negotiating process. There are several different levels of moral commitment among the parties to industrial relations. First, there is a commitment to the moral values of the organization which they represent; union negotiators are required to share the Labour movement's concern with political objectives and a broad allegiance to social reform; management negotiations are required to value efficiency, profitability and the pursuit of business objectives even, in some circumstances, to reject the union's political values. These are very hazy descriptions and it may be that the values of the different parties may encompass a range of views. The norms of union negotiators may permit some deviation to the left, so that commitment to Marxist views in an individual will be regarded as respectable, if eccentric, while on the management side deviation to the right is again permissible.

A second level of moral commitment among the parties to industrial relations may be a shared respect for the need to avoid mutual destruction, a perceived need to respect differences in outlook by preventing the confrontation of quite different value systems. It is this commitment which seems to underlie the conventions, procedures and rules of collective bargaining. In this sense, collective bargaining is that part of industrial relations from which the differences in moral values have been excluded. The rules and procedures of collective bargaining are an example of what Gouldner calls representative bureaucracy: they are shared and respected by the parties who have constructed them in order to avoid mutual damage. They are deemed to be necessary and legitimate and their observation rests upon a degree of moral force; it is important that agreements once made are respected, that undertakings once given are not broken, that conventions are observed and procedures are respected.

At this point, no doubt, many practitioners in industrial relations will be convinced that we are describing some academic Shangri-la. The more general view seems to be that industrial relations is characterized by anarchy and moral disorder. Thus in 1969 Jack Lee, then President of IPM, said in a speech to the Third London Personnel Management Conference:

> It is a terrible admission to make but I doubt if sanctity of contracts has any meaning at all in the British industrial relations scene of 1969.

More recently Alan Fox described the consequences of the

'low-trust' character of organized work as:

> suspicion, jealousy, the misreading of men's motives . . . inhibitions to co-operation; the blockages created in the handlings of differences . . . the blight on fellowship and compassion.[157]

There are two explanations for this difference of view: that on the one hand industrial relations rests upon a degree of moral consensus, and that on the other it is anarchic.

The first is adopted by those critical of capitalist or liberal-democratic society, that industrial relations is a structure built upon an unequal division of power imposed by owners and protected by the persuasion of workers that it is acceptable and legitimate. Industrial relations, in short, is said to rest upon the acceptance of suppression by those who are suppressed. The deception is said to have been supported by education, by the mass-media and by a complex intellectual process in which theories of democratic pluralism have been advanced with great subtlety to pull the wool over the workers' eyes by convincing them that the society that employs (exploits) them is in some sense theirs and that they have a moral duty to respect it and its laws and procedures. According to this explanation (to which we shall return in the last chapter) all that we have said about collective bargaining as a mechanism of social control is an acknowledgement of the extent to which it serves and protects the interests of those who have power. It is an explanation of what we have acknowledged, that collective bargaining tends to exclude basic questions concerning differences of values, that it bargains at the margins. Within this explanation, collective bargaining and its conventions are a means of trapping workers into an acceptance of the *status quo*.

The second and alternative explanation encompasses the contradiction between moral consensus and anarchy by different means. It rests upon an assumption that differences in fundamental moral values, or between contradictory ideological positions, are unresolvable except by force. The next step is more of a rational calculation than a moral precept, that the resolution of morally incompatible positions by force is not worth the damage that the application of force is likely to cause. Unless there is a preponderance of power on one side sufficient to destroy the opposition (in which case the coexistence of two morally opposed groups is not likely to be a continuing problem) then a confrontation between them is likely to impose unacceptable damage to both or the obliteration of one. In either case, the prospect of perpetual struggle seems unattractive. There is an associated moral argument to add to the persuasiveness of the purely pragmatic conclusion, that is, that application of force to an implacable foe may result in his destruction but cannot result in his conversion; shooting the opposition is a political rather than a moral solution. The conclusion must be that the opponents must learn mutual respect, withdraw from hostile intercourse and distance each other. But the opponents in industrial relations cannot have nothing to do with each other. They must therefore construct a relationship which facilitates cooperation (while accommodating conflict) without risking ideological exchange. The relationship will require a conventional respect for the singularity of each party's moral commitment by ensuring that those commitments never become the subject of exchange.

The moral and ideological baggage which is left outside the negotiating room is bound to influence the behaviour of the parties inside it and, conversely, the negotiating process may affect each party's moral commitment. If these influences did not take place, moral convictions would take on the character of dogmatic irrelevance to the environment and negotiations would become unrelated to the aspirations of the contending groups.

The second explanation is broadly the position of pluralists although pluralism is a concept which has suffered severely in its adaptation and transfer from political theory to industrial relations and it would be a foolhardy champion who threw himself into a defence of pluralist theory as currently outlined in industrial relations.[158]

For the sake of identification let us call the first explanation the fundamentalist position and the second the relativist position. Which is to be preferred? We are already provided with the means of escaping the question when we said that fundamental differences in outlook and values seem often to be resolved only by force. Indeed, both explanations seem to acknowledge this gloomy conclusion, the fundamentalist by a tendency for its adherents to take up a revolutionary position and the relativist by a commitment to a permanent state of stand off between the parties. From here on, it is perhaps a matter of temperament dictating choices. For my own part, peace seems generally to be better than war, particularly when, in this field, the outcome of war (or rather 'revolution') seems often to have been worse than the circumstances that occasioned it. There are other reasons for the choice. The argument for the fundamentalist position seems empirically untestable, it rests upon the sands of 'false consciousness' and 'social conditioning' and it shows scant respect for the judgement and intelligence of the working population which it purports to champion. The relativist position, on the other hand, seems to have succeeded in bringing about more change than it is sometimes credited with and it carries the consent (within limits which we shall soon explore) of the parties in employment. This brief judgement, incidentally, is not so much intended to convince the reader as to confess the author's prejudice in this matter.

What emerges is some acknowledgement of the moral

complexity of the world of industrial relations. The groups in industrial relations are likely to be committed to values which are both unifying and contending, thus:

1 there is likely to be some degree of commitment to consensus values in the society as a whole. Government agencies, unions and employers are likely to feel vague approval, in Britain, for democratic government (however defined), individual liberty, the rule of law and the avoidance of violence
2 groups are likely to be broadly committed to procedural norms, to 'respect for the rules', which they have helped to construct in defining their relationship with other and contending groups. In part, the commitment to these procedural norms follows from the general commitment to the more general social values but they are always under pressure and are likely to be constantly modified. They are subject to constant critical review and to frequent modification because their particular form at any time represents only partially the values of each group; they represent a compromise between its view of the justice of the relationship and the power available to press its view against its opponent. Both the world which the parties inhabit and the distribution of power between the parties changes
3 groups are committed to their own values and ideas of justice, often in contention against the values of other groups. The clearest example in industrial relations is between the outlook and goals of trade unions and those of employers but there are other examples in which different functions or departments of management may sometimes pursue contentious goals
4 individuals are committed to personal values.

Thus it is not uncommon for an individual to disapprove of his union's policy, to pursue it at some cost against the opposition of his employer, to accept procedural rules for the regulation of the resultant conflict, to disapprove of the procedural rules but to accept them because of his broad agreement about the need to support social values concerning the avoidance of violence.

In other words, our allegiance to values is usually contradictory, our behaviour is rarely coherent or consistent. Our allegiance to values or, at least, to the rules which we acecpt is also not always fervent. The traffic laws are a favourite example. No one fined for a parking offence is entirely filled with moral fevour in paying the fine or with moral guilt in avoiding it. In industrial relations, many of the rules are given a grudging, rational acceptance. Gouldner, again, explains why this should be; Some of the rules are coercively imposed, some are imposed by distant bureaucracies. Even those in the formulation of which our own representative organizations have participated have not always carried our own private consultation and commitment. In these cases we may accord them formal recognition, observing them because we acknowledge the propriety of the interest in them of 'our' union or management organization. Others may receive even less commitment when we accord rules a grudging, *de facto* recognition based solely on respect for the power which will be applied to those who break them.

Employment and industrial relations are areas in which strong moral convictions can be expected to coexist with considerable moral confusion and complexity. The employer's need to control his environment or, at least, to attempt to make it predictable, explains why he should wish to reduce this confusion to more orderly proportions. But simplification and order are difficult to achieve when the existence of collective bargaining, by importing different moral values (from however distant a source), causes so much of the confusion. The desire for moral order is one of the reasons for the employer wishing to avoid the collective bargaining relationship.

It is by now, at least in Britain, a very unfashionable approach. It rests upon the assertion of responsibility and moral leadership which was best represented in the paternalist pattern of employment. The obstacle to a return to this pattern, apart from a lack of moral confidence induced by the challenge of collective bargaining, is the formidable barrier of the law of union recognition.

But collective bargaining is not incompatible with employer responsibility at least in the field of welfare. It is not inconceivable that a change should take place by the employer attempting to achieve a higher level of moral commitment from this employees by demonstrating a higher level of moral responsibility towards them. Such attempts have been made in the past; they have become very unfashionable but some of them have been successful (IBM and Marks and Spencer are random examples). There are several reasons for suggesting a possible re-evaluation of employer responsibility.

The main barrier in the way of the exercise of moral responsibility by the employer has been the unions' justifiable claim to represent the interest of employees through collective bargaining. If the chronic addiction to incomes control continues it is likely to change the strength and nature of the collective bargaining relationship. If, in addition, the role of management and union becomes increasingly concerned with joint administration of the law and with consultation and negotiation over non-wage items in the contract, the concept of employee welfare is likely to be re-examined.

Managers have been taught to regard the pursuit of a unitary framework as impractical and mistaken. But Fox, who taught them this lesson, has now revealed that the pluralism which he persuaded them to accept was illfounded and deceptive and that 'high-trust' relationships need to be established in employment. He suggests that a more egalitarian society must be brought about in order to legitimate the relationship between workers and managers, He also argues that managers themselves might make some progress in achieving the greater commitment of their subordinates, that we should examine 'the managerial problems of promoting co-operative compliance and, if aspirations extend that far, evoking moral involvement'.[159] If Fox's impact on managers in the refutation of pluralism is anything like as great as it was in his advocacy of it, we are likely to see a return to an interest in the achievement of 'moral involvement'. At least, the subject of moral leadership and responsibility may be no longer pronounced as anathema.

Recently, a powerful piece of advocacy has been directed at persuading personnel managers to a new comprehension of responsibility. Kenny acknowledges that a great deal of the welfare movement:

> was associated with hostility to trade unions, palliatives for low wages and other devices to keep the worker in his place. Much of the human betterment movement carried, therefore, the seeds of its own destruction, and was swept aside with the growth of the trade union movement it had often tried to impede.[160]

But, he argues, many personnel managers have never abandoned a concern with human welfare and many of the current approaches to job enrichment and participation are entirely grounded in welfare assumptions and he concludes that the essence of personnel management is surely 'to see the place of work as a point of contact for solving the problems of citizenship in the larger society.'

One of the perennial dangers apparent in describing the approach of personnel managers to the problems of employment is their tendency to yaw from one course to its opposite: when pluralism is in, unity is out; when conflict is acceptable, harmony is rejected. It is to be hoped that a reassessment of managerial concern and responsibility will not lead to a rejection of reality. Such a rejection is least likely in the field of industrial relations.

CHAPTER 7

Industrial relations in the technical and commercial context

The influence of technology on work and on the behaviour of the worker has been acknowledged in a long tradition which certainly goes back as far as Adam Smith. The idea of alienation was developed by Marx to mean that highly specialized and routine tasks in the manufacturing process resulted in severe damage to the worker, damage which would result in his negative reaction. Durkheim's analysis of the division of labour contributed the notion of anomy, a state of moral withdrawal or vacuity which was brought about by over-specialized tasks. The notion of alienation has now gathered so many accretions of meaning that it has been described as connoting anything which the speaker dislikes in industrial society. It has certainly become a dominant feature of managerial thought; a good proportion of the theory and practice of personnel management is directed at nothing more than countering the supposed alienation of the industrial worker.

There is therefore no need to begin a discussion of the influence of technology upon industrial relations with persuasive explanations; its influence is widely acknowledged. But it is necessary to try to assess the nature and extent of the relationship between technology and industrial relations because there are quite wide differences of opinion about the way in which the one affects the other.

Silverman distinguishes between the major analytical conceptions which have been applied to the study of organizations. The context of his discussion is, of course, sociological[161] but it illuminates the different views which have emerged over the relationship of technology and industrial relations.

The first perspective which he examines is the view of organizations as systems, 'composed of a set of interdependent parts; organizations have needs for survival; and organizations, as systems, behave and take actions'.[162] Within this perspective conflict comes to be regarded as 'functional', that is, as bringing about adaptation within the organization which enables it to adapt to changes within its environment, to satisfy the demands of contending factions within the organization and to avoid rigidity and inflexibility. Goals are usually attributed to organizations and organizations are believed to act or to behave so as to achieve them. Earlier versions of systems theory, which regarded the organizational system as more or less finite or closed, have been overtaken by an 'open-systems' approach in which the organization is seen as influencing its total environment and being influenced by it in turn. The system's pursuit of its goals is also affected by internal control mechanisms or devices which contribute to long-term consistency and stability. Two processes have been described as influencing organization: morphostatic 'processes in complex system environment exchanges that tend to preserve or maintain a system's given form, organization, or state', and morphogenetic 'processes which tend to elaborate or change a system's given form, structure or state'.[163]

The systems approach to industrial relations has been enormously influential and, although systems theory in sociology has been long contested, in its application to industrial relations, signs of a critical reaction have been more recent. The influence of systems theory in industrial relations is explained partly by the greater naivety of industrial relations theorists who have almost always displayed a sturdy British contempt for theoretical pre-occupations of any sort, and partly by an acknowledgement of its very real advantage if only as an approach to teaching a complicated subject. Dunlop's introduction to industrial relations systems, for example, makes a clear explanation of the interaction of the major actors in industrial relations (workers, employers and the State) in an environment which influences them by way of technological, commercial and social forces. Systems theory also has the advantage of allowing for the influence of obviously powerful forces, such as technology, without appearing to become deterministic in a slavish acceptance of their absolute control. But the very clarity of the explanation which systems theory can offer may become dangerously attractive, both to teachers and taught. The model which is exposed to view may be conceived of as representing a reality which is much more difficult to comprehend, more subtle and more complicated. For this reason, a number of students may have been convinced that they understand industrial relations when, in fact, what they have understood is an obstacle to its comprehension. The cruder versions of systems theory have, for instance, been criticized for leading to an understandable impression that the system or the organization exists, lives, acts, wills, decides: that it is in every respect a sentient being. 'If one talks in terms of organizations behaving ... one runs the risk of attributing human characteristics to social constructs'.[164] Systems theory has also been criticized for its inherent conservatism and for leading to difficulties of definition.

Managers have been taught to appreciate that employment

relationships are not simply a matter of communication, leadership and motivation. Silverman sees the development of the idea of a socio-technical system as an extension of the human relations approach in a more sophisticated direction:

> attention could still be directed towards the work group, and the assumption of the 'beneficial' effects of strong work group ties still be made, but all this would have to take place within a framework which recognized that crude prescriptions about techniques would have to be replaced by a careful analysis of the ways in which behaviour could be shaped by different organizational settings.[165]

Technology has figured largely in the subsequent assessment of influences on behaviour, to the extent that Silverman regards W F Whyte as making 'the mistake of viewing behaviour and motivation as the outcome of technology'.[166] Leonard Sayles made a famous distinction between technological characteristics of production systems and patterns of group behaviour which were often associated with them. The four distinctive patterns of group behaviour, strategic, conservative, erratic and apathetic, which resulted from this analysis are relevant to the understanding of industrial relations in the place of work. The assembly line production process has come to be regarded as almost conditioning the response of workers who are exposed to it and, until recently, the effects have been commonly believed to be entirely negative. Thus a great part of industrial conflict in particular industries has been attributed to negative effects of the production process. Currently, the location most favoured as the embodiment of the dire effects of assembly line production is the motor industry:

> If you stand on the catwalk at the end of the plant you can look down over the whole assembly floor. Few people do, for to stand there and look at the endless,

> perpetual, tedium of it all is to be threatened by the overwhelming insanity of it. The sheer audacious madness of a system based upon men like those wishing their lives away.[167]

The high incidence of strikes in some parts of the motor industry has been explained as a consequence of the technology just as, when the high incidence of strikes in coal-mining commanded attention, it was technology which offered the most likely explanation.

Certain features of technology often emerge as a common theme in accounting for conflict. The technology is frequently described as producing some degree of psychological tension. This view is associated with the repetitive tasks required to be performed by highly divided, specialized, routine operations and there is a long tradition of criticism of their effects. Few have stood against this tradition and most of those who see positive characteristics in divided work on assembly lines have chosen to confine their enthusiasm to the compensations and rewards which it brings or have stressed the consonance of what it provides with what is expected by those who choose to undertake it. Baldamus goes further in isolating what he calls 'traction', the 'feeling of being pulled along by the inertia in a particular activity'.[168] Most commentators fall within Blauner's judgement, that:

> the consensus of the work literature is that assembly line work, especially in the automobile industry, is more disliked than any other major occupation, and the prime factor in dissatisfaction with the assembly line is the lack of control over the pace of production.[169]

Professor Joan Woodward made an important and influential contribution in the evidence she presented for distinguishing between major categories of production process, small batch, large batch, mass and process production. The implications for industrial relations management begin to be more clearly comprehended if we visualize a stable group of workers engaged in building a ship or a diesel locomotive and contrast their situation with that of workers employed in producing, say, washing machines or car bodies. In the first case the workers are literally on top of their work, in the second the work is on top of the workers. Large single units are worked *upon* by employees who may exercise more control over production processes. Assembly work is conveyed over employees and the pace at which the track moves controls their operations. Disputes on single assembly jobs or on small batch production often coincide with the end of the job (when the ship is nearing completion) or with a change-over in the batch. At these times workers may feel that their bargaining power is temporarily enhanced and that they have more cause for dispute over rates and times as they are changed at the end of the batch. The interruptions to task patterns and rhythms of work in small batch work are notoriously productive of conflict. It is the kind of situation in which management appears to be both distant and inconsistent, yesterday's urgent priorities are shelved to-day, the foreman has to cope on an hour-to-hour basis, the favourite slogan on the shop-floor is 'you don't have to be mad to work here, but it helps if you are'.

In assembly line production, on the other hand, the crises are not intermittent so much as chronic. Work is paced and determined not so much by the machine, or by the particular piece of work to be done, as by the organization and interrelationships of the specialized jobs undertaken within the plant and even outside it. Work is a question of orchestration, timing and co-ordination. This aspect both gives management an unusual interest in maintaining control over the work process and workers an unusual interest in denying it. Beynon's view, although it is exaggerated, is probably accurate in seeing Ford's as a constant battle ground in which conflict may arise, not over particular concrete issues, but at times when one group or another sees itself as enjoying a temporary ascendancy. Process industries are different again. Anyone who has visited, for the first time, a modern power station or an oil refinery, may have been impressed by the apparent absence of anyone actually doing any work. The plant controls the process, what direct effort there is is largely expended in the maintenance of the plant and the monitoring of its performance from control panels. There is a sense in which workers here neither control the job nor are they controlled by it, they seem to enjoy a passive relationship with it, they *tend* it rather in the way that shepherds tend sheep. The relationship is less critical and tense than many others involved in work and the workers may see themselves as members of less distinctive and characteristic groups than other groups of workers. Groups are not so clearly defined, the opportunities for intragroup contacts may not be frequent in a plant extending over several miles and there is no history and tradition of corporate worker loyalty and associations.

These considerations are reminders that the technology of the work process is rarely, if ever, a determinant of worker behaviour. Technology may be influential in several characteristic ways. Technology influences the length of the job cycle, the size of the work group, the nature of relationships, the opportunity for and frequency of communication between group members, the frequency with which jobs are changed, the degree and nature of skills employed, the mixture of prescribed and discretionary elements in work, the physical environment and physical effort in work and the occupational structure. These are powerful forces and they suggest the inappropriateness of generalizing about standardized approaches to industrial relations, collective bargaining or payment systems. As

Lupton and Bowey put it:

> in order to understand behaviour and in particular to predict the way in which employees will respond to any one type of payment system, it will be necessary to examine the state of these variables in the organization concerned.[170]

The examination will have to take account of other than technological factors and some which, although influenced by technology, have come to attain an existence independent of technological considerations. We have become more aware, in recent years, of the considerable influence of 'occupational community' on the behaviour of workers. As Salaman describes it:

> an occupational community means that people who are members of the same occupation or who work together have some sort of common life together, are, to some extent, separate from the rest of society.[171]

Among the determinants of membership of an occupational community are involvement in the work itself, the inclusive influence of the work and its organization (shift working, for example) and the direct control which work and its organization may seek to exercise over the lives of the workers. Salaman's work suggests what many have suspected, that it is a gross over-simplification to identify the pervasiveness of work with the actual enjoyment which workers experience in doing it. Many coal miners seem to loath pit work but to take great pride in being miners. The same contradiction seems to emerge in Beynon's work on Fords. Salaman's description of Hull trawlermen is interesting for this reason:

> To say that fishermen must be involved in their work is certainly not to say that they find it satisfying or enjoyable, but to suggest that it has considerable emotional signifi-

> cance for them. The nature of this emotional importance is difficult to establish, it probably varies over time. The involvement of a deckie learner differs from that of a veteran trawlerman. The trawlermen are committed by their work to a view of themselves and their mates, a definition of the world and their position in it, which cannot be simply sloughed off. They are enmeshed in a work-based world which, for all implications, constitutes *their* world—their only one.[172]

Salaman concludes that the most important features conducive to feelings of involvement in work are danger, skill ('the application of knowledge and expertise, relatively free from supervision'), the existence of extreme conditions (involving arduousness or great discomfort) and the importance of the work (that it 'is in some way concerned with core societal values').[173]

The authors of the affluent workers studies go much further in dissociating the worker from a determined response to his technological environment. They specifically reject the argument that 'technology imposes a pattern of work tasks and roles which in turn act as determinants of work attitudes and behaviour' because, they said, 'there was little association between the workers' immediate experience of their work situations as technologically conditioned and the range of attitudes and behaviour.'[174] They conclude that 'the basic shortcomings of the "technological implications" approach is that the attempt to provide explanations from the point of view of the "system" entails the neglect of the point of view of the actors involved', and that in modern 'mass society, the enterprise is often not an organisation of any great normative influence in the lives of its manual labour force.'[175]

Workers in these studies were reported to share a largely instrumental orientation to work; they undertook it for the money with which they could purchase satisfactions outside their working lives. These conclusions are inimical to a long tradition of managerial thinking, that work both *is* vastly influential and that it *ought* to be influential. The workers at Luton, the authors argue, cannot be described as alienated because they bring to their work a realistic expectation of what it will provide, money, not inherent job satisfaction. Managers and employers have always required a high degree of involvement of workers in their work and this commitment or moral investment in work has a tradition of some 200 years in which it has been emphasized as a duty. In this sense, any evidence of alienation in the workers becomes a serious managerial problem, not simply a problem for employees. It is not likely to meet managerial requirements for work performance for employees to develop an instrumental attitude to their work. From this point of view, the whole concept of alienation can be seen as a managerial idea, developed because managers' expectations of work involvement meet the obdurate resistance or realistic expectations among workers of what work is for; the idea of alienation develops to explain the gap between managerial requirements for workers' commitment and the instrumental attitudes of the workers themselves. The gap leads to intensified efforts by the managers to close it, they embark upon more and more sophisticated programmes for recruiting the whole-hearted involvement of the employers, they concentrate upon dealing with the problem of alienation. But the problem is essentially a subjective one, present in the minds of managers rather than of workers. Workers may not see themselves as alienated if their perceptions of the purpose of their work are very different from those of managers. Workers may see their work as instrumental to the achievement of other goals; their managers may expect them to find it intrinsically rewarding. Alienation becomes a managerial conception, indeed a managerial problem, and managerial action to solve it is likely only to exaggerate the ways in which the problem is formulated. So we disappear into an endless spiral in which 'solutions' serve only to make the perception of the 'problem' seem more acute, which demands the production of different solutions which, in turn, re-emphasize the problem of alienation.

It is not so simple because Salaman's evidence suggests that workers in occupational communities *are* involved in their work, that 'men in certain lines of work consider their participation in a work role is an important and meaningful aspect of their own identity, ie they are involved.'[176] The evidence about the attitudes and behaviour of railwaymen seems to be quite different from, if not contradictory to, the conclusions about the instrumentalism of the affluent workers.

The involvement of the railwaymen, has not been produced as the result of managerial appeals or by changes (cosmetic or constitutional) in the style of management or by the introduction of machinery for worker participation. It seems to require, as we have seen, some characteristics that most of us would say were best avoided, danger and arduousness. The involvement of the worker is not brought about by work that is simply enjoyable. Work which produces pride in the worker has rarely been regarded as fun, it has more usually been seen as hard and demanding, as toil which earns the respect of others for those who undertake it, requiring a mature adjustment to a harness which younger men may find irksome.

The development of occupational communities, Salaman suggests, may change with the age of the workers, developing more completely in, for example, the veteran trawlermen. It may be significant that work groups most likely to be acknowledged to possess a sense of occupational community, go through a process of learnership or career development in the job. Colliers traditionally were prepared for a responsible job at the coal face by a butty system of working as lad to an experienced man; even now they go through a formalized process of underground and coal-face training. In the railways, the new lad started as an engine cleaner, the lowest step in a lengthy process of up-grading through fireman to the coveted and vastly respected position of driver. In the steel industry promotion is still characterized by a rigorous system of seniority. In all these cases, status and respect is associated with maturity and to some extent with power; the senior's opinion of the aspirant's performance is important to the latter's progress, particularly where the process of slow initiation cannot be short-circuited. There is an almost primitive acknowledgement of the similarity between work and life, maturation in the one reflects growth in the other, the values of one become embedded in the other so that work is more likely to become life. Just as life is not always expected to be pleasant or satisfying, so work comes to be seen as important.

The sense of importance depends to a large extent on other people's opinion. Members of the same occupational community may share an understanding of the importance of what they do but it seems to depend upon outsiders' acknowledging the rightness of these judgements. Railwaymen knew they were important and that their work entitled them to the respect of others. The valuation of others is often reflected in relatively high earnings, secure employment or generous fringe benefits which are ungrudgingly provided as proper indications of status.

These feelings are generated in the first place by the technology of the work, but they are perpetuated and reinforced by social and occupational factors and by employment and payment systems. Subsequent changes in technology may have no immediate effect, a reminder that technology is not simply a determinant in matters of industrial relations, because the occupational community may continue to see itself in terms which it has been taught to accept and which it continues to teach to its members:

> Railwaymen's expectations of their work and their work situation, have been built up over time, developed and transmitted. They are now largely unrealized. Discrepancy between hope, expectation and reality is particularly acute for footplatemen, bringing with them changes in work relationships and activities, and changes in the organization of railway work.[177]

Salaman concludes that railwaymen:

> are, in a sense, trapped in a way of seeing themselves, in an occupation which has become an integral part of their lives, which has changed and is changing in ways that affect them deeply, because of their personal involvement, which they are unable to shrug off. And this, of course, is their personal tragedy.[178]

It is also ironic, if not tragic, that in one of those rare cases where an industrial society has succeeded in producing the commitment of the worker to his work, technical and organizational change should set about teaching him that it was a mistake.

This situation, in which an ingredient of cooperation which many managers would regard as priceless is being sacrificed, is not the result of stupidity or obtuseness. It is not only the result of changes in organization and technology. It is largely a response to a commercial imperative. Far from being an absolute determinant of behaviour in industrial relations, technology is itself frequently conditioned by financial considerations. Changes in technology are often introduced in an attempt to make a particular process less labour intensive and, in this sense, the influence of finance upon industrial relations is obvious, if long term. The whole character of industrial relations may, in the long run, be influenced by changes in the environment which are the result of financial planning. The demand for particular categories of labour, the demand for products, whether the enterprise is expanding or contracting will all deeply affect the climate of industrial relations and the choice of realistic strategies which are available to the unions and to management.

The short-run considerations for the financial influence of strategies in industrial relations seem to be much more obscure. We can acknowledge that the commercial environment, once it is known, has an obvious effect upon the conduct of industrial relations. The implications of financial planning and intentions for industrial relations strategies seem to be much more mysterious. The importance of the relationship between the financial direction of the enterprise and the conduct of its industrial relations seems hardly a matter that requires argument. A substantial cost element (that is, the wage and salary bill) which is susceptible to *some* degree of managerial influence and which can, apparently, have an immediate effect on product price, must be an important element in financial planning and control. But the literature of industrial relations is surprisingly reticent about the influence of financial considerations upon industrial relations management. In Professor Clegg's standard and exhaustive work on industrial relations, the only indexed reference to profit is to profit sharing.[179] It almost appears as though industrial relations is regarded as a rule-making process carried out in isolation from any contact with the financial environment.

Let us examine some possible explanations for this peculiar lacuna. There is, to begin with, the belief that there is a labour market which must be followed but which cannot be led. At the minimum level of influence to be exercised by the particular enterprise, the employer pays the 'going rate', accepts the Wages Council rates for the trade or follows the agreements of the relevant employers' association. At the maximum level of influence 'when an employer experiences difficulty in retaining or attracting people into a job, he may adjust its rate of pay, so changing the relationships between levels of jobs within the organization.'[180] Even then there are likely to be constraints upon the employer's freedom to adjust, because there are likely to be worker or union perceptions about the comparative value of jobs and because union power may be applied to restoring differentials which the employer has disturbed. These are examples of a market inertia which management may feel it is incapable of disturbing on any but a temporary basis; in the long run it simply follows the market. The belief in market inertia has been taken to the point at which it has been maintained that collective bargaining has no influence (or at most an insignificant influence) on levels of earnings.[181] If this is true it provides every excuse for industrial relations writers ignoring financial considerations because, apparently, while the market influences wages, wages are not influenced by bargaining so that presumably bargaining need not concern itself with its influence upon the market as it is determined by it; it is irrelevant. We should not arrive at this conclusion too hastily, since the protagonists of the 'market forces' argument are usually advocates of some form of intervention or control of collective bargaining because of the dire consequences of its uninhibited exercise. It seems difficult to maintain both that collective bargaining is irrelevant and that it is dangerous. But there does seem to be a pervasive view that the settlements and levels of the labour market are, in some way, beyond the control of collective bargaining and all we are concerned with here is to try to explain the apparent fracture between financial control and industrial relations management.

A second explanation concerns the institutional character

which has often been observed in the British study of industrial relations. The study of institutions and of techniques may have contributed to a certain isolation from reality and while that isolation has recently broken down with an acknowledgement of the importance of technology (and of the contribution which sociologists can make) it has not yet embraced the influence of the calculation of costs and profits. The approach has certainly given rise to an inescapable feeling that industrial relations behaviour is usually regarded as reactive rather than influential, that the environment must be regarded as given (if not understood) and that explanations concerning industrial relations must begin at that point. The explanation would include an unfortunate tendency, until recently, to ignore the firm and management's conduct of industrial relations.

A third explanation must lay some blame at the feet of economists and accountants. Economists seem to be preoccupied with the analysis of industry-wide statistics rather than with grubbing for data at the level of the firm or the plant and accountants display a wary suspicion (no doubt wisely) of activities in a field so random and unmeasurable as industrial relations. So we are left alone, undisturbed in the belief that commercial considerations are not noticeably relevant.

The practical effect has been a remarkable reluctance to determine financial objectives in collective bargaining. One suspects, with the recent activities of the Trade Union Research Unit at Ruskin, that unions are now rather better than managements at calculating profit levels, market elasticity and influences on real earnings in order to establish their strategies for collective bargaining: that unions, in short, may be more profit conscious than the employers. It may be that employers have not determined financial objectives in collective bargaining because they have not felt the need, believing that they will be driven into bargains that they cannot avoid and that the consequences will be financed by consumers, not by them. Under these circumstances, who needs to be aware of the financial implications of collective bargaining?

This state of financial irresponsibility on the part of employers has, of course, been held to be the cause of the inflationary problems which beset us.

> The new inflation arises from these facts: that in a modern mass society there is a tendency for wage increases to outstrip the increases in output per man; that the resistance to the translation of these wage increases into price increases, even on the part of apparently competitive industries, is not all that great.[182]

At this level, no one needs to be convinced of the relationship between economic considerations and industrial relations.

> If we do not over the next 12 months achieve a drastic reduction in the present disastrous rate of inflation by the measures outlined in this document, the British people will be engulfed in a general economic catastrophe of incalculable proportions.[183]

The consequence of acknowledging the relationship between industrial relations and the economy at large has been a succession of political attempts to exercise control over collective bargaining by one means or another. But this national, and often ineffective control, is imposed upon a situation in which the practice of collective bargaining seems to take place almost exempt from economic considerations, in which one writer could say of the conduct of industrial relations in the steel industry, 'some managers and observers of industrial relations do not appreciate the inter-action of long-term economic forces and collective bargaining.'[184]

There are numerous excuses for this state of affairs. Employers can shift the responsibility for a manifest unconcern with economic consequences (even for the firm itself) on to trade unions' intransigence in pressing excessive claims with unanswerable power. Trade union leaders, often the target for criticism in terms of irresponsibility can in turn point to the membership as determing the parameters of their own bargaining activity. It would be arrogant and uninformed for any observer to apportion praise or blame. Perhaps it would be most appropriate for an academic observer to suggest that some part of the responsibility might lie in regarding collective bargaining and industrial relations as a field of activity which can be described in isolation from an economic and commerical environment. Industrial relations is about the rules of work and the processes for determining its rewards. But work is made purposeful within an economic context and industrial relations cannot be detached from it. Some progress towards reality might be made by emphasizing the commercial constraints upon industrial relations as strongly as we have learned to emphasize the technological. Until the relationship is recognized at the level at which bargaining is conducted, we may have to continue to rely upon rhetorical political appeals and crude methods of central control as alternatives to bargaining in terms of economic realism.

CHAPTER 8

Joint regulations: scope and content of bargaining

Industrial relations is concerned with the rules relating to employment. The rules are frequently regarded as of two different kinds: *substantive* rules are those which establish norms or intentions in the form of specific conditions of work, and *procedural* rules which exist to adjust differences in the making of substantive rules and the relationships between the parties.[185] Substantive rules usually concern the payment for work, specifications about quantity and quality, the hours of work, differential or premium payments for overtime, shift-working, holiday arrangements and payments, sickness and accident payments, job entry, training, discipline, termination of employment and compensation for loss of jobs. Substantive rules may not cover all these items; British collective agreements have been criticized for the poverty of their subject matter, but they always concern pay and hours and they may concern a much wider range of substantive arrangements. The *content* of substantive arrangements thus varies considerably, that is, there are wide differences in the aspects of work which are the subject of substantive regulations. There are also considerable differences in the coverage or *scope* of collective bargaining and of substantive arrangements; some may cover a high proportion of the employees in a particular industry, others may concern a small fraction.

Both the scope and the content of collective agreements may be determined by the procedural agreement between the parties. Procedural arrangements determine the ways in which terms and conditions of employment are arrived at and the ways in which differences over the application of agreed terms and conditions are settled. Procedural arrangements may limit the range of subjective matter which lies within a substantive agreement and they may specify particular categories of employees who are within or outside the scope of the agreement. The scope of an agreement is often influenced by the bargaining rights which have been accorded by an employer in recognizing a particular union. The recognition rights of a union may be limited to specific bargaining units.

We can also speak of the scope of collective bargaining in general. Clegg distinguished between three kinds of rules (we have so far contented ourselves with two), substantive, procedural and disciplinary and, he said, there are three ways in which they are arrived at: by employer regulation (by the boss determining and administering the rules), by joint regulation or collective bargaining, and by statutory regulation. Industrial relations is concerned with all methods of rule-making but there is no doubt that collective bargaining has come to be regarded as occupying a most significant area within industrial relations and that it is vastly favoured as a method of job regulation. This favourable prejudice received its clearest expression in the Report of the Donovan Commission:

> Properly conducted, collective bargaining is the most effective means of giving workers the right to representation in decisions affecting their working lives, a right which is or should be the prerogative of every worker in a democratic society.[186]

But our preference for collective bargaining should not allow us to exaggerate its importance; it is not the only method of determining the rules of work although it is the most common method in this country.

Within the area of collective bargaining, agreements may be reached at different *levels*, so that the substantive arrangements for a group of workers may be arrived at nationally, for the industry in which they work. Workers may have their substantive terms settled by an agreement between the particular company and the unions concerned. Agreements may also be reached at the level of the plant or the department or even at the workbench. At the most localized level it would be rare for an agreement to include all the substantive items which governed the terms and conditions for the particular employee. The most local agreements are likely to supplement in some way the rules which are established by the national or the company agreement. Substantive rules will frequently be set out in a series of overlapping agreements, so that for some aspects of his conditions of employment a worker may look to his national agreement for the trade or industry (and to his national negotiators) while for others he will look to the plant or the department (and to his shop steward). There is nothing inherently irrational in this arrangement and in some circumstances agreements can be carefully tiered so that the lower agreement fills in ground left vacant by the higher agreement, the one exercising detailed discretion allowed it by the other. Unfortunately (at least from the point of trying to understand the situation) this logical arrangement is not characteristic of British industrial relations because both national and local agreements are likely to concern themselves with the same issues, and particularly with wages.

The pattern of substantive agreements in many industries has been that while the national agreement specifies payment in terms of rates per unit of time at work, actual earnings have come to be influenced by bargaining at the place of work and by incentive earnings, by allowances paid for various purposes and by overtime payments. The gap between earnings and nationally negotiated rates, insignificant before the second world war, has widened since its end. The following figures will give an indication of the nature of wage drift:

Table 2

Annual percentage changes in hourly wage earnings and hourly wage rates 1961–1974

	1 Average hourly wage earnings excluding overtime	2 Average hourly wage rates	3 Difference col 1 minus col 2
1961	+6.9	6.4	+0.5
1962	4.4	4.2	+0.2
1963	3.6	2.3	+1.3
1964	8.1	5.7	+2.4
1965	9.5	7.3	+2.2
1966	6.5	5.6	+0.9
1967	5.0	5.3	−0.3
1968	7.0	6.7	+0.3
1969	8.0	5.5	+2.5
1970	16.0	12.4	+3.6
1971	13.7	11.6	+2.1
1972	14.6	18.1	−3.5
1973	13.6	12.1	+1.5
1974	21.9	20.6	+1.3

Department of Employment *Gazette*, June 1975, Table 125, p595

A number of reasons are usually given for this gap between earnings and rates. It suggests the declining authority and relevance of the employers' associations and their role in national bargaining. Conversely, the growing power and importance of shop stewards and shop floor bargaining have contributed to this change. The preferences shown, for different reasons, for incentive payment systems has had a great deal to do with both these factors. There may also be some more subtle explanations which are difficult to establish with facts. Activities in collective bargaining have been widely reported in recent years and the British public (or the British press and television) have developed an extraordinary sensitivity to industrial relations. In addition, periodic attempts at incomes control have possibly contributed to a tendency to suppress the level of publicly visible bargaining to a point which is too low to satisfy the interests of either workers or employers. In these circumstances, invisible bargaining at plant level has to take place in order to bridge the gap between negotiated rates and an economically realistic level of earnings. The distortion has the function of disguising the actual level of negotiated increases which would have to be achieved if the gap did not exist. It also has the more useful function of allowing, in effect, a discretionary area of bargaining to those plants which can afford additions or to those union organizations which have the power to win them.

Wage drift has been defined as:

> the term used to describe changes in the gap between earnings and rates through time. It may be expressed as the relationship between changes in the gap and wage rates, or, alternatively, the difference between the rate of growth of earnings and wage rates. A distinction is also drawn in the literature between earnings drift which includes the effects of overtime payments, and wage drift which excludes them.[187]

The Office of Manpower Economics produced comparative data on wage drift in 13 industrial groups, see next page:

Table 3

	1967	1968	1969	1970	1971
Food drink and tobacco	−0.7	+1.6	+4.2	+5.0	+3.7
Chemicals and allied industries	−0.7	+3.7	+4.1	−9.4	−8.4
Metals	−2.1	−1.3	+2.3	+7.8	+3.9
Textiles	+2.1	+2.0	+4.1	−8.1	+0.8
Leather, leather goods and fur	−3.2	−0.3	+5.9	−6.1	+2.9
Clothing and footwear	+2.6	+1.0	+5.7	+8.2	−4.3
Bricks, pottery, glass, cement	−0.1	+2.2	+0.7	−3.0	+2.9
Timber, furniture	+2.6	−0.2	+2.8	+2.8	−5.1
Paper, printing and publishing	−0.5	+2.5	+5.1	−0.1	+1.8
Other manufacturing industries	−0.7	−7.5	+5.9	+8.9	−1.9
Construction	+0.2	+2.2	+3.0	+1.2	−0.1
Gas, electricity and water	+0.7	−1.0	−2.6	+4.2	+13.0
Transport and communication	−2.3	+1.8	+1.5	+2.8	+8.6

The Report concluded, on the evidence of changes in earnings, rates and drift over 10 years:

> that in the majority of the 13 industries there is a compensatory relationship between changes in wage rates and drift. That is, in most industries, in those years when the change in wage rates has been above the average for all industries, wage drift in that industry has been below the average for all industries and vice versa.[188]

The balance struck between nationally determined rates and locally negotiated incentives and allowances varies between different industries and between different occupations. Managers, professional and administrative people enjoy earnings which are barely affected by overtime, premium payments or incentives (whether their earnings are determined by collective bargaining or not). Manual employees in manufacturing industries, on the other hand, will have a higher proportion of their incomes based in relation to

Table 4

Components of average weekly earnings as percentages of total

	1 Overtime	2 PBR etc	3 Shift premium payments	4 All other pay
All occupations	10.6	6.6	1.7	81.2
Managerial (general management)	0.1	1.9	0.2	97.7
Clerical	9.2	1.0	1.1	88.7
Farming, fishing	11.2	5.9	0.4	82.6
Materials processing (excluding metals)	15.9	10.5	4.8	68.8

British Labour Statistics, Year Book 1973, Department of Employment, HMSO, 1975, Table 23, p55

variable elements in their work. Table 4 on the previous page gives some indication of these differences:

There are no precise explanations for these differences between 'tight' national agreements and 'loose' agreements which allow considerable local determination of earnings. Boraston, Clegg and Rimmer suggest that:

> historically, employers have been more willing to negotiate with unions about remuneration than about jobs. They have taken the view that, once the rate of pay was settled, the job to be done was for the manager to determine. Practically, it is easier to determine rates of pay in an agreement, especially an industry agreement, than to regulate jobs. An agreement can specify the rate for the job and the rate of overtime pay, but it cannot easily determine the amount of overtime working required by the job. Since in the past industry agreements have been prevalent in Britain, remuneration has been a subject for formal industry agreements whereas many aspects of the job have been dealt with by custom and practice arrangements at the plant.[189]

This is certainly true but those jobs which depend most upon discretion, individual differences in performance, personal abilities and trust, are the ones which are least affected by local additions to pay. As the last table suggests, although white-collar workers may be able to have considerable individual control of job performance they are not paid by reference to local variations: they are paid rates (or salaries) which largely determine earnings. But then their overall salaries are more likely to be individually rather than collectively determined. 'In a salary system increased rewards might accrue to an individual because he has passed some formal test of his capability to do a better paid job or group of jobs.'[190] In a manual wage, on the other hand, the negotiated rate (usually flat, that is, with no incremental additions) cannot be adjusted to variations in the job which must occur in the place of work. Salary systems, whether they are negotiated or not, are usually susceptible to adaptation to individual differences in performance. Negotiated wage structures are relatively inflexible and 'need' to be distorted by shop-floor additions and allowances.

The distortions to wage structures and the fragmentation of bargaining which follows has been widely condemned. The Donovan Report said that 'methods of wage payment and the ways they are applied have obstructed the development of orderly company and factory pay structures' adding that the central defect of our industrial relations 'is the disorder in factory and workshop relations and pay structures'.[191] Techniques of control have been widely recommended because, without them, 'industrial relations can border on anarchy', decentralization might 'degenerate into anarchy'. Clegg argued that 'defective management control over systems of payment by results has spawned opportunities for fragmented domestic bargaining with unrestrained fecundity'.[192] There have been frequent references to the relationship between disorderly payment systems and strikes:

> In the most strike prone industries frequent strikes over pay can be explained by pay systems fashioned by domestic bargaining and custom and practice, which allow wide fluctuations in weekly pay and encourage competitive pay claims from small groups.[193]

Donovan agreed:

> the conviction is borne out by consideration of circumstances in all four industries which suffer most from unofficial strikes—coal-mining, docks, shipbuilding and

ship repairing and motors. In all these industries work group bargaining is exceptionally strong, fragmented bargaining has been the rule, and wage structures have been notoriously anarchic.[194]

As the result of these dire warnings there has been a movement towards a greater degree of central control of wage bargaining particularly in the public sector. It has nowhere been clearer than in the coal industry. After nationalization and throughout the 1950s the coal industry was the most frequently cited as an example of the awful effects of anarchy in industrial relations. The most important determinants of face workers' earnings were colliery bargaining and colliery price lists. Disorder was reflected in a formidable strike record, coal-mining was the dominating influence in British strike statistics. The situation demanded improvement and it was generally agreed that improvement would depend upon greater control over local bargaining and allowances and more central influence on bargaining and wage payments. Coinciding with a general attack on incentive payment systems, piecework was regarded as the enemy; it was costly and it stimulated strikes: the elimination of piecework would reduce strikes. There was a more general requirement for control, 'after nationalization the Coal Board could not properly fulfil their responsibility for running the industry unless they could control wages costs centrally, and it was impossible to do that under the existing agreements.'[195] The day wage structure of 1955, the general strengthening of the industrial relations function, the centralization of the bargaining process and the power loading agreements of 1966 all followed the requirement for greater central control.

The results cannot have been entirely what had been hoped for. The following table shows the dramatic decrease in mining disputes as a percentage of all industry:

Table 5
Number of disputes

Year	Total disputes, all industry	Total disputes, mining	Mining disputes as % of total
1946	2205	1329	60
1950	1339	860	64
1955	2419	1783	73
1960	2832	1666	58
1965	2354	740	31
1970	3906	160	4
1974	2743	165	6

So far so good but if we take a different index of strike performance the progress of improvement becomes rather less certain.

Strikes in coal-mining have become longer and better organized. In 1972 and 1974 approximately 40 per cent of working days lost in disputes throughout Britain were lost in mining. In terms of lost production, when concern about industrial relations in mining was at its greatest, the industry never lost more than 2 per cent of its total production in disputes. In 1972 and 1974 the losses in disputes approximated to 20 per cent. The improvement in industrial relations suggested in Table 5 is illusory. The enormous increases in proportional losses has coincided with the results of cumulative efforts to establish greater control over industrial relations. Control has coincided with the greater organization of industrial disputes; where they were once sporadic, short, unofficial and relatively uncostly they are now long, organized, official and enormously effective. This is not a simple matter of cause and effect because many other changes have intervened but it is reasonable to suggest that the organization of conflict might not have been possible without centralization of wage structures and control because the NUM has emerged from changes introduced by management in industrial relations with much more power than it could have commanded in the old chaotic days of piecework. It appeared recently that management might be aware of the bargaining advantages of incentive bonus payments, but the NUM saw the danger and regarded the wish to return to them as an attempt to weaken the unions. Perhaps the NUM was right.

The general purpose of this cursory analysis is to suggest a proper wariness about demands for order in collective bargaining and about the dangers of fractionalized anarchy in wage systems. Line managers frequently refer to the advantages of incentive payments but rarely do they associate them with incentives to effort. The main grounds for their continuing popularity are all related to flexibility. Donovan acknowledged that incentives were popular, 'the participants in the current arrangements are . . . well satisfied with them' but went on to suggest that 'the advantages of conflict, flexibility and autonomy were more than offset by the grave threat that decentralization might degenerate into indecision and anarchy.'[196] But anarchy can have some advantages, as the example of the coal industry may illustrate. Incentives and fractionalized bargaining have some particular appeals.

1 They can help local managers to escape from the inadequacies of the central bargaining system, particularly when there is general pressure on the central bargaining system to suppress rates. The enthusiasm for the tardy introduction of incentives schemes in the NHS may in part be related to the rigid control of Whitley machinery and the related problem of low pay.
2 They can help local managers to offer competitive

earnings levels in stringent local labour markets when a general adjustment of rates would be too expensive.

3 They can be responsive to the particular requirements of local management and local labour.

4 They can facilitate the appropriate adjustment of earnings without attracting national attention, national comparison and national evaluation. It is more difficult, with fragmented bargaining and complex earnings composition, to talk in terms of a wages league. Comparisons are more difficult and, at least, there is a time lag between action, comparison and reaction.

5 They certainly facilitate shop floor participation in bargaining and they certainly contribute to the power of shop representatives (indeed a good deal of the energy put into suppressing them probably stems from a determination to curb the power of shop stewards). But they do not necessarily contribute to increasing the power of the union as an organized force.

6 They may help managers to escape from the control of incomes policy by reducing the negotiating process to a level of invisibility.

This alone is sufficient explanation for the unpopularity of incentive payments and fractionalized bargaining among public administrators. We have seen it suggested also that the achievement of central control in industrial relations is likely to be a bureaucratic requirement in the direction of public enterprises. It may well be the case that the 'personnel professionals' also have an interest in the pursuit of planned order and national and controllable wage structures; they may be effective weapons in their own internal struggles with production managers. Finally, it is proper to acknowledge that academic specialists in industrial relations contribute their own preference for orderly wages systems and bargaining structures since it is more difficult to understand the disorderly, because they must categorize before they can teach. All this is merely to suggest that the 'improvement of substantive arrangements and of ways of arriving at them may have to be judged by different standards when it comes to assessing their effects on industrial relations.'

There is no doubt that the whole weight of received opinion has been consistently in favour of measurement, rationality and a more consistent control of wages and collective bargaining. It is difficult to arrive at a judgement as to the effect of this accumulated wisdom. In its evidence to the Donovan Commission, the TUC estimated that earnings were arrived at by the following processes.[197]

			millions
National bargaining	ie	national machinery making the main agreement on an industry basis, closely adhered to at company level	7
National company bargaining		national machinery making the main agreement but coupled with bargaining with a company	6
Wages Councils			4
Company bargaining	ie	the main agreements made within company machinery	1
No bargaining	ie	employees not covered by any joint negotiating machinery	5
Total			23

If the campaign against the irrelevance of uncontrollable national bargaining and the chaos in which it has resulted had been successful, we would expect these proportions to have been substantially changed. Figures available for 1973 suggest that this has not taken place. The following table compares a percentage breakdown of the TUC's estimate for 1968 with the percentages of full-time adults affected by various types of collective agreement.[198]

TUC estimate	1968	1973
	%	%
National agreement only	30	40
National company agreements	26	25
Wages Councils	13	(14)[198]
Company, district or local agreement only	4	10
No collective agreement	22	25

The enthusiasm for productivity bargaining which overtook British industrial relations might have had an effect on the reinforcement of company bargaining as against national or national-fractionalized bargaining. The fact that this enthusiasm was short-lived and that productivity bargaining seems to have fallen out of fashion may explain why this change in distribution of the levels of bargaining has not taken place. There are some features of productivity bargaining which continue to deserve attention. It was hailed as a considerable innovation in collective bargaining (and for this reason we shall have to discuss its strategic implication in the next chapter), it represents a real attempt both to extend the content of collective bargaining and its control, and interest in it is always likely to be re-awakened by a continuing preoccupation with incomes control by the Government.

The National Board for Prices and Incomes (now defunct) defined comprehensive productivity agreements as those which 'cover a number of related changes, affect all or nearly all the manual workers in an undertaking whereas partial agreements normally affect only one practice, and often only a single group of workers.'[199] Other definitions have also emphasized both the element of considerable change and the wide coverage of productivity agreements. Thus Flanders said that:

> the principle common to all productivity bargaining is the furnishing of an economic inducement for an acceptance of change, but it can be applied to any rules and conventions regulating work practices, including—as in the Fawley example—systematic overtime, job demarcations, the employment of mates, union restrictions on supervision, or procedures for promotion.[200]

Jones and Golding add that:

> the prime purpose of productivity bargaining is to raise labour productivity and lower unit labour costs, and this is achieved by the exchange of alterations in working practices for increased leisure, higher remuneration for labour, more comprehensive fringe benefits and a general increase in the status of the manual employees.[201]

The methods by which increases in productivity and the reduction in labour costs have been sought have been by a reduction in manning (or an increase in the output without increased manning), by an increase in the pace or volume of work (by job elimination, methods improvement or an increase in the proportion of effective to available working time) and by more flexible working arrangements (the result of the interchange of jobs between previously discreet groups and of the reduction of demarcation boundaries protecting skilled groups from semi-skilled assistance[202]). Changes in flexibility were often hailed as some of the more dramatic achievements of productivity bargaining as they were sometimes accompanied by changes in the hierarchy of supervision (chargehands often disappeared as an entire supervisory level) and by the intrusion of non-craft supervisors into craft work.

The results included considerable increases in rates of pay

(to the extent that the productivity bargaining and its general repercussions have been blamed for the break away in negotiated increases which occurred in the 1960s and which has itself been blamed for consequent inflation.) But increases in rates were not always associated with proportionate increases in earnings; one of the objects in productivity bargaining was to impose greater control by narrowing the earnings gap. Rates were higher (increases of 20 per cent were described as average) but were financed partly by reductions in 'institutionalized' overtime, in allowances and in incentive payments which were often consolidated into the new rate. Employees were also persuaded to accept modest increases in earnings by the provision of greater security, reduced hours, better organization and, in some cases, by the metaphysical attractions of improved status.

The National Board for Prices and Incomes concluded that productivity bargaining had advantages for the following reasons:[203]

- they contributed to improved industrial relations
- they had achieved in 75 per cent of the agreements studies lower labour costs per unit
- they had not produced consequential effects of inflating in other companies
- they required and generally produced careful control to prevent the reintroduction of abandoned practices.

We might add that they often improved the bargaining, communications and representational structures in companies which engaged in them, they introduced a new element of reality into collective bargaining, and they may have contributed to the provision of more stable employment conditions for workers (at least, for those workers who survived their introduction).

The attack on productivity bargaining by surrogate defenders of the workers' interests was slow in developing but it was effective when it emerged because it dissolved some of the cloudier claims which had been advanced by management. Tony Cliff's[204] onslaught was clear and powerful and, incidentally, it revealed some differences in value which are always present in industrial relations but which are often politely suppressed in its discussion (for example, 'restrictive practices' which managers regard as wicked but which workers may regard as sensible and necessary, see below).

Productivity bargaining was said to involve the following disadvantages for workers:

- initial large wage increases were confined to profitable industries in which wages costs were low
- initial wage increases were often followed by lengthy wage stand-stills
- considerations of comparability were ignored and important ingredients in wages were forgotten
- increased flexibility meant harder work which productivity agreements did not adequately reward and flexibility broke up a necessary degree of stability in workers' organization
- productivity agreements often required the introduction of unhealthy and socially dangerous innovations, like shift working
- restrictive practices were valuable because they concerned job regulations and protection, and were a valuable erosion of managerial control over the use of working hours; they were often lost in productivity agreements
- productivity agreement tightened labour discipline
- there were often far fewer employees left in the organization to enjoy the advantages of a productivity agreement after it had been introduced.

It is doubtful if these and similar criticisms carried much weight in dissuading managers of the advantages of productivity agreements. Their association with incomes policy probably turned out to have given them a fatal encouragement to proliferate too quickly; one of the most serious reasons for the decline might have been that there was simply not sufficient managerial talent available to enable firms to negotiate them and to exercise the necessary degree of subsequent control.

The current decline in interest in productivity bargaining has left British collective bargaining in a suspended state while recent voluntary phases in incomes control, closely associated with the pieties of the social contract, have re-introduced a considerable degree of vagueness, even of hypocrisy, into the conduct of collective bargaining. Perhaps all that can be usefully done at the present time is to return to some general statement of managerial intentions and objectives in the negotiation of substantive agreements.

One statement came from the NBPI[205] on salary structures which, the Board said, should:

> serve the aims and purposes of the organization as a whole
> form an integral part of the organization's manpower policies
> be suited to a rational organization and be capable of allowing for its change and development
> attract the applications for employment of suitable candidates in sufficient number
> facilitate the efficient deployment of employees
> influence people who are suitable for the present and future needs of the organization to remain with it
> adequately relate to maintaining high performance by individuals
> meet all these aims at the least cost to the organization.

The Code of Practice[206] contained a statement of the general requirements or principles of payment systems, which should be:

kept as simple as possible, consistent with their purpose, so that employees can understand them

based on some form of work measurement where payment is linked to performance

jointly negotiated where trade unions are recognized

differences in remuneration should be related to the requirements of the job, which should wherever possible be assessed in a rational and systematic way in consultation with employees representatives

payment systems should be kept under review to make sure that they suit current circumstances and take account of any substantial changes in the organization of work or the requirements of the job.

One of the greatest difficulties concerns differences of remuneration. The matter of their determination becomes complicated because it cannot be decided by reference to any single criterion of measurement. Differences in pay are influenced by several different considerations. Market demand and market supply largely determine the fact that pop-singers get paid more than school teachers or nurses, but market forces are always present in influencing relative wages. They are also influenced by long-standing feelings about relative status.[207] They sometimes concern the length of time and the difficulty in learning the skills of a trade or profession. They may include an element of monetary compensation for tolerating difficult or dangerous conditions of work.[208] They are certainly related to feelings about justice but these may be differentiated between employers (who pay) and employees (who receive). In some jobs there is a direct consideration for the amount of goods that are produced or sold, or for maintaining the quality of the product. Payment systems may be shaped so as to encourage a process of growth or maturation of the employee. They may even take account of factors which have no direct connection with work or its evaluation, they may be adjusted to meet the extent of the workers' family responsibilities. The Pay Board summed up the matter by concluding that:

> relativities are . . . inherently complex, being influenced by economic, social and institutional pressures which are often difficult to reconcile. Two factors are of major importance: the labour market and fairness. In so far as pay relativities reflect differences in skill, responsibility and other features sought for particular kinds of employment, they help to distribute available manpower between jobs, occupations and industries in accordance with the varying demands for employees' services. On the other hand, people's views of the fairness of their pay in relation to that of others frequently lead to changes or pressures for changes in wage levels, and these may conflict with the operation of market forces. Fairness itself can be interpreted in many ways: it is not only subjective but its meaning is liable to change over time with changing circumstances.[209]

Fortunately, the employer does not have to wrestle with these impossible complexities when he is trying to determine what the objects of his payment system should be. In the first place, many of his choices have already been taken; there is a broadly determined pecking order which he knows he cannot disturb; his own influence is likely to concern detail rather than structural design. In the second place, unlike the Pay Board, he has the advantage of being able to think in terms of the objectives of his organization rather than of society at large. In the third place, he may derive a wry satisfaction from the realization that, in the area of collective bargaining, he can rarely make a unilateral decision.

This is a more genuine advantage than it may appear to be. The complexity and diversity of the elements composing wages make any objective or scientific attempt to determine their ideal relationships impossible to achieve. We can make distinctions along one dimension (market value, product value, degree of difficulty, amount of effort) but the result would be obviously unreal. When we make reference to measurements along a number of dimensions we obviously have to give some thought to the relative importance of the dimensions. This is precisely what is done in multi-factor job evaluation systems and the results are always a reflection of the relative weightings of the factors which have been included for measurement. This is not to say that job evaluation is worthless because, if the factors and their relative importance are agreed, the measurements are meaningful for making comparisons between jobs amongst those people who have agreed their constituent factors and their weighting; job evaluation becomes an acceptable vocabulary within which precise communication about comparisons can be made but the communication is possible only among those who have accepted the vocabulary. The application of job evaluation to the measurement of jobs for comparative purposes is a most important advance because it not only makes precise comparisons possible among those who understand and accept (for their purposes) the particular job evaluation system, but it also exposes to the scrutiny of others the values underlying their judgements.

The practical applications of job evaluation are summarized by the ACAS as helping to:

- establish acceptable differences in the wage rates between jobs, thus removing any existing anomalies and inequities in pay
- create simpler, more easily understandable, pay structures
- reduce the number of grievances over relative wages
- provide a yardstick by which grievances or claims about jobs can be judged and so help avoid arbitrary decisions

- lessen time spent on dealing with such grievances and claims
- fit new jobs into existing pay structures, thus easing technological and organizational change.[210]

Job evaluation is not scientific or entirely reliable but it certainly promotes the more logical and systematic comparison of jobs and to this extent it is an essential analytic tool. Its over-enthusiastic application can be dangerous. The more complex methods (complex in terms of the number of factors to be measured and in the apparent precision by which the comparisons are made) may lead to a belief that the results can be arrived at, assessed and discussed only by experts. Complexity of methods of measurement may also introduce psychological difficulties of exercising judgements over a confusion of factors requiring unduly fine judgement; in these cases the analyst is likely to become more and more subjectively convinced of the reliability of his own judgement as it becomes less and less reliable. Here managers may be heard to announce that it is utterly impossible for them to concede a re-grading of job X from grade 3 to 4 because the job evaluation evidence shows that in three out of 20 factors job X falls two points below the dividing line between grade 3 and grade 4. Points rating systems, particularly when they are imposed upon over-complicated grade structures, can magnify (and give the appearance of objective reality to) distinctions which are so fine that they were better not recognized at all. Difficulties of this kind are not endemic in job evaluation but where they appear they can impede the process of collective bargaining rather than assist it. Trade unions have one other reason for sometimes becoming sceptical when they are told that the 'values' underlying the job evaluation system cannot be negotiated. This is inevitable because agreement about them is essential to maintaining the validity of the vocabulary of comparison; if we do not agree about job factors and their importance then nothing can be compared with nothing. But this is no comfort to a union negotiator who is convinced that job A entails more effort than job B and who is told that effort is not relevant to the assessment of the jobs in question.

Generally speaking, the simpler the method of job evaluation, consonant with the requirements for its use, the better. Thomason provides a clear and full account of the main evaluation methods: job ranking, job classification, points evaluation, factor comparison, time span, staff evaluation, across-the-board evaluation and rational classification. Thomason also describes procedures to be followed and the problems in and approaches to the validation of job evaluation plans. He concludes that:

> it is virtually impossible to validate job evaluation findings either by reference to existing structures of payment . . . or by reference to general normative distributions obtained by questioning

but that:

> it is not necessary to make broad claims for job evaluation to establish its usefulness. In a society characterized by frequent changes in occupations, we need a set of new tools with which to analyse and reconstruct the situation. Amongst these are likely to be tools other than those of job evaluation. But it would be foolish to abandon those of job evaluation.[211]

Enthusiasm about job evaluation should always be curbed when it reaches the point of diminishing the importance of collective bargaining or of impeding its progress. This is an important qualification not because of any sympathy which we ought to feel for trade unions but because collective bargaining itself provides a remarkably sensitive method of producing comparative judgements about relative rewards for jobs. The difficulties involved in comparing one job with others are, to say the least, formidable. There is no available standard of justice or equity which can be used, comparisons are at best made on the basis of elements in the jobs which the observers have decided are important. Different observers may select different elements and attach relatively different importance to them. The great virtue of collective bargaining is that it *does* evaluate jobs by a remarkably complex process which produces results even though we cannot always explain it. Collective bargaining arrives at differential rates and rewards and it is capable of re-adjusting them when they are not perceived to be acceptable to those to whom they relate.

Collective bargaining produces acceptable results between groups holding very different perceptions of the meaning of concepts like 'fairness' and 'equity' and very different objectives for the outcome of the negotiating process. The objectives of unions and their members concern income and the reward of effort. The objectives of employers concern costs and the satisfaction of economic demands. The Pay Board said that:

> a wide range of meanings is attached to fairness in the context of relative pay. Sometimes concern is with the fairness of pay changes within a plant or company, sometimes with changes in or between industries. Not only is fairness interpreted subjectively but its meaning changes with circumstances. At one time a group may emphasize the arduousness and at another time the skill of its work in relation to that of other groups. Moreover, the individual may make his comparisons with others than those whom the representatives of his group cite in negotiations. Most importantly, one group's view of fairness may not be shared by the groups with whom the comparison is made.[212]

Comparisons are made easier by the construction of wage and salary structures so that, instead of a confusion of unplanned relations between rates of pay for large numbers of jobs, jobs are grouped and each group is given the same rate. Some sort of rational attempt to justify the relationship between the rates for the groups or grades is now possible and it is also easier to measure and make judgements about the relationship between one structure and another. In this way both internal and external relativities are more subject to rational control. Wage structures are usually relationships between flat rates for groups of jobs; salary structures often express a range or scale of salaries for each grade. This means that a salaried job holder may expect to receive increases in pay, up to the limit of his scale, whether he is promoted to a higher grade or not. The reasons for this progressive element in salary payment are obscure but they are said to include the need to reward maturity and experience and the employer's wish to reward service and to retain it. They are probably related to the affinity which was believed to exist between staff and owner and to providing a sense of climbing the hierarchy towards the top, a reflection of status in cash. They reflect a long-standing view that staff and professional jobs involve a career, a life's work, whereas manual occupations are jobs which command and require a less permanent relationship with their occupants. Judgement and discretion, both regarded as important elements in administrative work, increase with time whereas the abilities relevant to manual work (strength, fitness, perceptual skill, dexterity) decline.

Incremental salary systems may be fixed or variable. Fixed incremental scales seem to be characteristic of non-manual public employment (in which 2½ million employees, or 96 per cent of the total were on fixed scales governed by automatic progression) but to be less common in the private sector.[213] Fixed systems in which the individual climbs his scale by predetermined steps, are associated with the allocation of jobs to grades within groups or families of comparable jobs. A salary structure may thus be composed of three groups, say, administrative, production and scientific, each of which has a differential relation to the others and each of which consists of a number of grades, each containing incremental progression. Job evaluation may or may not be used to allocate jobs to grades. Fixed increments are not as flexible as variable progression because they are not as responsive to management's discretion in the reward for what it considers to be good performance or the withholding of reward for bad. It may be that the comparative inflexibility of fixed systems is associated with the deliberate upgrading of jobs. The Office of Manpower Economics concluded that:

> almost without exception unions state a preference for fixed compared with variable systems. They support open arrangements which are easier to regulate by collective bargaining and which limit management discretion, while expressing doubts about the fairness and reliability of performance assessment.[214]

The maintenance of salary progression for staff employees has come to be regarded as a traditional advantage which they enjoy over manual employees. Like many other long standing and unquestioned arrangements, it cannot be entirely justified by 'the facts' of work. The distinction may be one that comes under attack in the demand that staff status and conditions should be provided for manual employees, or that the conditions of all employees should be harmonized. There is not a great deal of evidence to suggest that incremental salary systems have been a casualty in these innovations because they are sometimes advanced with partial expectations, not always 'designed to give manual workers a similar status to staff, but rather to provide the practical conditions necessary to achieving the desired changes in working practices.'[215] A much more serious long term question was raised about the popularity of incremental salary systems and was contained in *The Attack on Inflation*, the Government's approach to incomes control: 'Already established incremental and wage-for-age scales are payable provided that this does not raise the overall wage bill by more than £6 per head.'[216]

The scope of collective agreements, although not confined to pay and hours, does not have uniform coverage in the area of fringe benefits. The General Household Survey in 1971 showed a considerable range in the number of employees in different industries who were covered by sick pay arrangements, from 95.7 per cent in gas, electricity and water, to 23.6 per cent in leather, clothing and footwear.[217]

British industrial relations, particularly outside the public sector, has preferred to regard sickness and accident pay, safety provision, redundancy protection and compensation, welfare provisions and to some extent training, as a matter for minimal protection by statute. The preference has not been explicitly expressed and it sometimes appears that, rather than a conscious choice between negotiation and legislation, the state has simply been forced to provide protection in a field in which both parties have neglected their responsibilities to employees and to members.

The lack of provision for these areas in national bargaining is, of course, not the whole of the story. There is a feeling that national agreements cannot adequately provide for conditions which vary and must be controlled at the place of work:

> if they are touched upon in industry agreements it can only be in the most general terms, leaving all the particular decisions to the plant: and whereas some plants work on overtime, many of them have no payment by results, and

more of them no system of job evaluation, virtually all plants of any size must have some problems of safety, health, general working conditions and discipline.[218]

The preference for local treatment takes two forms. Where non-payment issues are the subject of bargaining they become an important part of the representative work of shop stewards, a matter for plant bargaining which sometimes produces one of the immediate, 'perishable' issues which become an item in the figures of unofficial disputes: The second form of local treatment is a belief in British industrial relations that safety, welfare and training are distinguished from the 'proper' subject matter of collective bargaining because they are non-controversial, not as divisive and productive of conflict as wages. For this reason they have become grist to the mill of the joint consultative machinery. Joint consultative committees, particularly in large public undertakings, have complex representative structures within the consultative process, especially designed to deal with safety and health. There is no evidence that the separation of these areas from collective bargaining has done anything to extend the influence of trade unions in them or to enhance the protection of and concern for employees. If the joint consultative relationship has been generally ineffective, its preoccupation with safety, health and welfare may have served to protect employers from the influence of trade unions.

The scope of collective bargaining is defined by the procedure agreement between the parties. Procedural agreements establish the relationship between the parties, 'they establish a constitutional method of reaching substantive agreements and of resolving disputes about them'.[219] Procedure agreements not only lay down the rules which govern relationships, they define to some extent the scope and context of bargaining between particular unions and employers. The framework of collective bargaining is composed of formally recognized relationships for the joint regulation of employment conditions in distinct sectors of employment; the sectors are defined by procedure agreements between the parties. The 1967 Ministry of Labour Handbook still provides the most comprehensive guide to the number and scope of the particular procedures.[220]

The Donovan Commission was greatly concerned with the unsystematic and irrational nature of procedural arrangements in British industrial relations. The procedures which had defined the structure of collective bargaining had been laid down for a process of national bargaining between employers' associations and unions. It had subsequently been subjected to several strains. 'Many of these procedures have been subjected to strain by the transfer of authority in industrial relations to the factory and the workshop.'[221] The transfer of authority is the result not only of the access to negotiating power of shop stewards, or of fragmented bargaining and wage drift. The inadequacy of the industry-wide procedures arises partly from the fact that they were devised to fit industrial sectors of bargaining now supplanted by technical and structural changes, which have made their boundaries anachronisms. This was inevitable; industries cannot be accurately defined and change is bound to make even the best attempts inadequate. Apart from change in jobs and processes and the development of new industries which cut across the old boundaries, union development and recognition in new areas (such as white-collar employment) must inevitably disturb the old procedural divisions. Employers have contributed to untidiness because their recognition of unions for bargaining purposes has often been piecemeal rather than orderly.

In dealing with manual unions in the past employers have usually granted recognition only to unions strong

> enough to insist upon it, and the acceptance of a *fait accompli* of this kind has not given them much influence over structure, since that has already been established . . . But employers could, if they chose, exercise a good deal more influence over union structure in industries and services where membership is at present weak and recognition has not yet been granted.[222]

Influence over union structure would imply influence over the relationship between procedure and industrial organization.

The structure of national procedures is likely to be inadequate even if their divisions accorded precisely with divisions between industries. The process of amalgamation of trade unions and the more open policies which many have been driven to pursue guarantees the existence of multi-unionism and overlapping in the plant. The development of commercial organizations which spread across industrial divisions (not to mention national boundaries) underwrites the probability that existing procedures for collective bargaining will not accord with situations which concern either the employer or the unions. It is extremely doubtful if any systematic approach to procedural reorganization will ever achieve final rationality.

Even if it did there would still be problems. Procedural agreements not only accord recognition, they attempt to draw a boundary to de-limit the substantive area that is properly negotiable and they lay down rules which are a reflection of the respective power of the parties. The limits are never final and there is much to be adjusted at shop floor level which must be settled outside procedure. 'Industry-wide procedures leave a great deal to be settled in the plant, but the disputes procedures which commonly provide the only formal negotiating machinery available at plant level were not designed to provide machinery for the settlement of complex wage structures.'[223] It is not only a question of complexity but of arrangements challenged at shop floor level which procedures may never have been designed or intended to accommodate. Shop stewards' rights, discipline and dismissal are all areas in which national procedures often define rights less than those which have been won on many shop floors. There is a tendency for many procedures not to acknowledge areas of joint regulation which are quite common to the industry, employers preferring to withhold *de jure* recognition from an acknowledged fact in order to preserve at least a formal statement of managerial rights. National procedures are often general in that they fail to distinguish between different types of issues. Wage claims, disagreements over the assimilation of groups to grades within a wage structure, the interpretation of rules and challenges to disciplinary decisions may all have to be contained within the same general procedural framework.

There is a sizeable sector of industry which, although the firms within it are not bound by procedures for their industry, follow them. They may negotiate their own piece rates, even their own time rates, but they always bear a relationship to those established by the negotiating machinery for the industry or trade as a whole. There is a considerable industrial tail trailing behind the standards set by the negotiating pattern for many industries. In these companies and plants there may be no procedure and no acknowledged practice other than a general understanding that the terms for the trade will be accepted or reflected with due and customary allowances for company variations. Substantive matters will, in these circumstances, follow a well recognized pattern but, for the rest, there may be no acknowledged procedure. Grievance, job regulation, discipline, manpower allocation, training and a wide variety of other concerns may be a matter of customary arrangement or *ad hoc* settlement. Here this unregulated area, of indeterminate size in British industrial relations, may not be too different from many sizeable firms which regard themselves as comfortably ensconced within established industrial procedures. Many managers will describe the procedural arrangements which govern their relationship with unions entirely in terms of their commitment to national procedures. As far as they are concerned, industrial relations are entirely defined by the formal procedural relationship to which they have access. The extent to which these procedural arrangements leave prescriptions unspecified, job regulations ill-defined and avenues for grievance unexplored is, as far as they are concerned, a matter entirely outside the scope of industrial relations. In other words, there is a large sector of employment including, for example, catering and retail, in which employment conditions are barely touched by collective bargaining and, beyond that sector, there are other areas where national bargaining and national procedure has only a minimal influence.

Apart from this great penumbra there is a third sector where, for one reason or another, the particular employer has made himself responsible for his own affairs. This is the area of domestic bargaining: 'it is almost certain that domestic bargaining affects only a minority of firms, and it is possible that it affects only a minority of employees, even of manual workers.'[224] Even here, one has to distinguish between regulated and unregulated domestic bargaining. Regulated domestic bargaining may be closely defined by company procedure which may well be more closely defined in its scope and content than any comparable national arrangements. Company procedure, as in the case of Ford's, may be intensively codified and entirely independent of national arrangements made in the engineering industry. Company procedures may, in other circumstances, fill in the gaps left by national procedures so that the arrangements for regulating the rules of employment are a complex relationship between national and private networks of bargaining.[225] The unregulated area, in which there are no written or formally acknowledged procedures, can range between an extreme of employer domination which may be benevolently exercised or not, as in the retail trade, to a situation in which workers' bargaining power is considerable but which is not formally recognized 'where the plant procedure' (we might add, if there is any):

> does not allow for collective bargaining, shop stewards can still impose a form of collective bargaining; and where the plant procedure does not provide for collective bargaining over any particular issue of importance to the workers, their stewards may find a means of settling it with management in a manner which amounts to bargaining, or of deciding it for themselves by unilateral action.[226]

This is to suggest that the divisions between two systems of industrial relations, the formal and the informal, is rather too straightforward a division between control exercised by national procedures and chaos exercised by workplace bargaining. Workplace bargaining can be controlled and the distinction between order and chaos is likely to depend upon the distribution of power rather than the difference in the level at which bargaining is conducted and the extent to which national procedures are followed. The table on page 218 is an attempt to suggest some of the complications in the discussion of procedural control. The horizontal axis illustrates differences along a spectrum from total reliance on national procedures, through regulation partially by national and partly by company procedures (called here regulated licence), to independent company procedure (regulated independence), limited procedure and, finally, the absence of any procedure at all. The likely outcomes of these procedural variations are plotted against the single variable of worker strength and organization in the work-place. This is also a gross over-simplification, but less of one than distinguishing between the formal and the informal system. The table on page 218 leaves out very important variables. It takes no account of official union organization, centrality of structure and strength. It takes no account of company structure and the degree of autonomy left to local management. It does not include any reference to the influences of different employment sectors subsumed within a single company structure and it leaves out any reference to functional specialism within management. There seems to be no way of simplifying, in order to categorize, the number of influences which converge on the determination of procedure and the practical influence which emerges from it. If it were possible to do so the result would finally suggest some functional rationality in the outcome which might be totally unreal because it would leave out the effects of particular personalities, historical accident and institutional lethargy. The only defence of such vagueness is to say that it is better to suggest the complexity of reality in industrial relations rather than to observe it for the sake of heuristic clarity.

In the following table the definition of 'dependence' relates entirely to the relationship of company to national or industry-wide procedural arrangements. The company's dependence or freedom from worker influence is measured along the vertical axis:

Table 6

	Regulated dependence Dependence on national procedures	**Regulated licence** National procedures with company procedure	**Regulated independence** Complete formal company procedure	**Limited regulated independence** Partial formal company procedure	**Un-regulated independence** No procedure
Strong work-place employee organization	Fragmented, unofficial bargaining, filling in national procedural gaps	Some organised company bargaining with complex relationships between levels of bargaining and jurisdiction over joint rules. Procedural over-lapping	Strong company bargaining exercising large influence over terms and conditions. Regulated conflict	Limited regulation by collective bargaining. Constant challenge to managerial control and to procedural boundaries	*De facto* worker control. Limited managerial challenge to custom and practice. Management by persuasion of work groups
No work place-employee organization	Exercise of managerial prerogatives filling in gaps. Employer autonomy limited by employer associations' control	Company procedures likely to be tokens of benevolence; joint consultation, employer consultation	Benevolent paternalism. Participation rather than bargaining	Limited recognition granted to some emergent groups. Defensive bargaining	Total employer autocracy, benevolently or coercively exercised

CHAPTER 9

The negotiating process

Collective bargaining has been defined by Stevens as 'a social-control technique for reflecting and transmitting the basic power relationships which underlie the conflict of interest in an industrial relations system.'[227] The definition emphasizes important characteristics of collective bargaining, that it is concerned with the application of power in the adjustment of inherent conflicts of interest. Walton and McKersie define labour negotiations as 'the deliberate interaction of two or more complex social units which are attempting to define or re-define the terms of their interdependence.'[228] Collective bargaining depends upon interdependence but the relationship is also characterized by conflict generated by competition over resources or power. Collective bargaining is therefore a mixed relationship in which 'both parties stand to gain by cooperation to the extent of preserving the fact of the relationship. But there are also elements of competition involved.'[229]

Because collective bargaining is concerned with the determination of wages it has often been regarded as a market process. The Webbs were described by Flanders as being 'largely concerned with undertaking an economic evaluation of the economic consequences of collective bargaining which they treated throughout as an economic institution'[230] and Flanders went on to say that they were mistaken in regarding the process of individual bargaining giving way to collective bargaining:

> negotiation is not the same process as bargaining in markets. A collective agreement is not truly a collective bargain. Trade unions do not sell the labour of their members; nor do employers' associations, unlike individual employers, buy it.[231]

In Flanders' view collective bargaining is joint administration, synonymous with joint management. The legislative or rule-making aspect of collective bargaining has come to be emphasized in contrast to the economic or labour-price determining: 'collective bargaining is among other things a rule-making or norm-creating process of a bilateral kind'.[232] At the same time, much more stress is placed on the political processes of collective bargaining rather than the purely economic: 'collective bargaining, involving as it does the use of power as well as the making of rules, is really a political process.'[233]

There are two dangers in regarding collective bargaining as a legislative or rule-making process 'of a bilateral kind'. The first lies in an implication that the rule-making process goes on, or should go on in a stable enrivonment. Stability comes to be regarded as essential in terms of the procedural rules and in terms of the normative aspirations of groups which are related to the bargaining process. To put it more simply: it is seen to be important that the ground rules do not change and that the expectations of those for whom bargaining is conducted do not get too far out of line with the expectations shared by the bargainers. Flanders and Fox illustrate both these concerns when they say that major sources of disorder in industrial relations arise when, first, one group, against the resistance of another, seeks to change the procedural norms and nature of the system and, second, when the degree of tension between the prevailing norms and the aspirations of one or more relevant groups have become so great that it provokes challenge and conflict.

We have already suggested that the tendency to distinguish procedural from substantive rules is not particularly helpful and it may become obstructive to an understanding of collective bargaining if it sets up the latter as the proper subject of the negotiating process while reserving the former from joint regulation. Procedural rules may be regarded by one of the parties to collective bargaining as reflecting the distribution of power between them and their opponents. The parties may be concerned to change the procedural rules, if they regard them as unjust or coercive, particularly if the distribution of power should change. Such a state of affairs is not necessarily a sign or disorder (however that is defined) in industrial relations so much as a sign of necessary flexibility, essential for 'reflecting and transmitting the basic power relationships' between the parties.

Concern about tensions between prevailing norms and the aspiration of groups raises a question concerning the ambiguity with which the terms 'norms' and 'rules' are used. They are sometimes regarded as synonymous but a recent discussion has pointed to the importance of distinguishing between them; the norms 'regulate action within the production system, but have not yet been re-institutionalized within the industrial relations system; they are not yet rules.' Norms may only be exposed, as in custom and practice, 'when they are challenged, questioned or broken, that is when prevailing practices or norms become "issues".' In these circumstances, 'the ensuing negotiation (or rule-making) may lead to the formal acceptance of the practice. Usually, however, the processes of re-institutionalization are more complex.'[234] This process can, no doubt, become a source of disorder and the circumstances in which it is likely to arise will concern us when we are discussing industrial relations and social change, but for the most part the accommodation of the rules of the industrial relations system to the norms of the production process is the very heart of collective bargaining. It is not exceptional or disorderly, it is the thing itself.

The distinction between formal rules and norms regulating conduct in work emerges in the well-known phenomenon of custom and practice in industrial relations. The appeal to custom and practice is almost invariably a defence against threatened change. The defence often seems to rest on three grounds: that the practice which is being changed is long-established (is 'customary') and therefore has carried management's approval (at least tacitly); that change represents a kind of bureaucratic inconsistency: if it was right yesterday, it is right today; and that the change will be damaging to the group upon which it is imposed. Custom and practice may only emerge with any clarity when what is claimed to be customary performance is contrasted with innovation; custom and practice is as silent and unobtrusive as the sleeping dog until disturbed.

Brown points out that custom and practice may be introduced by management as well as workers, that its origins are often obscure but that 'even if their authorship were known it is doubtful whether this would be important because authorship is often divorced from subsequent enforcement.'[235] Commenting on the extension of custom and practice since the second world war, he says that:

> the widespread acceptance of C and P as a principle of legitimacy in itself, even though its customary basis is often bogus, can be explained to a large extent by managements' need to save face during their long retreat

a single precedent is enough to:

> create a position where the new-born rule is seen to be sufficiently legitimate to be fought for by the workers.

> Unless management is willing to embark upon an expensive confrontation the situation will be irreversible.[236]

He concludes that the ability to claim precedent, to convert an incident into a customary practice, depends upon the political ability of workers and their representatives, their power and the frequency afforded by the technical system of opportunities to use it. Custom and practice also depends upon the reluctance of management to exercise formal control and to extend procedural description to practices which it would prefer to ignore. It is probably greatly nurtured by the assumption of consistency which pervades managerial decision taking. Management presents itself as a rational bureaucracy; part of its claim to legitimacy depends upon its legislative activity, its expertise and its rationality. To the extent that this claim is advanced by management it may find it difficult to resist the argument that it should be consistent with its own decisions.

The second danger in regarding collective bargaining as a rule-making process of a bilateral kind is that it suggests the equal division of power between employer and union as a pre-condition for the existence of collective bargaining. Joint responsibility for the rules of industrial relations suggests the necessary maintenance of a balance of power between the parties to collective bargaining. If it is maintained out of a respect for the legitimacy or utility of the joint rule-making process, regardless of any shifts in the political or economic distribution of power between them, then it suggests a 'mature' relationship in which the permanent advantages of joint regulation outweigh the temporary expedients to be won by applying force to weak opponents. Undoubtedly, a collective bargaining relationship is often to be found in industrial situations where the bargaining relationships between the parties are responsible, stable and mature. That is true of many of the nationalized industries in this country, partly because the bargaining relationship is protected by statute and is made independent of changes in the market. But collective bargaining also exists in different circumstances where power is quite unevenly distributed, where control is more unilateral and where responsibility is barely jointly exercised. Harbison and Coleman's distinctions between 'armed truce', 'working harmony' and 'union-management cooperation' suggest varying degrees of joint control, mutual respect and maturity but collective bargaining may be found in each. Collective bargaining is a relationship which can be found in a variety of circumstances ranging from, at one extreme, unilateral control by the employer to, at the other, unilateral control by workers. The particular character of the relationship of collective bargaining will depend upon a number of variables including 'the context of the organization',[237] the respective power of the parties, their values and attitudes and the extent to which they see their environment as benign or hostile. The collective bargaining relationship may thus change along a spectrum between two extremes of unilateral control. If we see it in this way we avoid the dangers of identifying it with precise and perhaps unusual circumstances in which a balance of power exists and of having to regard departures from this state of affairs as a distinct phenomenon, something other than collective bargaining.

Collective bargaining is essentially fluid and dynamic. A definition which suggests rigidity and finality contributes to the attitude which persistently seeks a 'solution to the problem of industrial relations.' It would be better to regard collective bargaining as a process in which representative groups involved in employment seek temporary accommodations of their different interests. The accommodations are not final; at any time they are likely to reflect a distribution of power between the groups which may change and which may then result in a demand for a new accommodation. For this reason, the rules arrived at in collective bargaining may be of a particularly fragile kind.

Levinson broke down the environmental influences within which collective bargaining took place as economic variables (marker considerations for the product and for labour), political variables (concerning pressures on union leaders to compete with other unions in maintaining the strength of their unions as an institution), and 'pure power' variables (concerning the strength and stability of the bargaining institutions, the union's ability to strike and the employer's ability to hold out).[238] This at least suggests the complexity of collective bargaining but we should recognize that we continue to over-simplify it. Collective bargaining has developed in a voluntary system of industrial relations as a bilateral process between employers and unions. There are complications enough in trying to explain it in these terms but it becomes increasingly apparent, in advanced industrial societies, that it is no longer bilateral so much as triadic. Major negotiations must now take into account the Government, as a party, or they must take place within a context of rules or expectations established by the Government. But let us pretend that this complication does not exist, for the moment, while we try to understand the nature of collective bargaining as we comprehend it so far: as a bilateral process involving two institutions, employers and trade unions.

Despite appearances to the contrary, collective bargaining is essentially a collaborative relationship. Collective bargaining:

> *requires* that some agreement be reached between the parties. However prolonged the strike to settle disputes over divergent interests, some agreement must ultimately be forthcoming if collective bargaining continues. Thus neither party is independent under collective bargaining. Neither can perform its function without the other.[239]

Chamberlain and Kuhn describe this process of involuntary cooperation as 'conjunctive bargaining'. The relationship deals with 'matters of divergent interests, and each party secures its interest to the extent of its relative bargaining power. Coercion is the principle ingredient of conjunctive bargaining power.' The authors contrast this relationship with 'cooperative bargaining' in which each party realises that it

> can achieve its objectives more effectively if it wins the support of the other. This means that when one party is seeking a change the better to secure some objective, it is more likely to succeed in its design if it anticipates what objections may be raised by the other party, on whose cooperation in the matter the degree of its own success depends.[240]

This distinction is one of many that has been made about collective bargaining. More recently Deutsch has distinguished between destructive (or competitive) conflict and productive conflict resolution which involves cooperative problem solving and cooperative commitment.[241] In much the same way Walton and McKersie made a widely recognized distinction between distributive bargaining ('the system of activities instrumental to the attainment of one party's goals when they are in basic conflict with those of the other party') and integrative bargaining ('the system of activities which is instrumental to the attainment of objectives which are not in fundamental conflict with those of the other party and which therefore can be integrated to some degree').[242] Similar distinctions have been made between bargaining and problem solving approaches.

Walton and McKersie's full taxonomy is that labour negotiations consist of four sub-processes: distributive bargaining, integrative bargaining, attitudinal structuring and intra-organizational bargaining. This does not seem to be the most helpful of analytical frameworks, nor does the contrast between distributive and integrative bargaining which it contains. Bargaining, however essentially collaborative the relationship within which it takes place, *implies* a difference in interests and objectives. Collective bargaining is concerned to reach accommodations, often of a temporary nature, between different interests and expectations. In this sense collective bargaining is almost always what Walton and McKersie define merely as a sub-process; it is always distributive bargaining in which the parties are negotiating over the distribution of scarce resources, money, status or power. If distributive bargaining is the genus then there are at least two varieties of species in which a party may choose between different approaches to the end he seeks. Now it becomes sensible to discuss a competitive or a collaborative approach. The party to collective bargaining now, as a matter of strategy, selects an approach to the attainment of his own ends. The strategy will either be competitive (involving the use of tactics like threat, bluff, the application of power) or cooperative (in which again there will be a choice between available tactics, the emphasis on joint problem solving, teaching the opponent new skills, removing obstacles in the environment). Walton and McKersie's attribution to attitudinal structuring of equal logical status is mistaken because it appears more sensible to regard it as one of a range of *tactics* which may be chosen when a party has chosen a strategy of cooperative (in their terms, integrative) bargaining. There is a further confusion over the sub-process 'intra-organizational' bargaining because this represents neither strategic nor tactical concerns but rather an environmental characteristic of the total field within which bargaining takes place; it takes place within organizations rather than between them. In that it is an essential part of the negotiating process it can probably be explained in precisely the same terms as the external process which takes place between organizations.

It might be more helpful, therefore, to regard the collective bargaining relationships as a joint *process*, the *function* of which is the distribution of valued utilities, which each party determines by a process of internal bargaining and which each tries to attain by a choice of strategies and of appropriate tactics. Thus

Process	*Function*	*Objectives*	*Methods* (Each party's strategy)	*Tactics* (Choice determined by strategy)
Collective bargaining	Distribution of utilities	Determined by internal or 'intra-organizational' bargaining	A Competitive (what Walton and McKersie call distributive)	Bluff threat coercion control of information
			B Cooperative (integrative)	Problem solving teaching (what Walton and McKersie call attitudinal structuring)

The purpose of this aside has been twofold: the first to try to clear up some logical confusions that may have arisen in the analysis of collective bargaining, the second to clear the ground for stating that the view of collective bargaining to be taken here is that it is essentially a distributive relationship. It is concerned with the regulation of different interests and the pursuit of different objectives but it is a part of a wider relationship of employment which is essentially collaborative. The methods by which the regulation of conflict is pursued and by which accommodations are achieved can vary according to the circumstances and attitudes of the parties. their perceptions of other's positions and of the environment which surrounds them. We are concerned, in effect, with distributive bargaining and with the choice of approaches which each party makes to achieve its ends.

We shall look at this process under the headings of:

1 the preparation for bargaining
2 the purpose of bargaining for each party
3 the selection of means for achieving the purpose
4 the adjustment of each party's position
5 sanctions
6 third party intervention
7 finally, we shall look at characteristics which seem to be associated with effective negotiation.

1 The preparation for bargaining

The difficulties of determining objectives in industrial relations have already been discussed (in chapters 2 and 3). In the preparation for negotiation the ground may be laid out by the union's claim and management's objectives may be defensive, determined by the estimated costs of various degrees of concession as against the possible costs of refusing to satisfy the union's demands. Stevens suggests that the initial influence on the respective positions of the parties is the 'large demand rule' which declares that the demand of one party and the offer of the other 'are in excess of the least favourable terms upon which each party is willing to settle, and in excess of what each expects the agreed-upon position to be. Both parties know this.'[243] The initial positions cannot be arbitrarily determined; however, they are usually set within an 'area of interdependency' which, Walton and McKersie say, set out 'the most fundamental limit to the two party conflict. Beyond each of these outer limits one or the other parties would terminate the potentially advantageous relationship.'[244] The limits are influenced by market considerations by the understanding of the parties of going conditions, and of other influential agreements and by assumptions and expectations which are shared by the negotiators. We suggest (in chapter 3) that the process of transmission involved in the internal process of bargaining was heavily influenced by each negotiator's predictions and understandings of what might be acceptable to his opponent and of what would be totally un-negotiable under any circumstances. These expectations may be characterized by aspirational rigidity on the part of negotiators and by the aspirational optimism of those, like directors, more distant from the negotiating frontier. The influence of the negotiators, represented by the degree of control they are capable of exercising within the internal bargaining process (that is, within their own organization) contributes to a degree of conservatism in collective bargaining. 'There are certain things that are not asked for and certain things that are not said; if they are said it is as a deliberate tactical irritant rather than as a serious negotiating objective.'[245] The accommodations arrived at in collective bargaining cannot penetrate too far into the attitudes and perceptions protected from contact in the inner recesses of the organization. The agenda is therefore concerned with differences over common ground, an area, which is judged to be suitable for collective determination. Change and the importation of new items for negotiation are more often brought about by changes within each organization which require, after some tension, to be adjusted by the negotiators. Such a change can be seen occasionally when the agenda for negotiation is extended by political movements within the trade union. The productivity agreements at Fawley provided another example of the unusual extension of the range of collective bargaining, on that occasion brought about by management's extension of its strategic objectives.

The agenda is drawn up by mutual agreement between the parties, sometimes by rules established within their procedure agreement. There is a convention that the agenda is not extended to include other items once negotiations have begun, otherwise there might be no finite end to the bargaining process. Agenda items, on the other hand, are often shed, sometimes disappearing because of a failure to reach agreement and thence consigned to an indefinite postponement. Sometimes they are intended to be shed because, as Stevens says, the composition of the agenda may have tactical significance; weak items may be included to be deliberately jettisoned as trading items for items concerning targets which the party seriously wishes to achieve.[246] It has also been suggested that one party (it is more likely to be management) may include weak items which it intends to abandon simply to maintain the confidence of its opponent in the bargaining relationship. Similarly, one party (it is more likely to be the union) may include weak items in which it intends to succeed as some compensation, for purposes of internal bargaining, for a major item in which it expects to fail. In circumstances like these, which are no doubt rare, the mutual agreement in which the agenda is drawn may go beyond the point of public visibility.

The initial position of the parties are set within an 'area of interdependency', but Walton and McKersie point out that bargaining is normally confined to limits narrower than the extremities of this range because 'the parties enter negotiations with more limited expectations about where on the spectrum serious bargaining will take place.'[247] Each 'knows' that the declared target of his opponent, although not outside the area of interdependency, is not what his opponent seriously expects to achieve. We can imagine the initial area of interdependency, including a settlement range and, revealed in the later stages of negotiation, a contract zone and a manifest contract zone:

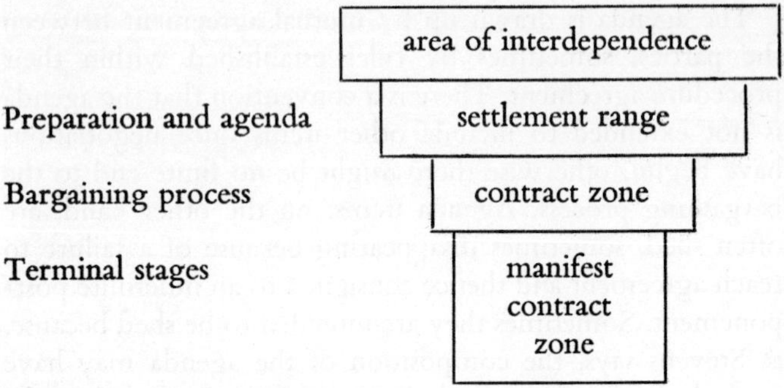

although the symmetry of this figure should not suggest that the successive adjustments of the parties' positions are balanced and equitable.

Walton and McKersie tell us that:

> In practice the target of one is usually selected in a way that represents the best estimate about the other's resistance point. Thus, for all intents and purposes, a party usually behaves as if his own resistance point and target describe *the* settlement range. Perhaps the most common configuration is one in which both parties (1) prefer and entertain hopes for positions which are incompatible but (2) are resigned to accept other less ambitious positions which are compatible.[248]

These circumstances are familiar to negotiators as the normal state of affairs from which bargaining begins. Each 'knows' that the other's position is to some extent unreal, and that the bargaining process (and the passage of time which it occupies) is necessary to the investigation of reality. It occasionally happens that the initial position of one party or the other represents the final position which he intends to adopt. Such a circumstance can arise in at least two ways. The first has been described as Boulwareism, the minimum demand or maximum offer. It has been advanced as an American 'philosophy' of management when, in an attempt to avoid the irrationality of horse-trading, management makes an objective assessment of what should be the substantive conditions, offers them and sticks to its offer. The weaknesses of this approach are that no single party is deemed capable of objectivity by its opponent and that the approach depends upon arrangements for accommodation alternative to collective bargaining. In practical terms, the success of this approach depends upon a consistent refusal to be drawn or forced into bargaining over the initial offer which is intended to be the final outcome. In that it is an alternative to bargaining, it may be compared to the strategy of those employers who refuse union recognition and avoid collective bargaining by providing employee conditions ranging between the adequate and the superlative. These are exceptional arrangements and they can only be exceptional because they depend upon exceeding employment standards which are set by collective bargaining elsewhere; peace is maintained as the result of warfare on another part of the front.

The immutability of the initial bargaining position may also be made to be dependent on some kind of commitment to a position which the opponent knows cannot be abandoned, 'an irreversible sacrifice of freedom of choice'.[249] One of the functions of internal bargaining, and of the distance that separates the policy makers from the front-line negotiators, is that it enables such a commitment to be claimed; the union can say that it is too late to reverse its members' decision (either because of administrative deficiency or because of their sluggish intransigence); management can say that the Board is incapable of reversing a decision which has tied its negotiators' hands. Commitments are best made visible to a real and immovable object in the environment, otherwise they are likely to be interpreted as bluffs; the process of revealing them as such is part of the process of negotiation. But commitment, or the process of 'locking oneself in', can endanger the success of the negotiating process in reaching accommodations. The rational commitment, as Deutsch says, is 'that a bargainer will gain an advantage if he can commit himself irrevocably, so that the last clear chance of avoiding mutual disaster rests with his opponent.'[250] He goes on to point out that:

> locking oneself into an irreversible position in order to gain an advantage is rarely more beneficial than co-operating with the other for mutual gain, and it has the prospect of leading to a mutually destructive contest of willpower.[251]

In these circumstances, the only alternative to mutual destruction or impasse may be for one party to assist his obdurate opponent to unlock himself by a series of helpful rationalizations intended to demonstrate that he is not really abandoning positions by avoiding them. These are the cooperative moves which are more characteristic of the final stages of negotiation than they are of the openings.

2 The purpose of negotiations

The purpose to be achieved by negotiations can be regarded as offensive or defensive, as a series of changes which one party wishes to achieve or as a series of adjustments which it wishes to make to its opponent's intentions. The manner in which purpose is determined may vary between autocratic decisions (on the part of the union executive or the board) and open consensus arrived at within the organization. At any position on the spectrum between these extremes, and at the extremes themselves, purpose is likely to be influenced by a process of internal bargaining which has already been discussed. Winkler has pointed out that there may be some utility in preserving distance and some obscurity of communication between the decision making body (in his case, the board) and the negotiating representatives. There have been other suggestions that the decision function and the negotiating function are clearly differentiated even while negotiations are in process, that management takes its decisions privately while receiving communications from the negotiators.[252]

The opportunity for determining purpose by a process of internal bargaining is probably affected by the structure of different organizations and by the status that has been achieved by their different parts. In some managerial organizations the personal department is influential, while in others line or technical management may be untrammelled by advice. In some unions, the membership gets what it is given and does what it is told. But it seems likely that objectives will be both more realistic and more acceptable if they have been arrived at by a process of internal bargaining than if they have been unilaterally determined by one section of the organization concerned.

The purpose is not likely to be determined by reference only to the requirements of the organization; it will be influenced to some extent by predictions about the acceptability of these requirements to the opponent. In this sense the impact of bargaining is felt before bargaining begins. This is a conservative influence in the negotiating process which both explains its success and its limitations. The influence is transmitted by the negotiators, whose experience and expertise gives them some control over the determination of objectives.

Walton and McKersie say that the target points (the most favourable outcome) are determined by the highest estimate of what is needed, the most optimistic assumption about what is possible, and the most favourable estimate of the party's own bargaining skill. Resistant points, on the other hand, result from the lowest estimate of needs, the most pessimistic assumptions about possibilities and the least flattering assumptions about skill.[253] There is likely to be a difference between the determination of objectives in negotiations over substantive conditions and in grievance bargaining. The former are more likely to concern conflicts of interest, the latter conflicts of right. In substantive negotiations both parties are likely to concede that there is a real difference in interests and perspectives and that the winner is likely to be chosen by the favour of prevailing circumstances and by the influence of power. In grievance bargaining on the other hand, where the issue is likely to concern the 'correct' application of an agreement to an individual or group or the 'just' interpretation of a rule, management is more likely to see itself as having a dual (even a contradictory) role in which it must behave as both advocate and judge. In an attempt to resolve these difficulties, domestic grievance procedure is arranged hierarchically so that advocacy can be conducted by a level of management subordinate to that which is required to decide. In these circumstances management may conceive the purpose of bargaining to be less self-interested or one-sided than it would do when bargaining over a wage claim. Management may see the purpose as more objective, as an attempt by rational means to reach a correct decision in which the arguments of its opponents have a much more constructive purpose than are acknowledged for them in wage negotiations. The fact that management perceives these differences does not necessarily mean that its objectivity is necessarily acknowledged by the union. In grievance bargaining, management's pursuit of its interests are constrained by a body of rules which it is in management's interest to maintain.

Management's detailed objectives in collective bargaining may be distinguished from its overall purpose in maintaining the collective bargaining relationships, in which it is important to maintain mutual cooperation and inter-dependence. At the very least, mutual cooperation and inter-dependence is necessary to the joint regulation of differences between workers and unions on the one hand and management on the other; joint regulation is usually preferable to uncontrolled hostility.[254] For the most part, management has an interest in the maintenance of collective bargaining and the interest is worth paying for in the form of costs of accommodation within the collective bargaining process. This means that management may subordinate the pursuit of its specific negotiating objectives in order to maintain its overall purpose in collective bargaining; immediate gains may be sacrificed for long-term advantages, including the maintenance of the collective bargaining relationship itself. But it is important that management knows what it is doing and does not rationalize the justification of short-term losses in the pursuit of long-term disaster.

3 The selection of means for achieving the purpose

The means for achieving the purpose of the parties in collective bargaining are either coercive or influential: calculated to constrain the opponent, to force him to alter his own objectives or to accept others or persuade him to alter his outlook and expectations. The approaches are not simple alternatives; a negotiator may alternate between one and the other or even apply both concurrently. Again, the bargainer's skill may be directed at convincing an opponent that he has been persuaded when in fact he has been coerced; force may be more effective when disguised as persuasion.

A Coercive approaches

(i) *Power*

It is widely acknowledged by now that collective bargaining is, among other things, a relationship of power and that the distribution of power between the parties can vary. The importance of power has been acknowledged by sociologists who have turned their attention to industrial relations because power is a concept with which sociology has been deeply concerned. Despite this attention or because of it, 'power' is used in a very nebulous fashion. It can refer to many relationships of coercion in which preferred intentions are abandoned, but the bases of coercive force may vary considerably and coercive force may be applied in a variety of different forms. Deutsch distinguishes between six different types of power:

1 coercive power 'which uses negative incentives such as threats to physical well-being . . . to influence the other'
2 reward or exchange power 'which employs positive incentives . . . in exchange for what is desired from the other.
3 ecological power 'which entails sufficient control over the other's social or physical environment to permit one to modify it so that the modified environment induces the desired behaviour'
4 normative power 'which is based on the obligations that the other has to accept one's influence as a result of the social norms governing the relationship'
5 referent power 'which uses the other's desire to identify with or be similar to some person or group in order to alter his attitude and values
6 expert power, 'which is grounded in the other's acceptance of one's superior knowledge or skill.'[255]

Power represents the ability of one party to overcome the resistance of its opponents in carrying out its intentions, but the ability rests upon different sources of coercion. Some of Deutsch's sources of power come dangerously close to confusing it with authority. Dahrendorf makes the distinction between the two quite clear: 'While power is merely a factual relation, authority is a legitimate relation of domination and subjection. In this sense, authority can be described as legitimate power.'[256] The distinction is an important one in collective bargaining for, while management exercises authority in the employment relationships (where the claim to superior knowledge and skill, as Deutsch defines expert power, is in fact a basis of management's claim to exercise legitimate authority), the collective bargaining relationship takes over in the area where management's authority has, to some extent, broken down. Collective bargaining is concerned with areas in which management's authority to make or interpret rules has broken down or is being challenged. Management is about authority, collective bargaining is about power. Management, in response to the challenge to its authority which is inherent in collective bargaining, will attempt to rely upon or restore its authority. One of the several complexities in the collective bargaining relationship is that management brings to it an authoritative role which it must necessarily defend by the application of power. But the application of power simply serves to question further the legitimacy of management's authority. The collective bargaining relationship thus continues to erode management's claim to exercise legitimate authority, not because unions become stronger but because the nature of the relationship demands power which inevitably undermines authority. The more intense the scrutiny, the fewer clothes the emperor is observed to wear.

There are more practical problems concerning the application of power in collective bargaining. It can lead to a spiralling situation of endemic conflict which is fought out quite independently of the issues which gave rise to it; conflict becomes an end in itself. Deutsch points out that power confrontations concentrate power in the most militant of leaders within each organization:

> Within each of the conflicting parties, there is increasing pressure for uniformity of opinion and a tendency for leadership and control to be taken over by those elements

> that are militarily organized for waging conflict through combat and taken away from those that are more conciliatory.[257]

There are likely to be further deteriorations in the relationship. Communications between the parties become weak, unreliable or unusable; messages are misinterpreted so as to reinforce stereotypes of the enemy and so that a cooperative move by one party may be ignored or misinterpreted by his opponent. Each side convinces the other that only the application of more force can be effective. Continuous increasing of the conflict may lead to a suspension of the normally accepted rules of behaviour: 'it permits behaviour toward the other that would be considered outrageous if directed toward someone like oneself.'[258]

The outcome of such a situation is likely to be the total defeat of one of the parties but this can be a hollow victory for the other. Defeat may carry with it demoralization or the sullen determination to win next time, whatever the issue. The application of power also becomes a part of the rational determination of costs: 'Some companies have been known to revise their offer downward after a long strike, saying that the ability to pay which existed prior to the strike had been depleted by the strike.'[259] Striking may also harden a resolve not to concede simply in order to avoid an acknowledgement of the usefulness of striking.

This recital of dire consequences suggests that the bargaining process is not simply a matter of applying power by both sides in order to determine who wins. Collective bargaining *is* about power but it is often concerned to avoid its use. It is never entirely absent from the scene, however, if only because alternative methods may be insufficient to change the perceptions and expectations of the party and because the bargaining process requires that their perceptions and expectations must change in order to arrive at a settlement. 'Sanctions applied by the party seeking substantive change may provide a show of strength or an indication of determination and thus function as an integral part of the bargaining process.'[260]

(ii) *Threat*

Words like 'show of strength' or 'determination' imply a preparedness to apply power which may stop short of reality. Power is inseparable from collective bargaining although bargaining may be concerned to avoid its use. The relationship is often established by references to its availability in the form of hints, threats or bluffs. These references may be necessary in order to introduce a greater element of reality into the bargaining process, to establish, for example, that a party cannot be coerced into accepting a bargaining position if it has sufficient power to avoid it. Again, it may be necessary for one party to make it clear that its demand for a position can be backed by force and that its opponents' expectations would be more realistic if they were changed to accommodate this fact. Threats are references to power.

The promiscuous use of threats in the negotiating process is dangerous. They are likely to impede progress in the terminal stages of negotiation towards a manifest contract zone or to an agreement when the negotiating process is likely to depend upon cooperative gestures and responses, not only because they provoke counter threats and competitiveness but because they may be judged to be illegitimate at that stage. The size as well as the timing of a threat is also likely to be important. A threat, to be effective, must be realistic in relation to the power to which it refers and in relation to the threatener's preparedness to apply that power. A threat which is manifestly unrelated to power is a bluff. A threat related to a disproportionate application of power may also be perceived to be a bluff or at best to be counterproductive:

> The credibility of a threat or promise will decrease as its magnitude increases—particularly if a threat or promise of less magnitude is seen to be more than enough . . . if I am convinced that it is really going to hurt you more than me if you carry out your overblown threat, I may provoke you to do so.[261]

Schelling points out an exception to this rule in the advantage enjoyed by an irrational opponent. If a man rings my doorbell at midnight and threatens to blow out his (or my) brains with a pistol unless I give him a cigarette the credibility of his threat is vastly enhanced if he is obviously drunk.[262] This is a vivid illustration of the notorious difficulty of negotiating with a stupid opponent. But we should not necessarily conclude that the best industrial relations specialists are idiots.

Specificity in threats may be dangerous in that they require precise performance; vagueness, on the other hand, may imply a lack of real intention or of real power. Threats cannot be applied too frequently without devaluing their currency; if they are to be made they must occasionally be carried out or they become bluffs.

(iii) *Bluffs*

But bluffs are not useless in altering the outlook and expectations of an opponent as long as they are perceived as threats and not bluffs. To be effective, bluffs must be perceived by the recipient to relate to power and the willingness to use it. There are two ways to expose the weakness of a bluff. The safest is to possess information about real power and intention and this is partly why the negotiation process is frequently concerned to obtain and evaluate information. The other way, in the language of poker, is to 'call' it. 'Calling' instantly reveals the difference between bluff and threat but the process involves risks for both parties. The judgement will be influenced by the available information about the opponent's position and by judgements based on experience. and evaluation of his behaviour. Once again, inflated or disproportionate threats are likely to be interpreted as bluffs and they can lead to difficulties in the control of negotiations, particularly between inexperienced negotiators. Bluffs are threats which are not related to power or which lack the intention to apply it. Bluffs which are perceived as threats are indistinguishable from them whether they are related to power and intention or not so that the effect of a successful bluff is the same as a threat. The utility (and the dangers) of 'locking-in' in presenting bluffs as threats has already been discussed.

B **Influential approaches**

Coercion is not the only way in which a negotiator adjusts the outlook and expectations of his opponent. The use of coercive approaches can contribute to growing hostility until the relationship between the parties is out of their control and negotiation is impossible. Force can also cause unacceptable damage, incur costs greater that the expected advantageous outcomes to be achieved by negotiation. For these reasons other methods of influencing the opponent's behaviour may be used:

> these other ways either attempt to influence the other's subjective probability that a given course of action will lead to a given consequence, or they attempt to alter the other's appraisal or evaluation of the consequences that are expected to follow from the different courses of action.[263]

(i) *Attitudinal structuring*

We are presenting attitudinal structuring as one of a choice of approaches or strategies to the achievement of the bargainer's goals. It is meant, however, precisely as Walton and McKersie defined it (although they regarded it as one of four distinct sub-processes of labour negotiations) as 'the system of activities instrumental to the attainment of desired relationship patterns between the parties'.[264] It may be intended to produce friendliness rather than hostility, trust rather than suspicion. It may require the subordination of immediate advantage for a more progressive change in the relationship between the bargainers. It may range between the more superficial approaches of friendliness and affability to the concession of debating victories and the apparent humiliation of the party's fortunes in the eyes of his opponent. Whatever the posture which is adopted, in that attempts at attitudinal structuring are intended to increase the influence of one party over the other, they are often deceptive. They imply the exercise of considerable control by negotiators over their own behaviour in order to bring about more favourable sentiments in their opponents. The inexperienced negotiator who believes that successful negotiation requires the exploitation of every tactical advantage is likely to be a threat to the successful structuring of attitudes in his opponent. The belief that negotiations are debates to be won is likely to result in the increased intransigence of the opponent as his contradictions and illogicalities are exposed. Successful attempts at attitudinal structuring may require the opposite of what is commonly regarded as sound negotiating behaviour, for it may be deemed wise to invest the opponent with more power, wisdom and intelligence than he possesses in order to promote his favourable feelings.

The assumption (which has a long record of human observation behind it) is that sentiments and feelings are likely to influence judgements and decisions. Attitude adjustment is intended to produce favourably biased judgements and decisions on the part of the opponent. It may involve a deliberate attempt to prevent the development of hostile sentiments. Tactics which are rationally directed at eliciting more information may have unplanned consequences. The result may be that the opponent's behaviour is provoked to a point where it is beyond his rational control. Tempers are lost. In these circumstances progress in negotiation may be impossible and it will be necessary to restore a more orderly atmosphere and calmer attitudes. These are the occasions when familiar ground is re-covered, statistics are regurgitated and old arguments are rehearsed again. The explanation is simply that boredom and excitement are mutually exclusive states.

(ii) *Integrative bargaining*

Walton and McKersie define this as 'the system of activities which is instrumental to the attainment of objectives which are not in fundamental conflict with those of the other party and which therefore can be integratrated to some degree. Such objectives are said to define an area of common concern, "a problem".'[265] The approach has also been called problem-solving. It may occur as a phase or development in most negotiating situations when the parties are moving away from earlier hostile stages in which the high costs of not conceding claims have been stressed, to a more co-operative phase when the low costs of concession are emphasized. The parties, or one of them, now begin to search for impediments to progress which can be jointly attacked; the approaches are more consultative and co-operative.

The formal structure of negotiation and psychological process of group reinforcement which bargaining encourages are impediments to the development of these approaches, although they do not totally inhibit them. The very formality of the setting can assist development. Formal negotiating conferences create:

a situation which all concerned recognize as to some

> extent artificial. The ritual which surrounds a conference emphasizes the fact that all are performing roles. As a result, a hostile interchange which occurs will not be taken personally; officials who have in effect to live with each other can divorce what they do and say on behalf of their organizations from their relationship as individuals.[266]

Hyman adds, later, that conference ritualism means that:

> the hostility which a negotiator may be obliged at times to express on behalf of his organization cannot be allowed to form the basis of overt personal enmity towards an opposing representative. Such enmity would normally make intolerable the personal position of an official who must regularly interact with his opposite number.[267]

The structure of negotiation does not prevent integrative bargaining from taking place but it does mean that collective bargaining is often perceived as essentially hostile or competitive and, therefore, as inhibiting the development of integrative or problem-solving approaches. The result is that management has continually been concerned to find alternative frameworks which will stimulate and encourage more cooperative relationships between the parties. The earlier enthusiasm for productivity bargaining suggested that it was just such a framework, that it might provide a totally new approach to bargaining and a major innovation in industrial relations.

(iii) *Participation*

Management inevitably regards collective bargaining with some ambivalence because it represents a challenge to its authority and because it is a process which it cannot control, the outcome of which it cannot predict. But management has an inescapable interest in maintaining control over its employees by one means or another, by the exercise of authority, by persuasion or by achieving their involvement. Management certainly needs to attempt to keep control over its communications with its employees. For these reasons management seeks to establish communication channels which are free of the uncertain inputs and unpredictable outputs of collective bargaining and which offer some prospect of direct communication with employees. One of the first alternative channels to command general interest was joint consultation which received enthusiastic support from many quarters throughout the 1950s. Enthusiasm has now been abandoned because the channels were so clogged with management communicating information about past events and so concerned to avoid conflict that they were perceived to be irrelevant to the pursuit of interests other than management's. There were also problems concerning the executive inactivity of consultative committees (they talked but they never did anything) and the difficulty in bridging a communication gap between worker representatives and their constituents. Consultative committees declined into apathy or they were abandoned.

The interest in controlling communication did not decline: it turned to the applications of more sophisticated techniques. Some evidence and a great deal more rhetoric suggested that if the employee is made to feel a part of his organization, made to believe that he can influence his decisions, then he will cooperate more fully in activities necessary to achieve its goals. The question is, who is influencing whom in these participatory approaches to management? French suggested that there was a need to distinguish between what he called 'psychological participation' and 'objective participation.' ' "Psychological participation" is the extent of influence on a jointly made decision which the participant *thinks* he has. "Objective participation" is the amount of influence on the decision which he *actually* has.'[268] In developing participatory approaches, management is often concerned to increase psychological participation while at the same time decreasing objective participation. Participation is invited to overcome problems which managers define as problems. The intention is to create what Fox defines as a unitary frame of reference. The point may be made by the following quotation:

> From the economic point of view (participation) is regarded as a powerful factor for improving the productivity of undertakings because it can stimulate a spirit of initiative and responsibility among the workers, enable the management to benefit from the practical experience of the rank and file, and improve cooperation between the two levels.[269]

Although that quotation could well be an account of western management's expectations of participation, it does in fact describe official expectations in a communist country (in order to facilitate the deception, 'participation' has been substituted for the original 'labour democracy').

The particular approaches to participation which are recommended change from time to time; their underlying purpose remains the same. Commenting on the current revival of interest in employee participation, Ramsay says that:

> the calls for an extension of worker participation in decisions far from being a new phenomenon, have appeared in waves of popularity . . . Essentially these periods follow growing pressure on the legitimacy of management authority from below, and represent an attempt to regain control by making a show of appearing to share it.[270]

(iv) *Improved understanding*

Improving the understanding of the opponent (which often means altering it in a manner favourable to one's own position) can take place both outside and inside the bargaining relationship. Outside, it includes a general approach to influencing and educating opposing institutions so as to bring them to a wider understanding of facts and techniques or to a more sympathetic outlook. Inside, it is an 'attempt to alter the other's appraisal or evaluation of the consequences that are expected to follow from the different courses of action.'[271] The approach can be made by efforts at helping the opponent to understand alternative situations or by teaching him about new possibilities. An impasse may be avoided by suggesting a course of action of which the opponent was ignorant and by providing him with the necessary learning and technique in order to pursue it. Deutsch suggests that the opponent can be helped to remove some of the obstacles in his environment which prevent him from moving in an acceptable direction.

4 The adjustment of each party's position

If negotiations are to result in an agreement the positions established by one or both parties at the outset must be abandoned. This movement from mutually unacceptable positions to a contract zone and to an agreement is accompanied by changes in the perceptions which each party has of its opponent's intentions; each party shifts the other, is shifted in turn and adjusts his own outlook on his opponent.

The adjustment of positions is the result of each party learning more about the environment within which negotiations are conducted as the result of the negotiation process itself. Contact and communication with the opponent provides information about his situation and ultimately, perhaps, even about his intentions. Facts and evidence are revealed which enable each party to make more accurate estimates of the real influence concerning, for example, the solidarity of the union membership, its relationship with other unions, the depth of feeling about perceived inequities, the reality of these feelings and the determination and power to do something to correct them. Management, while it is making and evaluating these discoveries, is itself under pressure, by overt or subtle means, to reveal information about its cost structure, the true commitment of senior management, its anxiety to settle or its propensity to incur costs of a failure to agree. Each party is gathering information, evaluating it, unwillingly providing information and deliberately providing information in order to influence its opponent's judgement. The evaluation and the control of information is of vital importance:

> it is not necessary for the objective conditions to change; it is only necessary for the perception of those conditions to change in order for a negotiator to alter his position. In contract negotiations, objective knowledge virtually never becomes complete.[272]

Information is of two kinds or it ranges between two levels of reliability. Information may reliably relate to the environment, to situational conditions. 'The situational conditions are the facts which make up the environment within which negotiations take place . . . The process conditions are the influences which the parties can bring to each other within the negotiations.'[273] The two cannot be clearly isolated from each other because while some situational conditions are clearly perceived by both parties (the requirements of government incomes policy, for example), other conditions in the environment, equally real, are communicated by one party to the other and may or may not be perceived as real. The party which receives information about what he cannot see for himself has to make a judgement about whether those conditions really exist in the world or whether they are part of a process tactic used by his opponent.

Continuous judgement and evaluation is essential. Each

party not only has to sift information which his opponent reveals, it has also to discover or provoke more information than is being volunteered. Various tactics have been described which are deployed purely to elicit information. One party may engage in a finesse in which he asserts information in the hope that it will be corrected by an opponent. A negotiator may appeal to the least experienced member on the opposite side in the hope that a temporary lack of control by the leadership will allow information to flow. Walton and McKersie describe the tactics of ' "exaggerated impatience" which make it appear as if the negotiators were rushing headlong into the final stages' so as to 'force the inexperienced negotiator into prematurely revealing the bargaining room he has allowed himself.'[274] A negotiator (as long as he has sufficient influence in the internal bargaining process) may actually arrange for evidence of changes in the environment (the situational conditions) to be made and to be publicly visible to his opponent. Personal abuse may be used so as to provoke a loss of control in the opponent which may result in the provision of more information. Although negotiations are not debates, indulgence in long, tortuous and rigorous arguments may be engaged in so that, in the process of rebutting them, an opponent may produce information to refute points. All these are subordinate devices, tactics deployed to produce information. They suggest the paramount importance of the negotiator retaining control of his own behaviour and directing it to the goals which he wants to achieve. Complex and lengthy negotiations can result in a loss of sense of direction and a tendency, particularly among inexperienced negotiators, to confuse tactical victories with strategic success.

The provision and evaluation of information assists the parties to perceive each other's positions more realistically. A process of 'reconnoitring the bargaining range' begins in which more collaborative gestures are made. But the process continues to be one in which rationality, argument and persuasion are sometimes insufficient to bring about necessary change and adjustment. Power may have to be applied either to change the faulty evaluation of an opponent concerning its availability and the willingness to apply it, or to change his perceptions of reality, to change the equation upon which he has operated concerning the costs of a failure to agree.

The processes of internal adjustment may be crucial in moving the parties towards an agreement. It can take place as the result of the effective exercise of control upon the negotiator by his organization or by the negotiator upon his organization. In these circumstances the obstacle to the agreement resides within the organization rather than in the opponent and a series of meetings in recess will have to occur before movement can take place in resumed meetings between the parties. Occasionally, adjustments are facilitated when the negotiators begin to see their own organizations as the principal threat to agreement so that the solidarity of the negotiators, across the frontier, is enhanced; they reach private understandings in an effort to assert their own control.

Towards the terminal stages of negotiation, communications become both more open and more subtle. Non-verbal communication, sign language and silences all assume significance. The negotiator's knowledge and experience of his opponent are likely to be crucial: 'Mutual familiarity ensures that the subtle processes of probes and cues can be compressed into a few brief exchanges . . . and that either side can tacitly convey a complex position in a few sentences.'[275] Sometimes the recognition of an area of intractable difficulty preventing progress which both parties want to make will result in purely semantic exercises to obscure its importance. The language of a potential accommodation will become deliberately vague and ambiguous as part of a necessary price for reaching an agreement (although, often, the price may have to be paid subsequently in re-defining a position of conflict which the agreement has failed to regulate; but at least the conflict will have been deferred while other advantages of accommodation have been achieved).

In these final stages, the problems of 'how to come clean without commitment' have been partially resolved as the result of clearer perceptions as to the true commitments of the parties. This may be the result of each party being forced, under pressure from its opponent, to see and express its own objectives more clearly:

> Your chances of influencing another to do what you want are considerably enhanced if the other clearly knows what you want him to do. Too often, particularly in situations of conflict, there is a tendency to express our attitudes toward the other or to state our own objectives rather than to indicate what we specifically want the other to do.[276]

The mutual adjustment of the positions of the parties is the result of subtle and complex processes. They require time to elapse before they can be effective. Negotiations are necessarily protracted. They are also, necessarily, formal. We have already observed the utility of formal negotiations in protecting the negotiations from personal involvement in hostile exchanges. Hyman points out that:

> the refusal to move towards compromise in domestic discussions is one means whereby each party can attempt to convince the other of its own determination and hence, hopefully, induce the maximum concessions from its opponent.[277]

He adds that procedure has other advantages: it exercises the formal obligation to exhaust procedure before sanctions are applied; it offers practical gains for the union (as least, in wage issues) and it can be a safety-valve.

5 Sanctions

Negotiations do not necessarily end in agreement. In some circumstances they may have to be interrupted before they can be resumed. Interruptions usually take the form of industrial disputes, strikes or lock-outs. Industrial disputes are inseparable from collective bargaining for the following reasons:

(i) Collective bargaining depends upon the distribution and application of power. If, for one reason or another, power is never applied, the belief in its existence wanes. In circumstances of procedural or legislative constraint which forbid disputes, divisions of interest which are associated with power are unable to find realistic expression in the collective bargaining relationship. The inevitable result is guerrilla warfare, unorganized rather than regulated conflict. Some observers believe that the consequences to society and to industry are likely to be more damaging. The collective bargaining process runs the risk of being undermined as the constituents of employment come to see it as irrelevant and unproductive. Union leadership and managerial responsibility become difficult to maintain and the result is the 'two (or more) systems' of the Donovan analysis, fractionalized bargaining and a break-away from control.

(ii) Industrial disputes demonstrate force, conviction or necessity which must be accommodated and recognized in the bargaining process. If bargaining has failed to perceive realities, industrial disputes may be the only means of changing the perceptions of the parties so that an accommodation can be achieved. Disputes may serve to change the parties' understanding of reality and may be the only way in which negotiating objectives can be shifted so as to make an accommodation possible. Collective bargaining may not be fair or just but disputes help to ensure that it reaches accommodations to powerful interests when they possess sufficient conviction about injustice to apply the power available to them to correct it. Disputes impart convictions and the power to maintain them to the bargaining process.

(iii) Disputes may improve the negotiating value of one party to its opponent. 'Identifying an external enemy usually increases the internal solidarity of a group.'[278] The more representative of its constituents a negotiating body becomes the more useful it is to its opponent. The costs in increased negotiating effectiveness (to the opponent) are balanced by the greater utility and authority of deals when they are made. This is related to Lewis Coser's argument that, in conflict relationships, each party has an interest in promoting the effectiveness of his opponent.

(iv) Disputes may serve to correct an imbalance within each negotiating organization. In terms of the processes of internal negotiation, a situation in which the negotiating representatives of the organization are deemed to have been accommodated too successfully to the opponent may be corrected only by a dispute. This may happen when senior management refuses to allow its negotiators to concede under pressure. It often occurs when stewards or other representatives of the rank and file take strike action in order to influence their own official negotiators; in these circumstances, sanctions may be applied to the organization's negotiators in order to bring them to a more 'realistic' or representative position. Disputes can be a method by which the organization seeks to control its own negotiators.

Strikes have come to assume a position of great importance in the public discussion of industrial relations in this country. This discussion illustrates the way in which the conduct of those engaged in industrial relations is controlled or influenced by appeals to wider social criteria. The social significance of industrial disputes or, as it is often defined, 'the problem of strikes', is certainly relevant to the discussion of industrial relations but we shall postpone its discussion until the next chapter.

(v) Disputes do not take the form only of strikes. Strikes have sometimes been regarded as the most severe form of industrial action to be taken by workpeople but this judgement may have to be revised. 'Cut-price' industrial action which requires no finance from union funds to support it, and which may entail little loss of earnings among the workers involved, may be more protracted than a strike. Various forms of restrictions of effort may change the analysis of collective bargaining in terms of measurable power because these apparently more mild sanctions appear to be limitless in their extent; as they cost little to apply they need never be withdrawn. They can also cost a great deal to the employer because they may disrupt the production or distribution process very severely. This changes the relative application of power by both parties in the classic analysis of which each party withstands the cost of sanctions applied by its opponent while each incurs costs until, finally, the issue is re-appraised in more realistic terms so that sanctions lead to an accommodation. In limited sanctions, the opponent incurs costs and the party applying the limited sanction incurs none.

The only courses of action for the party facing a limited sanction short of a strike is to concede or increase the conflict by applying further power. In practical terms this means that the employer, faced by a restriction of effort, may terminate contracts or apply a lock-out. The discussion as to whether the dispute is now a strike or a lock-out is likely to be interminable. Whatever the particular verdict, if the original sanction is sufficiently severe, it is hard to see what else the party facing the sanction can do if the dispute is to be in any sense controllable within a joint process of accommodation. The difficulties are compounded by the exclusion of these affairs from procedural descriptions; there is nothing that procedure can do to contain these circumstances because the sanctions are difficult to define or accommodate within a formal, procedural relationship.

It is not, however, a one-sided relationship, although managers often see this as a new phenomenon directed against them by workers. Managers have always been able to exercise limited sanctions short of a lock-out by the simple exercise of the managerial prerogative to take and enforce decisions about the organization of work. In the old engineering procedural agreement this procedural right was formally acknowledged. It was countered, where there was sufficient power in the workshop, by precisely the same application of a counter sanction intended to lift the conflict to a more visible and controllable level. There is a difference (in fact, there is bound to be a difference) between what procedure allows and the realities of behaviour:

> In theory, trade unions are obliged to acquiesce in a wide range of managerial decisions while pursuing any objectives through procedure. In practice, companies are normally cautious in insisting on their formal rights. The extent to which an implicit *status quo* provision has been allowed to operate can also explain why trade unions in engineering have continued to tolerate—under very difficult economic conditions—provisions enforced in a lock-out when over 25 per cent of workers in the industry were unemployed.[279]

It is not possible for procedure to account for or prescribe the applications of limited sanctions by either side in the place of work. Hyman is right to say that 'a certain tension seems inherent between the prescriptions of procedure and the realities of collective bargaining.'[280] The tension is resolved, in some circumstances, by responding to a limited or 'informal sanction' (which procedure cannot recognize) by the application of a formal sanction. Management responds to a go-slow by a lock-out, workers respond to a change in work pace by a strike. The function of what at first sight appears to be a dangerous increase of conflict out of control is to promote unregulatable conflict to a level at which control is possible. Where this 'promotion' of conflict does not occur, other means of resolution may have to be found. One of them is, of course, concession. Another may be the intervention of third parties.

6 Third party intervention

(a) *Conciliation*

The attempt to resolve disputes by the introduction of third parties may take one of three forms. Conciliation was introduced by the Conciliation Act of 1896. First the Ministry of Labour, then the Department of Employment and now the Advisory, Conciliation and Arbitration Service are able to offer their services to parties in dispute as long as one of them requested assistance and as long as both parties had exhausted whatever procedural avenues were available to them. Conciliation officers listen to what both parties have to say, attempt to clarify the understanding in each of the other's position and explore the possibilities of bringing those positions together. It represents an attempt to explore the bargaining range when other means of doing so have failed. 'The object of conciliation is to try and help the parties in a dispute to find their own solution to it—not to put a solution before them.'[281] It is, as Thomason describes it, a process in which the conciliators, either officers of the Service are able to offer their services to parties in dispute reach a settlement by using any agreed procedures, and, whether such procedures exist or not . . . help them to come to a resolution of their difficulties.'[282] The conciliation function is provided by the ACAS in disputes in which collective bargaining has failed to reach a resolution and in which one or more of the parties have requested it. Conciliation can also be provided in cases of alleged unfair dismissal as a preliminary, if unsuccessful, to the case being heard by an Industrial Tribunal. In both cases of conciliation, there is a convention that the process is privy to the parties and that no account of it is available in any successive attempts at resolution or decision.

(b) *Mediation*

Although a feature of industrial relations in the USA for some time, mediation is relatively new to Britain. It seems to have been recently favoured by the ACAS. It requires reference by the parties to a mediator whose function is to bring the parties to an agreement. It is distinguished in practice from conciliation by the fact that it is a more three-cornered process in which the mediator searches for possible solutions which the parties negotiate over in the expectation of an agreement; it is more purposeful and less tentative. The mediator does not impose a solution, he explores and proposes possibilities which the two parties must accept or reject.

(c) *Arbitration*

Arbitration was provided under the Conciliation Act of 1896 and the Industrial Courts Act of 1919. Apart from the intervening vicissitudes of war and the Industrial Relations Act 1971, arbitration has been a voluntary process both in terms of access to it and in the acceptance of its decisions. In arbitration before single arbitrators, or before single arbitrators aided by assessors, the parties must have agreed to seek arbitration. The process is not a formal one although procedural conventions have evolved. The arbitrator's function is to listen to the arguments and evidence presented by each side and to reach a decision within the terms of reference which he has been given. There is nothing in law or in the method of access to arbitration that imposes an obligation on the parties to accept the decision of the arbitrator but there is a strong convention that they should do so. This no doubt stems from the view that arbitration represents finality which both parties have chosen to seek and that there is, therefore, something contradictory about re-opening a debate about whether the decision is acceptable or not, that it is a return to the frying-pan from which both parties have agreed to leap. Although the parties are under no formal obligation to accept an arbitrator's award there is an almost unbroken convention for its acceptance by both sides. References to arbitration quadrupled in the first few months of the existence of the ACAS.

This increase is partly explained by the reputation of the previous agencies (the Ministry of Labour and the Department of Employment) being damaged by their association with the current versions of incomes policy. The ACAS is regarded as an independent agency and it seems anxious to avoid involvement in issues which involve the interpretation or implementation of Government policy. The Employment Protection Act established a Central Arbitration Committee to take over the work of the Industrial Arbitration Board. The Committee makes arbitration awards enforceable through the contract of employment over claims for the observance of recognized terms and conditions of employment.

The matters which have just been described might be called the public access to arbitration: they are available usually as a last resort after procedural exhaustion or deficiency. Private access to arbitration may be provided by the domestic procedure agreement for a particular trade or industry. It can take several forms:

(a) the decision to go to arbitration may be binding (by prior commitment within their procedure agreement)
(b) the binding decision may operate when the procedural

hierarchy of negotiations has been exhausted, when the issue has been referred from bottom to top when there is nowhere else to go

(c) the automatic reference to arbitration may take place at the point in procedure at which a failure to agree is registered (unless a matter of more general application is involved)

(d) the reference to arbitration may rest upon the prior agreement of the parties faced with a failure to agree

(e) the issue, when it is referred to arbitration by whatever method of reference, may be the subject of an arbitration decision which is binding upon both parties. This follows the logic of the ACAS's preference for an acceptance by the parties of the arbitrator's decision

(f) the arbitrator's judgement may be given the force of a recommendation which it is for the parties to accept or reject; the arbitrator's decision is not binding upon them. This on the face of it looks like a contradiction of the ACAS's logic concerning the necessary finality of arbitration. It is not necessarily so. It may represent the extent to which the parties to the procedure agreement are prepared to go by way of a prior commitment to arbitration. It may, in some circumstances, reveal a realistic understanding of the extent to which over-reliance on arbitration can rob the union of a right to strike which it sees as essential to the maintenance of collective bargaining and its own independence. Procedure which compulsorily directs the parties to arbitration and which commits them to accept its findings is likely to be too severe and restrictive; in these circumstances, it is hardly possible for a union to engage in an official and constitutional strike. The consequence of such procedural rigidity may produce more, rather than less, unregulated conflict and industrial action

(g) the composition of the arbitration body (or person) may

be defined within the procedure and it may constitute a standard machinery for the industry. Railways, coal and the Civil Service have standing arbitration arrangements

(h) the arbitration arrangements may be left to be arranged *ad hoc* or by the ACAS. In these circumstances the private route to arbitration may take the parties into the field of public provision of facilities.

A useful summary of the forms of conflict regulation provided by third parties was provided by Dahrendorf:

Type	*Invitation of third party*	*Acceptance of third-party advice*	*Description*
A	None	None	Conciliation
B	Voluntary	Voluntary	Mediation
C	Voluntary	Compulsory	Arbitration
D	Compulsory	Voluntary	Arbitration
E	Compulsory	Compulsory	(Suppression)

There is no doubt that the extension of the arbitration can contribute to the greater regulation of conflict in industrial relations. But support for its infinite extension should be limited. It cannot be substituted for collective bargaining, except in circumstances of more general social change, which will be discussed in the next chapter. It may be more effective in relation to conflicts of right rather than conflicts of interest. Some managers believe that there may be a tendency for unions to refuse to negotiate a settlement over wages in the belief that intransigence will be rewarded by an arbitration decision which is forced to exceed the last offer. Arbitration is also less likely to be successful over complex issues in which the judgement is forced, by specific terms of reference, to say yes or no to a particular question.

Singleton says that 98 per cent of the industry level procedure agreements studied provided for third party assistance which, in 21 per cent of them, was automatic on a failure to agree. But, he adds, the general view of employers' associations was that little use was made of these provisions because of an emphasis on domestic settlement.[284]

(d) *Enquiry*

The last version of third party intervention to be considered is by the method of public enquiry. The Industrial Courts Act of 1919 provided the Minister with the power to set up a Court of Enquiry to investigate the facts of a dispute so as to inform Parliament of the facts concerning it. The procedure is not frequently invoked and it is more usually confined to large scale disputes which have captured public or Parliamentary attention. The establishment of a Court of Enquiry does not, unlike the other processes we have discussed, depend upon the approval of the parties and its real function is to establish facts so that a better understanding of them may help the parties to proceed to a settlement. Enquiries also allow the public observation of particular disputes so that the conduct of the parties is exposed to public standards; they break down the 'professional' isolation within which negotiations are conducted and which may not always contribute to rationality or justice. Enquiries and their results have no compulsive force except that of informed opinions but that may be sufficient to encourage the parties to negotiate a settlement.

The process of enquiry has been informally extended by the ACAS by the establishment of panels of investigation but here the investigation is established with the consent of the parties. The dispute about mechanical rectifiers (or engine tuners) at British Leyland, Cowley, resulted in the appointment of a three-man panel of investigation.[285] The dispute between the British Steel Corporation and the Blastfurnacemen's Union at Llanwern has also led to the appointment of a panel of enquiry.

7 Effective negotiation

There are two difficulties about attempting to lay down prescriptions for the achievement of effective negotiations. The first is that they are bound to be naive; the process of negotiation is complex and subtle, rules for its improvement are necessarily crude. The second is that the criteria of effectiveness will change with the perspective of the judge. It may be possible to suggest some characteristics which improve the efficiency of the negotiating process in the sense that it may better serve to meet the joint interests of the parties who resort to it. Effectiveness may be judged to be increased by the removal of unnecessary and accidental obstacles in the way of the parties reaching a joint accommodation which they would both regard as a desirable end.

With these reservations in mind, let us examine some possible precepts concerning first the environment of negotiations and, second, the relationship between the negotiators:

1 *The environment*

(a) *Adequate procedure*

The advantages of procedural regulation and improvement were given at least sufficient emphasis in the Report of the Donovan Commission. Their contribution to effective negotiation is that they:

> can establish accepted standards of conduct and influence behaviour. They can give early warning of developing problems and provide experience in devising methods of dealing with them. They put a premium on rationality and fairness and a discount on arbitrary action. They can affect the whole style and tone and morale of an enterprise.[286]

(b) *Open internal negotiations*

The formal and informal relationships between the bargaining parties are not the sole determinants of effective negotiations. If negotiations are to be purposeful, to relate to the organisation's wider objectives and to the aspirations of its members, then there must be adequate provision for internal adjustment within each organisation. Within trade unions this requirement is often subsumed under the heading of union democracy. The facilitation of internal adjustment in employer organizations may be more complex. It suggests the importance of the relationship between functional departments (like personnel and industrial relations) to the executive and to line management. It requires that autocracy should be tempered, if not by revolution then by the recognition of the need for flexible response, of the importance of expert advice and the need to heed it without being dominated by it.

(c) *Reduction of conflict scale*

Negotiators can handle small scale conflicts more easily than large confrontations. The escalation of the size of conflict can entrench positions and demand that principles should never be abandoned and that faces must be saved. The negotiators can find themselves dealing with issues remote from those originally presented and with issues that are fundamentally un-negotiable. These are circumstances in which protracted disputes may take place before a negotiable agenda can be reconstructed. Protracted procedures or a lack of readiness in one party to deal with issues raised by the other can inflate the size of conflict. There have been memorable instances when the intervention of government, by one means or another, has increased the scale of conflict to un-negotiable proportions.

2 *Relationships between negotiators*

(a) *Co-operative negotiation*

Negotiations may be more effective when they are concerned

with a cooperative effort to solve problems rather than with a competitive struggle to achieve victories. The scope for cooperative negotiation is probably limited. It may be limited in time, in the early stages of productivity bargaining, for example, before distributive bargaining emerges. It may be a joint and passing response to an outside threat which both parties perceive in common. It may also be the result of a strategic ascendancy which one party has been able to establish over the other. If the ascendancy is not based upon an inbalance of power it is likely to be fragile.

(b) *Stability of negotiators*

Negotiators are better able to understand the nuances of the relationship between them when they know each other, when experience has taught them to read each other's behaviour. They are also able to judge each other's representative authority, to assess how far they can reliably be expected to speak for and carry the approval of their organization. Frequent changes in the personnel of a negotiating team is unsettling to effective negotiations.

(c) *Rationality*

Negotiators are better able to understand opponents when their behaviour is controlled and purposeful, directed at the achievement of some perceptible goal. Irrational or emotional behaviour, whether deliberately or accidentally demonstrated, is best met with a controlled response.

(d) *Experience and training*

Effective negotiators seem to emerge and survive, others subside. There may be no way to imitate and shorten a process of natural selection but there is little doubt that some of the skills of negotiation can be developed by training. The difficulty of simulated games or role playing situations is that they lack the urgency, even the terror, of reality.

Role playing can, however, improve a sensitive understanding of realities and expectations in another organization. Training can improve knowledge of the economic and procedural environment and of the negotiation rules.

(e) *Moral reinforcement*

There is a danger that negotiators come to respect only the pragmatic and the powerful; the negotiating relationship can become cynical. A negotiator may permit deterioration of the relationship simply by abstaining from the expression of disapproval for a violation of normal conduct or of disorderly behaviour. Disintegration of the relationship or of the rules may appear to be sanctioned by customary practice. Deutsch suggests that adherence to the rules is more likely when the rules themselves are known, are clear and consistent, are not perceived to be biased, when violations are apparent to others, when adherence to them is socially approved and violations are condemned and when their acceptance has been rewarded in the past. [287]

CHAPTER 10

Industrial relations and society

The British method of conducting industrial relations is not unique but neither is it typical. All other industrialized countries engage in a higher level of legal regulation even than that which has been achieved in Britain since 1971. Some other countries, those devoted to central planning of both the economy and the society, control industrial relations to an extent which renders their industrial relations unrecognizable from our own perspective, so that trade unions are best understood as 'transmission belts' linking the government to the workplace. The characteristic feature of British industrial relations is collective bargaining which, never entirely free from legal control, has always depended to an unusual degree upon relationships established and maintained by the parties, employers and trade unions.

We have seen that collective bargaining has been defined as a mechanism of social control. Collective bargaining controls or at least influences social change. But any mechanism of control will break down if the forces which it seeks to moderate are too great or if the speed with which they change is too rapid. Collective bargaining is therefore influenced by social change. It is subject, as we have seen, to influence from a number of quarters, from the technical nature of production processes, from the expectations and attitudes of people at work, from political values and from changes in the law. The safest prediction in an analysis of any aspect of social affairs is that they will change. The difficulty about converting social analysis into social science is, of course, that the nature of the change can never be accurately predicted. We shall conclude this particular study of industrial relations by trying to take some account of the influences which are likely to introduce changes into British industrial relations; we cannot know what those changes will be.

The amount of criticism directed at the conduct of British industrial relations in recent years is probably unprecedented. There have been occasions in the not too distant past, when employers and politicians were convinced that the country was teetering on the brink of revolution (often between 1910 and 1920 and again, probably with less reason, in 1926) but this, it could be said, was in an immature stage of development in industrial relations (or of capitalism). The present criticisms are much more specific and they do not concern the behaviour or expectations of men in society of the working class or of the employers: they are about the technical efficiency of collective bargaining as a mechanism of control. There are at least three basic criticisms:

- that collective bargaining is economically inefficient
- that the procedural machinery of collective bargaining is inadequate
- that collective bargaining produces an unacceptable level of conflict; there are too many strikes.

A more general concern has also developed in recent years about the relationship between the mechanisms of industrial relations and the aspirations of groups within society. This concern can be expressed in two contradictory statements:

1 that the framework of industrial relations imposes a degree of consensus which makes representation of

the social aspirations of groups impossible and which prevents the achievement of necessary change

2 that behaviour in the context of industrial relations threatens social order and social stability.

We shall distinguish these two areas of criticism of industrial relations as technical and social.

1 Technical criticisms of industrial relations

(a) *Economic inefficiency*

The view, advanced by many newspapers and supported by a large section of the public, that collective bargaining and industrial disputes are inflationary and damaging both to union members and to society, has received powerful support from distinguished academics. Writing in 1972, Professor B C Roberts summarized the case as follows. The level of industrial conflict has grown in recent years but has brought no gain in the living standards of workers, apart from that which can be attributed to growth in productivity. While it has done no good to workers it has harmed the nation as a whole and it has imposed suffering on innocent bystanders such as the consumers. A *laissez-faire* theory of economic competition and power bargaining was irrelevant to present circumstances and the substitution of the application of countervailing power between giant interest groups was too damaging to be contemplated. The extension of collective bargaining 'to every section of the community as technical, professional and administrative employees up to the highest level organize and turn to the methods employed by the other trade unions to protect their occupational and social activity' would impose intolerable strain upon society.[288] Professor Phelps Brown says that 'under full employment the balance of bargaining power has swung too far towards the employee' and that the result has been inflation.[289] Collective bargaining, he says, 'made less difference than popular belief or the experience of recent years would suggest . . . The great rise of the general level of real wages was provided almost wholly by the rise of productivity and owed little to any changes in the division of the product enforced through collective bargaining.'[290] Collective bargaining has had some effect on particular groups; wages under collective bargaining may be 20–25 per cent higher than they would otherwise be but the relative advantage enjoyed by the worker is not achieved at the expense of the employer, it is achieved at the expense of the consumer 'and nowadays by the consumer we must understand, for the most part, other workers.'[291] The result is inflation and 'a continual disturbance of relativities, and an embittered endeavour to re-establish them.'[292] In consequence collective bargaining has ceased to be a form of self-government in industry . . . .

> It has become all too much a competitive scramble between groups, where what each gains for the time being is at the expense of the rest; and each trade union becomes increasingly indispensable to its members as a safeguard against being left behind by the others in a *bellum omnium contra omnes*[293]

The view seems to be generally shared:

> 51 per cent of the British population feel that the rise in world prices, import prices, world shortages or the price of raw materials carry responsibility for the price increases which most disturb them; while 50 per cent blame labour costs, wage or salary claims or increases, trade union demands or strikes.[294]

This is an area which has engaged the attention of expert economists and others are well advised to observe the usual advice given to hasty fools. Some economists believe inflation is caused by government economic policy rather than by wage claims. Some of the arguments appear to be self-cancelling. If collective bargaining has little or no effect on wages in general, but a considerable effect on the wages of those able to engage in it, if it does redistribute wages among workers, then the best advice to a worker is surely to join a union which is an effective bargainer. Again, although it is possible for bargaining both to have no effect on wages and to be inflationary at the same time, the relationship between both assertions requires some careful attention. The effect of wages on inflation, like all arguments about chickens and eggs, is likely to be complex. The difficulty about validating the arguments about collective bargaining is, as in so many aspects of social relationships, that it is impossible to calculate what wages would have been without collective bargaining. Finally, the critics of the economic consequences of collective bargaining, when driven to propose alternative methods of wage and salary determination, usually arrive at some arrangement for central administration which is either coercive or based upon a method of job evaluation more grandiose than those which produce a sufficiency of problems when they are confined to the level of the enterprise or the factory.

(b) *Procedural deficiency*

This aspect of collective bargaining has already been discussed. The reform of procedures can, no doubt, make a significant contribution to more efficient industrial relations but it would be dangerous to conclude that a high degree of formality is synonymous with stability and a low level of disputes. The Donovan Commission was possibly wrong and probably guilty of exaggeration when it described factionalized bargaining as 'the root of the evil.' The level of strike activity which so much concerned the Commission was easily surpassed when attempts were subsequently made to establish industrial relations on a more formal basis. There are also suggestions that one of the variables contributing to higher levels of industrial disputes is the size of the establishment and the extent to which procedures are bureaucratized.

(c) *Strikes*

This is probably the biggest single factor contributing to public concern about industrial relations in this country. The concern seems to remain constant despite great variations in the incidence and severity of disputes. From 1960 to 1965 the number of strikes remained reasonably constant, the number grew from 1965 to 1970. In 1972 and in 1974 the number of working days lost was higher than in any year since 1926 (the figures largely accounted for by national stoppages in the coal industry). The estimated number of stoppages for 1976 was the lowest for 10 years and there was a decrease of about 45 per cent in the loss of working days.

The number of disputes, the total number of working days lost, and the percentage of working days lost in official disputes are as follows:[295]

Table 7

	Number of strikes	Total number of working days lost (000s)	%age of working days lost in official disputes
1965	2354	2925	20.8
1966	1937	2398	48.9
1967	2116	2787	14.1
1968	2378	4690	46.9
1969	3116	6846	23.6
1970	3906	10980	30.2
1971	2228	13551	74.2
1972	2497	23909	76.2
1973	2873	7197	27.9
1974	2922	14750	47.7
1975	2282	6012	19.1
1976	1990	3286	14.4

The incidence and the severity of disputes varies considerably between different industries:

Table 8

Standard Industrial Classification	(Averages 1966–1973) No of stoppages per 100,000 employees	No of working days lost per 1,000 employees
1 Agriculture, forestry, fishing	0.8	27.5
2 Mining and quarrying	60.2	4,305.5
3 Food, drink and tobacco	10.9	198.1
4 Coal and petroleum products	12.2	243.4
5 Chemical and allied industries	11.0	136.8
6 Metal manufacture	32.8	761.8
7 Mechanical engineering	30.5	623.5
8 Instrument engineering	13.2	292.3
9 Electrical engineering	20.2	721.4
10 Shipbuilding and marine engineering	47.7	1,820.4
11 Vehicles	40.0	2,105.3
12 Metal goods	19.6	283.7
13 Textiles	10.1	161.1
14 Leather and fur goods	5.0	17.6
15 Clothing and footwear	5.0	90.1
16 Bricks, pottery, glass, cement	15.1	320.2
17 Timber and furniture	11.2	99.8
18 Paper, printing and publishing	6.6	104.9
19 Other manufacturing industries	18.6	516.9
20 Construction	18.6	538.1
21 Gas, electricity and water	3.7	139.5
22 Transport and communication	21.2	975.9
23 Distributive trades	1.6	6.5
24 Insurance, banking, finance and business services	0.3	46.4
25 Professional and scientific services	0.6	40.3
26 Miscellaneous services	1.1	9.5
27 Public administration and defence	2.6	130.9

The generalizations which we make about our strike record is not justified by the facts. In a study of the distribution and concentration of industrial stoppages in Britain, the Department of Employment concluded that 'Great Britain does not suffer from a problem of widespread industrial stoppages, but rather from a concentration of stoppages in a relatively small number of establishments.'[296] In the period 1971 to 1973 (a period not notable for its low strikes figures) an average of 97.8 per cent of establishments or plants were not affected by stoppages in any one year. The small proportion of establishments which were most affected by strikes accounted for a disproportionately high percentage of strikes and working days lost.

Table 9

The most severely affected

These figures are taken from the DE *Gazette*, November 1976)

	5% of affected establishments	10% of affected establishments
Accounted for	24% stoppages	35% stoppages
Accounted for	67% of working days lost	79% of working days lost

The most important cause of disputes is pay, and the proportion of disputes concerned with pay has been rising in recent years. The number of disputes over discipline and dismissal and over manning and work allocation seems to have been falling.

The figures in Tables 10 and 11, p 276, are taken or derived from Tables 1 and 2 in The incidence of industrial stoppages in the United Kingdom, DE *Gazette*, February 1976

Table 10
Percentage of the number of stoppages by cause

	1966	1970	1974	Annual average 1966–74 No of stoppages	No of working days lost
Pay	46	64	65	57	84
Hours worked	2	1	2	2	2
Redundancy	3	3	3	4	2
Trade union matters	7	8	6	8	4
Working conditions	7	6	5	6	1
Manning and work allocation	18	7	9	11	3
Dismissal and discipline	13	9	8	12	4

A recent limited analysis of stoppages in relation to size of plant suggests that the number of stoppages and the incidence of stoppages increases with plant size.

Table 11
Incidence of stoppages by size of plant
Annual average 1971–1973 *manufacturing industry*

	No of stoppages per 100,000 employees	No of working days lost per 1,000 employees
11–24	8.0	14.8
25–99	19.2	72.4
100–199	23.0	155.0
200–499	25.4	329.1
500–999	29.7	719.4
1000 or more	28.7	2046.1

Public concern about strikes is often expressed in terms of comparison with the strike record of other countries. The comparisons are usually made with countries which enjoy a lower incidence of disputes (invariably Sweden and West Germany) rather than with countries like the USA, Italy or Australia. It is noticeable, as with the other strike figures, that public concern is unabated by improvement and seems to maintain a constant level of agitation whether the figures rise or fall. I believe we were just as worried about strikes in the 1950s as we are now. To this extent the English disease may not be an inordinately high strike record but an hysterical anxiety about strikes which amounts to hypochondria. Here, for what they are worth, are figures of international comparisons.

Table 12

	Days lost per 1,000 people employed			
	1965	1970	1974	Average for 10 years 1965–1974
UK	220	740	1270	743
USA	860	2210	1480	1305
Australia	410	1040	2510	913
Belgium	40	830	330	334
France	100	180	250	274*
W Germany	—	10	60	50
Ireland	1720	490	1260	1018
Italy	540	1730	1800	1665
Japan	360	200	450	243
Sweden	—	40	30	46

*The average for France excludes the figures for 1968 which have never been available

The Department of Employment concluded that 'the averages show that throughout the 10 year period under review the United Kingdom has had slightly higher than the median number of days lost per year for the 18 countries listed.' The Department adds that 'with the single exception of Ireland, the average number of days lost per 1000 employees per year in each of the countries listed for the years 1970–74 is higher—in most cases considerably higher—than for the years 1965–69.'[297]

Many observers would agree that the severity of strikes in this country is normally exaggerated although there is no doubt that the size and length of strikes have increased in the last six years. A cynic might suggest that we did not face a really big strike problem in this country until we tried to do something about strikes. Knowles, and more recently Hyman, pointed out that many more days work are lost through other causes, including absence due to sickness and injury. Turner said of the motor industry that the estimates frequently made of production lost by strikes are of differences between planned and actual output and many optimistic assumptions may be involved in arriving at the planned figure. T I Richardson (industrial relations manager at British Leyland, Cowley, 1966 to 1970) wrote that:

> the factory where I worked had . . . an inbuilt loss of production of 11 per cent which had nothing to do with industrial relations problems, except to create them. That is, the factory was capable of producing only 89 per cent of the programme for which it had been laid out and manned because of failures in machines, supplies, etc. The figure of losses was consistent through the years 1965 to 1970 and in only one of those years was it exceeded by losses due to industrial action.[298]

The explanations offered for our concern with strikes are various. The most rational is that the precarious nature of the British economy focuses attention on any lost production, particularly in exporting industries where the balance of payments is likely to be affected. Hyman suggests that our concern is prompted by the media's transmission of the employers' sensitivity to attacks on their own interest. It may be that there is a moralistic element in our attitude; losses of production caused by the common cold are, in a sense, inevitable, but strikes are wilful acts and therefore believed to be both avoidable and wicked. Attention may also be drawn to strikes because they sometimes provide a first class excuse for poor managerial performance; strikes, like the weather, are believed to be beyond the control of man.

Various explanatory perspectives have been taken on strikes. They may be regarded as manifestations of conflict which is believed to be inherent in industrial society. There are several different versions of this view, some of which are mutually exclusive. A functionalist approach, sometimes associated with a managerial version of pluralism, would regard industrial society as composed of many competing interest groups which, from the perspective of management, are best allowed to pursue their objectives through machinery which, while allowing the expression of conflict, also regulates it. From this point of view strikes are a necessary and legitimate expression of divergent interests, can contribute to effective adjustment and change and ought, presumably, to be welcomed. In practice, the theoretical enthusiasm of pluralists for conflict is often muted when it comes to strikes. Marxists (and the many derivative groups) take a different view; while agreeing that conflict is inevitable, they argue that it is a consequence of a fundamental division between classes based on the ownership of the means of production by capitalists and their subordination and exploitation of employees. A third view is more narrowly confined to explaining strikes as an implication of collective bargaining which itself is characteristic of a particular pattern of industrial relations; strikes, like wars, are negotiations conducted by other means.

A different perspective sees strikes as the result of some kind of breakdown. The dominating idea here is that society is essentially cooperative and that consensus is a normal state of affairs. Disputes are therefore aberrations which have to be explained. The explanations may take different forms. One common version is a conspiracy theory, that strikes are the result of the work of 'wreckers', 'politically motivated men' or agitators. Another, much more respectable version, is that strikes are the result of procedural deficiency and that the incidence of them could at least be reduced by managerial improvement, by repair of fragmented bargaining processes or wage structures or by the restructuring of trade unions.

A third perspective suggests that strikes are the result of tension release, that large scale manufacturing processes produce a variety of psychological tensions (variously described as the result of alienation, anomy or stress) which require negative reactions against the employer as a form of therapy for the worker. One form of negative reaction is the strike; others may include absence, termination of employment, lateness or sabotage. In an extreme form, this view may regard all strikes as symptomatic manifestations of psychological disorder so that wage claims and strikes in support of them are really attributable to different root causes; strikes are never what they seem. Lewis Coser properly warned of the dangers of dealing with realistic conflicts as though they were concerned with problems of emotional release. At the same time, it would be unwise to forget that emotional problems, generated inside or outside work, can be a cause of industrial disputes and that there is sense in good, old fashioned managerial virtues like counselling, good supervision and effective communication.

A fourth perspective explains strikes as part of a rational strategy on the part of the strikers, a strategy in which strikes become part of a range of sanctions available to workers in pressing their case against managers. Strikes may be constitutional (justified within agreed procedure) or unconstitutional; official (approved of by the union executive) or unofficial. Professor Clegg points out that 'it is probable that most strikes have been both unofficial and unconstitutional ever since industry bargaining procedures were instituted.'[299] For strikes to be unofficial does not necessarily mean that they take place in the face of union disapproval. Strikes are often over before the union is aware that they have occurred. Strikes usually start as unofficial and are sometimes given the tardy blessing of legitimacy later. In perishable disputes, in which the grievance requires an instant response if it is to be removed, an unofficial strike may be a rational and a necessary reaction. Unofficial strikes may be manifestations of internal union tensions; in the nature of things, the 'strike at Pilkington's' could not have been official. The unofficial strike may also be an important part of the apparatus which assures some real measure of union democracy.

The explanation of strikes is likely to depend upon the perspective of the explainer. It is also likely to be too crude because strikes are always complex. The causes of a particular strike may include any or all of the following circumstances.

1 *Primitive industrial relationships*
It is dangerous to take an evolutionary attitude to the development of industrial relations but there is no doubt that in some industries or enterprises, the first response to an expression of divergent interests is to fight. The participants learn from each other that the only purposeful reaction is the application of force.

2 *Procedural deficiency*
Some strikes occur because procedure is too lengthy or is inadequate in that it leaves no real alternative for settlement.

3 *Insecurity in employment*
Strikes may be seen as a necessary defence against uncertainty.

The threat takes two main forms. Fluctuation in earnings was emphasized by Turner, Clack and Roberts as a probable cause of high strike levels in the British motor industry. The threat to jobs can also cause strikes either by promoting defensive strategies like work-ins or by attempts to delay the end of the job when its completion is in sight.

4 *Imposed change*

Strikes may be a response to a unilateral attempt to impose changes in patterns which are believed to be established formally or by custom and practice.

5 *Rational strategy*

Strikes are necessarily connected with collective bargaining. Collective bargaining does not invariably require strikes, in fact, collective bargaining normally seeks to avoid strikes, but it cannot be effectively conducted without the possibility of strike action. In some cases, collective bargaining may depend for its outcome on a strike.

6 *Management deficiency or initiative*

Managers may cause strikes to occur as a deliberate strategy. They may bring about strikes accidentally by their intransigence or their hostility. More frequently, as Richardson suggested, they cause strikes by technical or organizational deficiency.

7 *Union organization*

The cumbersomeness and complexity of union organization has often been singled out as a cause of strikes. In particular, multi-unionism can cause strikes although Clegg suggests that this is a contributory rather than a direct influence.

8 *Revolts against union leadership*

Critics frequently despair of the apparent failure of unions to direct and control their members. In March 1977 we saw examples both of a union forcing its members back to work

(NATSOPA in a dispute between its members and *The Times* newspaper) and of a union failing to do so, at least initially (AUEW in the toolmakers' strike at British Leyland). Strikes against the union leadership, whatever their immediate effect on production, are the only real corrective against the incorporation of unions and the deterioration in the value of collective bargaining that it would produce.

9 *Inter-group tensions*

Many, perhaps most, strikes about wages are attempts to change or restore relativities. Some other strikes are caused by rivalries and tensions between groups of different status, seniority or race.

10 *Government intervention*

Some strikes are caused by governments, the actions of which may be perceived as a direct challenge to unions (the Industrial Relations Act, 1971) or as a continuing and irksome constraint (the Social Contract).

11 *Demonstrations*

Strikes may be called as gestures, usually limited to a day, or token stoppages. They are intended as symbolic demonstrations in order to focus an expression of concern.

We have already noticed that strikes are not the only, and not necessarily the most effective, sanction available against management. Limitations or restrictions of effort, the withdrawal of cooperation, the refusal to work overtime, working without enthusiasm, going slow or working to rule, all represent control by the worker over his work which he is able to apply.

These are some of the major technical criticisms of British industrial relations: that it is damaging in one or more of the respects we have examined. There are deeper criticisms. Once again, they concern in the main collective bargaining.

2 Social criticisms of industrial relations

A view often expressed by left wing critics of trade unions

and collective bargaining is that industrial relations promotes consensus and discourages social change. This criticism derives from difficulties in Marxist theory of accommodating to or explaining the role of trade unions in capitalist societies. Trade unions came to be seen as essentially capitalist institutions, developed to engage in economic relationships with employers and conceded recognition and legitimacy by employers in order to help to promote an orderly and regulated management of conflict. Trade unions are at the same time organizations of workers so they have to be conceded some respectability, within a Marxist framework. They are said to be capable of providing workers with experience in association and organization and their sporadic confrontations with employers, limited though they may be, contribute to the self-consciousness of workers as members of a class and teach them organization. Unions may then be regarded by Marxists as useful training agencies and as proper associations for those who share an 'objective' understanding of the nature of capitalism to work within in order to achieve higher levels of confrontation with the employers and with the State. Unfortunately for the Marxists, trade unions remain a constant source of despair, at least in the United Kingdom. Trade unions have shown singularly little interest in pursuing the class struggle to the point where capitalist society is challenged and overthrown, or even drastically altered.

There are many explanations for this disappointing state of affairs. They include the notorious (in more ways than one) influence of 'false consciousness'; that the workers have become lulled and deceived into adopting an 'incorrect' understanding of their own true position in capitalist society. The methods by which this deception is said to have been practised are, again, various. They certainly include 'the media' which filters, selects and indoctrinates in the interests of the employers who control it. They include the inherited apparatus of power represented in the State, applied through education and the law which is said to have indoctrinated workers into a mistaken belief in the sanctity of liberal or bourgeois values. Most important, in the present context, they include the trade unions. The unions are corruptible, they suffer from oligarchic tendencies which serve to centralize power in bureaucratic processes of control in which the membership becomes a distant threat to the interests of the officers. The unions are also engaged in negotiating and reaching accommodations with employers; it is their function to understand their opponents and their understanding is so readily achieved that they forget the interests of their members. As the unions become important in the collective bargaining process, so they are more readily incorporated in the apparatus of the State, invested with rights, privileges and status which it becomes necessary for them to defend. The only hope of redress in this unbalanced process of accommodation is for pressure from the rank and file to swing back the balance. But the rank and file are, in the nature of things, organized only for specific sectional purposes, active only to redress particular grievances. Collective bargaining, both at the level of national bargaining and at the level of the shop floor, simply teaches the working class what the employers want it to know.

One of the more recent and perhaps one of the more influential exponents of this view is Alan Fox who, attacking the concept of pluralism which he did so much to propagate, says that the unions are under an illusion of sharing in the balance of power. In fact, he says, the unions are incapable of challenging the power of management because it is unequally distributed and because the unions are composed of 'men who have already been socialized, indoctrinated and trained by a multiplicity of influences to accept and legitimize most aspects of their work situation.'[300] The unions, in turn, 'help to socialize their members in what it is sensible for them to expect from their work and their life',[301] the lower ranks accept what collective bargaining gives them 'because they are either socialized to see it as legitimate, inevitable and natural, or resigned to submit to it as an expression of power which they cannot challenge except at disproportionate cost to themselves.'[302]

The accusation of 'indoctrination' is unanswerable because it is untestable and unprovable. It is no good asking workers or their leaders whether it is true or not because, by definition, they cannot tell us, they have been indoctrinated. This makes the argument a tough nut to crack because it subsumes all behaviour as evidence of its own truth. Once 'false consciousness' has been uttered as an explanation, rational discourse must cease. To say that workers show every sign of being broadly satisfied with their unions, or with 'the system', or that collective bargaining seems to do what workers want it to do, is simply to provide evidence for the existence of 'false consciousness'. The strength of the argument becomes a weakness in the theory, for any explanation which transcends the possibility of contradiction becomes worthless.

There are other grounds for dismissing this particular criticism of collective bargaining. The very evidence which is so distressing to the right wing critics suggests that collective bargaining *has* brought about more social adjustment in favour of employees than the left is ready to concede. But collective bargaining may well have prevented that total transformation in social relationships which some elements in the left deem to be both necessary and inevitable. Collective bargaining does depend upon a degree of normative consensus between the interest groups which, in their opposition, agree to accept a modified relationship of hostility and a mutual regulation of their conduct. Each concedes advantage to the other in a mutual avoidance of the risk of mutual destruction. Collective bargaining probably does tend to 'economism', to transform un-bargainable confrontations over ideological differences into negotiable issues over cash, hours and conditions of employment. To that extent, it may be true that collective bargaining has sapped the revolutionary vitality of the British proletariat (except that we cannot know how much revolutionary vitality would have existed in the absence of collective bargaining; we have only the fervent belief of some and remarkably little evidence to guide us). Collective bargaining may have produced social cohesion rather than destructive class conflict, convergence rather than class war, negotiation rather than revolution. If so, it is a result which most of us, owners, managers, workers or citizens, find acceptable. Collective bargaining represents a rational choice for determining relationships which most of us would make 'socialized' though we may have been.

It is not an inevitable relationship, not one that we can safely assume will persist in the face of every pressure. There were signs, in the response to the Industrial Relations Act, of precisely the reaction of which the Webbs had warned: that legislation conceived by one group to be directed against it in the interests of another is likely to break down any constitutional consensus. Collective bargaining cannot handle widely divergent values, which is precisely why Marxists argue that it produces consensus. A broad measure of normative consensus is necessary to support collective bargaining and it can be threatened by the emergence of new values held by some groups in society or by a reaction provoked by a threat to traditional, long established norms. Collective bargaining may only survive in a reasonably stable society, a society in which it is believed to be perfectly proper to 'socialize' its members into accepting unquestionable values which are believed to be important for the very reason that they inhibit violent conflict. But those values can begin to break down if stability and expectations are threatened by external changes, by attacks on positions always held to be legitimate, by the disappointment of 'reasonable' economic expectations.

Fears are often expressed that social stability is threatened, if not by 'extremists' then by concerted selfishness, that collective bargaining is now required to satisfy economic expectations which are less 'reasonable' than they once were. Recent evidence suggests that this is not so:

> In a sense what is remarkable about out present society is that people are so content with their situation and that their demands are so limited, rather than that there is so much pressure on pay . . . . In practice people remain prepared to accept major differentials in earnings without worrying whether these are justified or not.[303]

Daniel goes on to suggest a number of implications which help to assess the level of stability in our society. First, he says, in the face of so many 'predictions of a collapse of basic order because of the extent of people's demands and feelings of injustice, it is salutary to be reminded that as far as the mass of the people are concerned things change very slowly and very little.'[304] Second, there is no sign of a widening of the horizons within which pay comparisons are made. Third, there is little evidence of a demand for income redistribution or of feelings of general injustice; people require steady economic growth and rising living standards and, although this may be no great comfort in present circumstances, it is 'less generally disturbing than the idea that we are on the brink of large scale disturbances because of a general sense of injustice about differentials.'[305] Fourth, while there is no great change in people's expectations, the scope for them to get what they want has altered because of changes in the structure of industry and employment. This often means a continual disturbance and unsettlement in the work environment which constantly initiates claims followed by demands for comparability of treatment. Daniel concludes that:

> the only way out of this constant upward bidding of earnings and the wage drift it generates is a reformed system of payment, such as measured day work, less prone to generate continuous pressure and conflict; and agreed and rational systems of determining differentials, such as systematic job evaluation; and the more sensitive and imaginative management of change.[306]

The mechanisms of industrial relations are a highly articulated and complex process of reaching adjustments in the many different expectations of those involved in work. The achievement of collective bargaining is that it succeeds in reaching acceptable accommodations between people with differing perceptions and differing objectives. Substantive and procedural regulation could be achieved by different methods but alternative methods would be likely to be attended by one of two persistent weaknesses, each of which collective bargaining avoids.

The first method would be by central regulation of wages. We have moved, historically, in this direction by the introduction of statutory incomes control. There seems to be a general acknowledgement by now that, except as a short-term measure, statutory control is crude in that the norms it imposes are inflexible and unrelated to changes and differences in the employment situation. To the extent that statutory control becomes more eomplex it becomes more difficult to monitor and apply; it also presents the constant possibility of confrontation between government and a union with sufficient power to present its particular 'special case'. Statutory policies, therefore, are inseparable from an ultimate problem of political authority; they enlarge industrial into political crises.

For this if for no other reason, the current enthusiasm for the control of collective bargaining rests on voluntary agreement, on the commitment of the trade unions. In 1975–76, the trade unions showed a remarkable degree of responsibility for the Government's £6 limit on wage increases. On 6 April 1976, the Chancellor proposed a 3 per cent limit (which roughly equated to a limit of £2 per week increases) in return for a series of income tax allowances or high tax payment thresholds. This offer of a fixed deal gave the TUC and the unions about two months to reach agreement among themselves and with the Government. It also advanced the concept of a social contract further in that it substituted, as bargaining items, real items of taxation policy for the earlier vague statements of good intentions. It represented the furthest point yet reached in which the trade unions are invited to enter a firm contract with the Government. It has, apart from the pros and cons of the particular terms of the contract, great attractions for the trade unions. They are able to exchange the previous consultative relationship in which they, like every other powerful interest group, were asked for their view on public policy, for a bargaining relationship which helps to determine the course of public policy. It gives the trade unions the prospect of real influence over public affairs; it enhances their prestige and their power. It also gives them a new responsibility for adhering to the version of incomes policy which is incorporated in the agreement. In this way, a new relationship with the Government is established which extends collective bargaining to a national level of policy determination. This process could be regarded as the final acknowledgement of the importance of the trade unions in the democratic process of government. It could also be regarded as the beginning of the end of collective bargaining and, with it, of the representative influence of trade unions.

Whatever the nature of the deal that emerges from such

associations between government and trade unions, the unions accepted a negotiating relationship. We have seen that the argument of 'incorporation' suggests that by entering into agreements with employers, unions are forced to abandon their ideological independence, to shelve and forget non-bargainable issues and, finally, to become responsible for the execution of the agreements which they enter. We suggested that this view was exaggerated, that the vitality of the unions had not been sapped and that to the extent that the unions did contribute to a control process which modified their independence, they contributed to the maintenance of political and social values which we, or most of us, believed were important. The accusation from the left of incorporation is a serious one, however. Trade unions in this country have been constantly threatened by a tendency to join the establishment, to become enmeshed in the honours system, to become 'responsible' and hence to appear to stand surrogate for the interests of employers. These are threats which the collective bargaining relationship imposes on the unions: that, indeed, is the value of collective bargaining. But collective bargaining also transmits correctives. The rank and file and their workplace representatives are excluded from control and to some extent from responsibility. The unaccommodated power which they can apply requires that the unions maintain a role which is representative of their interests and their expectations. Unions are valuable in the process of social control to which collective bargaining commits them only to the extent that they remain representative institutions. The constant threat of 'incorporation' must be continuously resisted if the unions are to be able to contribute to the maintenance of social order.

A functionalist explanation might suggest that this is a delicately balanced state of affairs which, like the economist's equation of market forces, must inevitably continue, that an invisible hand corrects one tendency by another. This is not so. The present situation suggests that the usefulness of the trade unions as instruments of social control could be entirely destroyed.

If the necessary accommodation of unions to the interests of employers presents dangers, the accommodation required in negotiation with government presents entirely different problems. Winkler and Pahl in a powerful description of current developments towards a corporate state (or, in more emotive language, towards fascism) suggests that one of the characteristics is the creation of delegated authority by government.[307] Non-governmental agencies are given the responsibility for executing aspects of government policy and, in the process, the agencies are freed from legal constraint and public or parliamentary scrutiny. They suggest that the unions have already begun to act as delegated authorities; Denis Healey's version of incomes policy took the process to an unprecedented point.[308] The unions are now required to accommodate to government, rather than employers. The tendencies were already apparent in the complications which attended collective bargaining in some nationalized industries when their management, sooner rather than later, had to be brushed aside in order to arrange negotiating access to the Prime Minister. Incorporation of the unions with government imposes new dangers over and above those present in bargaining with employers. The accommodations which are arrived at with government leave the unions responsible for their execution, as any bargaining process does. But the responsibility now carries political overtones of legitimacy. Rank and file opposition becomes less respectable, to the point where it can be labelled sabotage. The coercive power which unions have always possessed but which they have often been unable to apply now enjoys a new authority. Rank and file opposition is no longer directed against the union hierarchy or against the employer, it is necessarily directed against the Government. It was dangerous when a single pay claim in a particular industry was directed at government policy; the danger is likely to be chronic when every minor infraction can be regarded as undemocratic and has to be corrected by the union as agent for government policy.

Rank and file opposition will in these circumstances face an obstacle of legitimate authority which is represented by their own union. The very same process begins in which free collective bargaining and representative union opposition is conceived to be unnecessary because the Government's policy represents the will of the workers expressed through their unions which are responsible for its execution. At the same time, the practical possibility of rank and file opposition to the union is weakened by changes in the law, made ostensibly to strengthen the union movement. After the 1974 Act, the unions emerged with much greater strength but the amendment in 1976, which removed the right to refuse to join a particular union on any reasonable grounds and the right not to be excluded by way of arbitrary or unreasonable discrimination, left their members much weaker. It is hard to avoid the conclusion that trade unionism has been strengthened, not out of any libertarian concern but to make it a more effective instrument of the State.

The process has begun but so far the work group and its steward representatives have remained outside control, have remained a 'problem'. The majority recommendations of the Bullock Committee represent the means by which the strengthening of the trade unions for administrative purposes might be completed.[309]

Everyone must by now be familiar with the proposals; they have been well-publicized. The majority report proposed that workers should be given representation equal to shareholders on unitary boards of companies employing more than 2,000 people All directors would share the same responsibilities but they should be widened to include the interests of employees as well as shareholders. Boards should consist of two groups of directors of equal number plus a third group of directors who might possess special expertise. The third group would be co-opted with the agreement of a majority of each of the other two groups; it would be composed of an odd number more than one and it would form less than one-third of the total board. The Report calls this arrangement the $2x + y$ formula.

Employee representation on boards is to be arranged through a single channel of representation through the trade union machinery. Any independent trade union recognized by a company as representing at least 20 per cent of the company's employees would be able to request a ballot of the workforce. The ballot would seek a decision in principle on employee representation at board level. If at least one third of those eligible to vote (all full-time employees) were in favour, the company would be obliged to concede board level representation. Shop stewards of recognized and independent unions would then establish a joint representative committee to negotiate with the board the size and structure of the new board and to decide how worker directors were to be selected: shop stewards are 'the key figures in a system of board level representation' (p 111). Employee directors would normally be employees of the company but they could, in some circumstances, be full time union officials. There should be no 'special provision for those who chose not to join a trade union and who are thus unable to speak with a collective voice.' (p 112).

The Committee proposed that an Industrial Democracy Commission should be set up. Its functions would be to monitor and report on the effectiveness of board level representation, to investigate and recommend following disputes over the allocation and occupation of seats on boards, to provide information, advice and codes of practice and to give rulings on the size of companies and the percentage of employees for which a union is recognized.

The arguments and assumptions upon which the proposals rest are less well known than the proposals and it is worth attempting to summarize them.

1 Trade union involvement is fundamental to the success of the nation's economic strategy. It is necessary to forestall resistance to change and to capture the positive contribution which employees can make in combating stagnation (p 22).

2 'The coming of age of democracy in our society is a process that inevitably affects the whole of people's lives; it cannot be excluded from the workplace.' (p 22). This is the familiar argument used to discountenance opposition; the march of progress is inevitable so objectors should get out of its way.

3 Participation is desirable to avoid waste of the talent that is necessary to achieve great fulfilment and the greater efficiency that it can bring to companies. (p 45).

4 The involvement of employees in decisions before they are taken 'would have a significant influence on the decision that was reached and because of this would share responsibility for what the board had decided. Managers would no longer have to begin negotiation with the trade unions in an atmosphere of suspicion about an unfamiliar policy agreed by a board representing only the shareholders; they would be implementing a policy agreed between the representatives of employers and shareholders jointly at board level.' (p 49).

5 There is a large measure of coincidence between the interests of shareholders and employees. Proponents of representation believed that it is likely to lead to 'a strengthening of the private sector from which investors as well as employees can benefit.' (p 52).

6 The proposals will reinforce the legitimacy of management. In the future there must be 'a new legitimacy for the exercise of the management function within a policy framework agreed jointly by the representatives of capital and labour. We believe that this new legitimacy is essential for the long-term efficiency and profitability of the private sector and for the ultimate success of the economy itself.' (p 95).

7 The Report attempts to meet the objection of the EEPTU that participation in management and collective bargaining will not mix. The Report says that it agrees with Donovan that collective bargaining is the best means of giving workers the right to representation in decisions affecting their working lives. But, it continues, the integration of employee representatives into a representative system based on trade union machinery will ensure that there is no conflict and, further, that there is great value in seeing shop stewards as 'the key figures in a system of board level representation' (p 111).

This last point is much more like an assertion than an argument and the objectives which the Report seems to be concerned with (admirable in themselves, no doubt) must raise the suspicion that the intention behind the proposals is, if not to weaken collective bargaining, at least to change its nature. The Report is anything but the revolutionary manifesto that some of its critics have taken it to be. Its founding arguments suggest that, under a radical disguise, it is concerned to turn collective bargaining into cooperative bargaining, it is concerned with problem-solving, with producing peace and a more orderly and well-mannered trade union structure.

There are many and well-known practical criticisms of the Bullock proposals which it is not our immediate business to explore. The dilemma seems to be that, if they were implemented, their failure on practical grounds might lead to economic disorder while their success might lead to social disaster. The proposals can be read as adding significantly to a process which, by way of union recognition, the closed shop and the social contract had left only the rank and file and the shop steward beyond the control of incorporation. The incorporation of the shop steward might complete a process of transforming the unions into more effective administrative instruments of the State.

These are tendencies which the unions are not likely to resist. The TUC's recent reversal of its traditional scepticism towards participation in the management of enterprises suggests that it is pursuing voluntarily the ends which governments seek to impose. The difficulty is that the advantages of collective bargaining as a mechanism of social control are not identified by any group other than Marxists, who generally deplore them. Collective bargaining generates a chorus of criticism precisely because it offers a measure (limited though it may be) of independence and of power to groups who are able to use it to further their own interest. It is important for society that this should be so. But those committed to the economic management of an increasingly complex and centralized society cannot tolerate the existence of a limited degree of unmanageable conflict. The economic criteria by reference to which decisions are made suggest that collective bargaining is 'inefficient' and this conclusion demands that collective bargaining must be controlled.

If these demands are met and collective bargaining is curtailed, the dubious economic advantages are likely to be outweighed by heavy political costs. It is difficult to define totalitarian regimes because they take on so many different characters, but the feature which they all seem to share and which becomes a defining characteristic is their inability to tolerate independent trade unions and free collective bargaining. The centralized administration of wage bargaining, with the ready acquiescence or executive cooperation of the trade unions, is likely to have several effects. Trade unions are political institutions intended to pursue ideological objectives but their social function is not always the idea of their function which is held by their members. Members join for instrumental reasons. Unions are social and political institutions but the members may see them as economic institutions essentially concerned with the protection or advancement of their pay and conditions of work. If the unions become less relevant to the membership, in economic terms, the strength of the unions is likely to be weakened and their social and political influence will be diminished. If the unions begin to appear to control wages rather than enhance them the process of decay is likely to be hastened.

The reduction of the unions' bargaining functions will also have adverse economic effects. The merit of the 'two systems' of industrial relations which so distressed the Donovan Commission was that it enabled detailed local adjustments to be made to nationally negotiated standards. It was complicated but flexible. National wages control is likely to be simple and extremely inflexible. It is likely to generate, as it has always generated, in some industries and in some regions, considerable pressure for adjustment from both workers and management. In the long run the pressure will either destroy the policy of wage control or, as this is less likely where the policy is policed by the unions, it will have other consequences. The pressure for adjustment may be suppressed, probably at considerable economic cost and certainly with an unacceptable degree of political, moral or legal coercion. The pressure for adjustment may have the result of so complicating wage payment methods that real wages and labour costs are reduced to the level of invisibility. In this case, wages control becomes ineffective and the system of industrial relations become unnecessarily complicated. But the worst consequences are likely to be political. Apart from the real dangers of coercive legislation (which, as we may already have begun to see, is presented in a totally different light when it is approved by the unions) the threat to the democratic process lies in the weakening of the representative strength of the trade unions. Democracies depend upon the existence of pressure groups. Pressure groups are important only when they represent real interests. The trade union movement is probably the most important political pressure group in an industrialized democracy. It cannot represent if it is required to be so entirely responsible as to be the agent for government policy. Political democracy not only depends upon collective bargaining, it is similar to collective bargaining in that both depend upon the continuous relationship between different and often mutually contradictory interests. The accommodations (grudging though they may be) which both the democratic and the collective bargaining process usually achieve, cannot be brought about if the representatives of one interest group simply abandon their position and march over to the other side. The interest remains to be satisfied. The result is likely to be chaos or coercion.

Whether the conduct of industrial relations moves towards chaos or coercion is, at this time, impossible to forecast. The pressures on the institutions of industrial relations seem to be unprecedented. Various explanations of the nature of these pressures are available. One suggests that the increased involvement of the State in the management of the economy and in the direction of state-owned industry means that it can no longer stand aside from the market or from collective bargaining. In this case, the planning directives of the State will inevitably incorporate wages and the representation of workers' interests, once conducted within collective bargaining, will now come to be encapsulated by the State so that any independent union opposition becomes, as in Eastern Europe, unnecessary, illegitimate and seditious. A second explanation suggests that collective bargaining has been all too successful in bringing about social change, that workers have come to enjoy an unparalleled access to power and that the chronic decline in company profit levels of the 1970s points to a change in the distribution not only of power but of wealth. A third explanation goes further in arguing that present circumstances reveal a final crisis of capitalism (there have, of course, been many 'final' crises before but it is always possible that the latest is the last). Post-capitalist society can take many forms but it seems probable that collective bargaining and the associated characteristics of a political democracy will not be among its most prominent features.

The new relationship between the State, employers and trade unions, whatever its implications for industrial relations, raises important questions concerning the constitution and the law. The political questions raised by the miners' strikes of the 1970s and by the legitimacy of the Industrial Relations Act and of the opposition to it were fundamental and are likely to appear again in different form. Questions concerning the nature of law, the arguable necessity for its foundation in consensus and the degree of that consensus, came to the surface with the Industrial Relations Act and have not permanently disappeared with its repeal. The Budget of April 1976 raised issues of a constitutional nature concerning the responsibility of Parliament for public fiscal policy. Generally:

> the temptation and apparent obligation to use law grows as people demand more of the State as a regulator of economic activity. But law requires reserve powers of enforcement, and as pressure groups within society have become more powerful *vis-à-vis* the State in modern industrial societies, law has become an increasingly difficult

instrument for the State to utilize. Even when a broad consensus is achieved, some groups may be able to challenge successfully the specific implementation of law. This is, of course, the central problem not only of a capitalist but of any pluralist society, and the dilemma it presents has rarely been satisfactorily resolved.[310]

These are wide and heavy issues, remote from the conduct of industrial relations as it is understood by those engaged in it as managers. It may be that, as the legal and political setting of their work develops, managers and unionists will develop new relationships with the State which will provide them with both power and representative influence. It may be that the employers' organizations will be stimulated by a new measure of authority and influence already being demonstrated by the Confederation of British Industry. It is also probable that the State's greater involvement in the administration of industrial relations will be sufficiently remote or inefficient to afford considerable discretion to the managers, unions, work groups and employees who, in getting things done, always have to work out the pattern of their own relationships.

There are more immediate and practical changes which are imminent or present in contemporary industrial relations. Incomes policy, whatever its form, to the extent that it reduces the concern of collective bargaining with earnings may serve to re-focus it upon issues which it has too long neglected. Gottschalk has suggested a number of issues of long-term significance which have emerged in British industrial relations in recent years. They include the extension of information available for collective bargaining:

> the extension of the bargaining agenda, a reappraisal of the facilities for conciliation and arbitration, the impact of growing unionization among white-collar and managerial employees, and the challenge of resolving the problem of

minority group relations at the workplace.[311]

Incomes policy has, on occasions, had an effect in extending the range of bargaining into the negotiation of substantial changes in the organization of work. In 1976 the NUM responded to incomes control by a diversification of strategy in expressing a concern with earlier retirement. There are other arguments and other pressures to suggest that:

> the frontiers of joint decision-taking must be extended to meet them. One way of putting this point in a practical way is to say that it is now time to end what has been termed 'the money solution' in British industrial relations. By this is meant the tendency of both sides to assume that all demands and criticisms can be bought off or deflected, if only people are given an opportunity to earn enough money.[312]

A discussion about industrial relations has finally taken us into an argument about the political process. That is entirely as it should be. It is certain that many people will take very different positions about the character of collective bargaining or the importance of statutory control and that too is as it should be. What seems certain, however, is that industrial relations is inextricably connected with the political process. It would be dangerous to argue, as many pluralists have argued, that there is a close analogy between the governmental and the managerial process and, because of the similarity, that industrial relations is essentially a political process. It is not governmental, the rules it produces are of a very fragile and temporary nature, the authority which it concerns is not conceded to be legitimate by many of the subjects, there are no oppositions and no alternate governments and the power which is applied is essentially economic rather than political. Yet there are many similarities between industrial relations and politics. Some of them are superficial;

the representatives seem to behave in a political way, there is a great deal of what is now called 'politicking', trade unions engage in the paraphernalia of politics with elections and ballots and, most important, the trade unions are an important ingredient in the Labour Party. What truly establishes the relationship between industrial relations and the political process is that work, subordination and authority, wages and conditions, employment and unemployment, welfare and industrial safety, make up so much of the lives of the majority of people who are the citizens of the political state. The health, happiness and expectations of these people are influenced, if not determined, by the processes of industrial relations. The conduct of industrial relations has also come to be seen as closely related to the economic health of the community (indeed, we have suggested that the relationship is too close for political comfort).

All this means that it is unreal to confine the study of industrial relations to its principal institutions, or to the rules. or to the rule making and negotiating processes which relate the institutions. These are all important features of industrial relations but once they have been described it is important to recognize that industrial relations is about change and the adjustment of the perspectives of different groups in society.

ABBREVIATIONS

ACAS	Advisory, Conciliation and Arbitration Service
APECCS (APEX)	Association of Professional, Executive Clerical and Computer Staff
ASTMS	Association of Scientific, Technical and Managerial Staffs
ASBSBSW	Almalgamated Society of Boilermakers, Shipwrights, Blacksmiths and Structural Workers
AUEW	Amalgamated Union of Engineering Workers
BMA	British Medical Association
CAC	Central Arbitration Committee
CIR	Commission on Industrial Relations
C and P	Custom and practice
CPSA	Civil and Public Services Association
DE	Department of Employment
EET and PU	Electrical, Electronic, Telecommunications and Plumbing Union
HMSO	Her Majesty's Stationery Office
ISTC	Iron and Steel Trades Confederation
NALGO	National and Local Government Officers Association
NATSOPA	National Society of Operative Printers, Graphical and Media Personnel
NBPI	National Board for Prices and Incomes
NCB	National Coal Board
NUA and AW	National Union of Agricultural and Allied Workers
NUDBTW	National Union of Dyers, Bleachers and Textile Workers
NUGMW	National Union of General and Municipal Workers
NUM	National Union of Mineworkers
NUPE	National Union of Public Employees

NUR	National Union of Railwaymen
NUTGW	National Union of Tailors and Garment Workers
PEP	Political and Economic Planning
SOGAT	Society of Graphical and Allied Trades
TGWU	Transport and General Workers' Union
TUC	Trades Union Congress
UCATT	Union of Construction, Allied Trades and Technicians
UKAPE	United Kingdom Association of Professional Engineers
USDAW	Union of Shop, Distributive and Allied Workers

FOOTNOTES

1 CHILD J, *British Management Thought*, Allen & Unwin, 1969, p 102
2 FLANDERS A, *Industrial Relations: What is Wrong with the System?* Faber, 1965, p 10
3 CLEGG H A, *The System of Industrial Relations in Great Britain*, Blackwell, 1970, p 1
4 De VOS G, *Conflict in Society*, ed de Rueck and Knight J, J & A Churchill Ltd, 1966, p 68
5 Commission on Industrial Relations *The Role of Management in Industrial Relations*, HMSO, 1973, pp 4–5
6 *Ibid*, p 39
7 *Ibid*, p 38
8 SMITH E Owen, *Productivity Bargaining, a case study in the steel industry*, Pan, 1971, pp 24–25
9 CIR, *op cit*, p 6
10 CIR, *op cit*, p 5
11 CIR, *op cit*, p 6
12 CLEGG H A, *The System of Industrial Relations in Great Britain*, Blackwell, op cit, 1970, p 170
13 *Ibid*, p 178
14 SPECTOR C, *Management in the Printing Industry*, Longmans, 1967, p 110
15 HILTON W S, *Industrial Relations in Construction*, Pergamon, 1968, p 182
16 *Personnel Management*, March 1963
17 For example, the Ford dispute in 1970 and the coalmining dispute in 1974
18 CIR, Report No 39, *Communications and Collective Bargaining*, p 12, HMSO, 1973
19 *Ibid*
20 *Ibid*, p 2

21 Arthur Marsh has been heard to say that when anyone uses the term 'principle' in collective bargaining the wisest thing to do is to run for cover because the speaker intends to do someone a serious injury

22 BOWEY Angela M, *The impact of new management control techniques on industrial relations*, a paper read to a Social Science Research Council seminar on management aspects of industrial relations, London School of Economics, May 1974

23 *Ibid*

24 Office of Manpower Economics, *Incremental Payment Systems*, HMSO, 1973

25 National Board for Prices and Incomes, Report No 132, *Salary Structures*, HMSO, 1969

26 CIR, Report No 89, *Retail Distribution*, HMSO, 1974

27 CIR, Report No 69, *Small Firms and the Code of Industrial Relations Practice*, HMSO, 1974

28 CIR, Report No 85, *Industrial Relations in Multi-Plant Undertakings*, HMSO, 1974

29 The terms used by the CIR were, in fact, 'internal growth' and 'external growth' by the merger with or acquisition of new companies. These terms do not seem as satisfactory as linear and lateral because there is nothing to prevent external growth leading to the acquisition of a company in the same product field, that is, into further linear development. The CIR's terms were not logically exhaustive

30 CIR, Report No 85, p 11

31 *Ibid*, p 29

32 *Ibid*, p 43

33 *Ibid*, p 43

34 Commission on Industrial Relations, Report No 11, *Hoover Ltd*, HMSO

35 CIR Report No 85, p 30

36 *Ibid*, p 36

37 WALTON R E and McKERSIE R B, *A Behavioural Theory of Labour Negotiation*, McGraw Hill, 1963. This provides one of the best discussions of the negotiating process. What they describe as 'intra-organizational bargaining' is discussed in a

chapter entitled Internal adjustment in Anthony P D and Crichton A, *Industrial Relations and the Personnel Specialist*, Batsford, 1969. There is also a discussion in a thorough survey of the field of the negotiating process by Andrew Gottschalk, A behavioural analysis of bargaining, in *The Sociology of the Workplace*, edited by Warner M, Allen & Unwin, 1973

38 FLANDERS A, *The Fawley Productivity Agreements*, Faber, 1964

39 Described as such in Anthony and Crichton, *op cit*

40 WINKLER J T, The ghost at the bargaining table: directors and industrial relations, *British Journal of Industrial Relations*, Vol XII, No 2, July 1974, p 194

41 *Ibid*, p 197

42 *Ibid*, p 201

43 *Ibid*, p 212

44 ANTHONY and CRICHTON, *op cit*

45 WINKLER, *op cit*, p 202

46 GOTTSCHALK, *op cit*, p 5

47 WALTON and McKERSIE, *op cit*, p 68

48 For the very same reason this is the title of Winkler's paper, *op cit*

49 POOLE Michael, A back seat for personnel, *Personnel Management*, May 1973

50 To be sure, one of the two organizations studied by Poole exhibited a low level of personnel management development and responsibility and his criticisms are very relevant to the facts he observed. It is not the facts which are to be questioned so much as the conclusions

51 GOTTSCHALK, *op cit*, p 51

52 BEYNON H, *Working for Ford*, Penguin, 1973, p 102

53 In that this view is the basis of McGregor's Theory X it has led to a fashionable reaction in favour of Theory Y, a false premise and a false promise which will be discussed later

54 DAHRENDORF R, *Class and Class Conflict in Industrial Society*, Routledge & Kegan Paul, 1959, p 249

55 GOULDNER A W, *Patterns of Industrial Bureaucracy*, Free Press, 1964, p 160

56 ROY D, Making-out: a counter-system of workers' control of work situation and relationships, *Industrial Man*, ed T Burns,

Penguin, 1969, p 364

57 BENSMAN J and GERVER I, Crime and punishment in the factory, *American Sociological Review*, 1963

58 For example, BALDAMUS W, *Efficiency and Effort*, Tavistock, 1961, LUPTON T, *On the Shop Floor*, Pergamon, 1963

59 GOULDNER A W, *op cit* p 236

60 The reasons for the confinement of academic industrial relations to formality, from which it shows recent signs of emerging, have been discussed to a limited extent in chapter 1. They probably derived from a need for distinctiveness (academics are at least as concerned with status as the people whose behaviour they study) which tended to discount the disciplines of sociology and psychology. They were also associated with a necessary reaction against the human relations emphasis on emotional responses which explained the conflict in terms of underlying issues which were never manifest. The reaction went too far. Academic attitudes are susceptible to the same explanations as those which academics apply to the shop-floor.

61 TURNER H A, The morphology of trade unionism, *Trade Unions*, ed McCARTHY W E J, Penguin, 1972, pp 105–6

62 *Ibid*, p 98

63 *Ibid*, p 99

64 MARTIN R, Union democracy: an explanatory framework, *Trade Unions*, op cit p 197

65 TURNER H A, *Trade Union Growth Structure and Policy*, Allen & Unwin, 1962

66 *Op cit*, p 195

67 CLEGG H A, *The System of Industrial Relations in Great Britain*, *op cit*, p 105

68 *Ibid*, p 80

69 LANE T and ROBERTS K, *Strike at Pilkingtons*, Fontana, 1971, p 52

70 MARTIN R, Union democracy: an explanatory framework, McCarthy W E J, *Trade Unions*, Penguin, 1972, p 191

71 *Ibid*, p 193

72 *The Miner's Next Step*, the Unofficial Reform Committee, Tonypandy, Robert Davies & Co, 1912, p 9

73 McCARTHY W E J, *The Role of Shop Stewards in British*

Industrial Relations, HMSO, 1968; McCarthy W E J and Parker S R, *Shop Stewards and Workplace Relations*, HMSO 1968; Goodman and Whittingham, *Shop Stewards in British Industry*, McGraw Hill, 1969; Marsh A I, Evans E O and Garcia P, *Workplace Industrial Relations in Engineering*, Kogan Page, 1971

74 The Donovan report point 'more of a lubricant than an irritant' has become something of a cliche. Evans E O , Cheap at twice the price? Shop stewards and workshop relations in engineering. *The Sociology of the Workplace*, ed Warner M, Allen & Unwin, 1973, p 82

75 TURNER H A, CLACK G, ROBERTS G, *Labour Relations in the Motor Industry*, Allen & Unwin, 1967, p 222

76 Goodman and Whittingham, *op cit*, p 16

77 CIR Report No 17, *Facilities Afforded to Shop Stewards*, HMSO, 1971

78 TURNER, CLACK & ROBERTS, *op cit*, p 222

79 BEYNON H, Working for Ford *op cit*, p 73

80 See the discussion of the steward's code of ethics in Beynon, pp 121–126

81 *Ibid*, p 170

82 *Ibid*, p 173

83 Goodman and Whittingham *op cit* p 122
Turner, Clack and Roberts describe the establishment and operation of 'The big six' committee in the British motor industry in the 1950s, *op cit*, p 220

84 CIR, *op cit*

85 TURNER, CLACK and ROBERTS, *op cit*, pp 221–222

86 ANTHONY & CRICHTON, *op cit*, p 49

87 LANE T, *The Union Makes us Strong*, Arrow Books, 1974, p 266

88 *Ibid*, p 274

89 BAIN G S, *Trade Union Growth and Recognition*, HMSO, 1967

90 BAIN G S, and PRICE R, Union growth and employment trends in the United Kingdom, 1964–1970, *British Journal of Industrial Relations*, November 1972

91 The figures are taken from the Report of the 107th Annual Trades Union Congress, 1975 and are for the year 1974. Membership of the AUEW includes the Construction Section,

the Foundry Section and TASS

92 BAIN G S and PRICE R, Who is a white-collar employee?, *British Journal of Industrial Relations*, November 1972

93 LOCKWOOD D, *The Black Coated Worker*, Allen & Unwin, 1958

94 GOLDTHORPE J H, LOCKWOOD D, BECHOFER F and PLATT J, *The Affluent Worker: Industrial Attitudes and Behaviour*, Cambridge, 1968, pp 112–114. The authors exempt the craftsman from their findings. Their general view of 'instrumentalism' among affluent workers has been criticized by G Mackenzie in *The Social Analysis of Class Structure*, ed PARKIN F, Tavistock, 1974

95 *Ibid*, p 176

96 LANE T, *op cit*, p 278

97 *Ibid*, p 279

98 DICKENS L, UKAPE: A study of a professional union, *Industrial Relations Journal*, Autumn 1972

99 LOVERIDGE R, Occupational change and the development of interest groups among white collar workers in the United Kingdom, *British Journal of Industrial Relations*, November 1972

100 BLACKBURN R M, *Union Character and Social Class*, Batsford, 1967

101 *Ibid*, p. 18

102 WEBB S and B, *The History of Trade Unionism*, Longmans Green, 1920, p 1

103 *Trade Unionism*, TUC, 1966, p 33

104 FLANDERS A, What are trade unions for? *Trade Unions*, ed McCarthy W E J, Penguin, 1972, pp 22–23

105 PAYNTER W, *British Trade Unions and the Problem of Change*, Allen & Unwin, 1970

106 KAHN-FREUND Otto, *Labour and the Law*, Stevens, 1972, p 270

107 DONOVAN, p 54

108 Kahn -Freund points out, however, that legal protection is not a simple alternative to bargaining strength. "Even the most efficient inspectors can do but little if the workers dare not complain to them about infringements of the legislation they are seeking to enforce. The Truck Acts and other protective

legislation began to be effectively enforced when membership in trade unions gave the workers the strength to insist on the maintenance of legal standards". (Kahn-Freund, *op cit*, p 10)

109 Industrial Relations Act, 1971, Section 1, p 1

110 *Ibid*, Section 41, p 43

111 ANTHONY and CRICHTON, *op cit*, p 277

112 KAHN-FREUND, *op cit*, p 29

113 *Ibid*, p 51

114 WEDDERBURN K W, *The Worker and the Law*, Penguin, 1965

115 *Ibid*, p 162

116 WEDDERBURN, *op cit*, p 82

117 Trade Union and Labour Relations Act, 1974, Schedule 1, Section 6, p 33

118 KAHN-FREUND, *op cit*, p 30

119 Department of Employment *Gazette*, August 1976, p 881

120 Department of Employment *Gazette*, May 1976, p 453

121 *The Guardian*, 7 September 1976

122 *Ibid*

123 This danger seems to have been acknowledged by Harry Urwin (TGWU) speaking for the General Council in the same debate

124 *Industrial Relations Review and Report*, February 1976

125 The word 'specified' was substituted in the 1976 Amendment for the word 'appropriate' in the 1974 Act. Before the Amendment it would have been possible for someone to argue that, although not a member of the union signatory to the closed shop agreement, he was a member of an appropriate union. The Amendment leaves it to the signatory union to permit membership of a specified union

126 *Industrial Relations Review and Report, ibid*

127 FELS Allan, *The British Prices and Incomes Board*, Cambridge University Press, 1972, p 6

128 BALFOUR Campbell W, *Incomes Policy in the Public Sector*, Routledge & Kegan Paul, 1972, p 237

129 *The Attack on Inflation, The Second Year*, Cmnd 6507, HMSO, 1976

130 National Board for Prices and Incomes, Report No 123, *Productivity Agreement*, 1969

131 FELS, *op cit*

132 CHILD J, *The Business Enterprise in Modern Industrial Society*, Collier-Macmillan, 1969, p 51

133 GASKELL P, *Artisans and Machinery*, Frank Cass, 1968, p 170

134 SUTTON F X, HARRIS S E, KAYSON C, TOBIN J, *The American Business Creed*, 33, Harvard, 1965

135 BERLE A and MEANS G, *The Modern Corporation and Private Property*, Macmillan, 1932

136 BURNHAM James, *The Managerial Revolution*, Putnam, 1941

137 CHILD, *op cit*, p 47

138 POLLARD S, *The Genesis of Modern Management*, Edward Arnold, 1965, p 195. Reinhardt Bendix gives an excellent account of the development of this moral appeal in *Work and Authority in Industry*, Wiley, 1956

139 SMILES S, *Self-Help*, John Murray, 1908, p 111

140 FORD H, *My Life and Work*, Heinemann, 1922, p 13

141 *Op cit*, p 19

142 HUMBLE John, Social responsibility audit, *Foundation for Business Responsibilities*, p 2

143 COPEMAN G, *Employee Share Ownership and Industrial Stability*, IPM, 1975

144 The clearest argument that free enterprise is inimical to social good can be found in the recent works of Kenneth Galbraith

145 GRANT M, *The World of Rome*, Weidenfeld & Nicolson, 1960, p 112

146 HUMBLE, *op cit*, p 3

147 COPEMAN, *op cit*

148 HUMBLE, *op cit*, p 3

149 NICHOLLS T, *Ownership Control and Ideology*, Allen & Unwin, 1969, p 141

150 CHILD J, *British Management Thought*, Allen & Unwin, 1969, p 32

151 CRICHTON A, *Personnel Management in Context*, Batsford, 1968, p 330

152 The alternative would be to believe that education can have no influence upon the outlook of those submitted to it. Whatever the merit of this argument, it can hardly be expected to be held by the writer, who earns his living in an institution of higher

education

153 CLIFF T, *The Employers' Offensive*, Pluto, 1970, p 3

154 There is a case for making Marxism a compulsory study for industrial relations managers, partly because of its influence and partly because it is conceptually difficult and comparatively rigorous—on the good old fashioned ground that education should not be enjoyable

155 MARSH A I, *Disputes Procedures in British Industry*, Royal Commission Research Papers, HMSO, 1966

156 GENNARD J and LASKO R J, Management behaviour towards strikers, a paper given at a seminar at the London School of Economics, 1975

157 FOX A, *Beyond Contract: Work, Power and Trust Relations*, Faber and Faber, 1974, p 317

158 I would hasten to explain that this comment is not directed at Professor Clegg, whose defence of pluralism (*BJIR*, November 1975) is clear and succint. This is not the place to attempt the analysis of a complex problem. It must suffice to suggest that pluralism is a theory of government; there is no clear analogy with government in the field of industrial relations: to regard the employer as exercising a governmental function is to invite fallacy and confusion

159 FOX A, *Man Mismanagement*, Hutchinson, 1974

160 KENNY T P, Stating the case for welfare *Personnel Management*, Vol 7, No 9, September 1975

161 This remark should not be taken to imply any obscurity in the way in which the discussion is conducted. Dr Silverman's analysis is presented with admirable clarity

162 SILVERMAN D, *The Theory of Organizations*, Heinemann, 1970, p 27

163 BUCKLEY W, *Sociology and Modern Systems Theory*, Prentice Hall, 1967, p 58

164 SILVERMAN, *op cit*, p 29

165 *Op cit*, p 100

166 *Op cit*, p 102

167 BEYNON H, op cit, p 109

168 BALDAMUS W, Tedium and traction in industrial work, *Men and Work in Modern Britain*, ed Weir D, Fontana, 1973, p 80

169 BLAUNER R, Work satisfaction and industrial trends in modern society, *Class Status and Power*, ed Bendix and Lipsett, Routledge & Kegan Paul, 1967, p 479

170 LUPTON T and BOWEY A M, *Wages and Salaries*, Penguin, 1974, p 79

171 SALAMAN G, *Community and Occupation*, Oxford University Press, 1974, p 19

172 *Ibid*, p 53

173 *Ibid*, p 121

174 GOLDTHORPE J H, *et al*, p 181

175 *Ibid*, p 185

176 SALAMAN, *op cit*, p 119

177 *Ibid*, p 69

178 *Ibid*, p 71

179 I should hastily acknowledge that this comment also applied to another work, *Industrial Relations and the Personnel Specialists*, by Anthony P and Crichton A

180 LUPTON and BOWEY, *op cit*, p 15

181 The argument was succinctly expressed by Professor Phelps Brown in *Collective Bargaining Reconsidered*, University of London, 1971, and it has been forcefully expressed by *The Economist* from time to time; for example, "British trade unions nowadays certainly cause their members' real incomes to be lower than they would be if trade unions did not exist". *The Economist*, 10 October 1970

182 JONES Aubrey, *The New Infiltration, the Politics of Prices and Incomes*, Andre Deutsch, 1973, p 30

183 *The Attack on Inflation*, Cmnd 6151, HMSO, 1975, p 12

184 SMITH Owen E, *Productivity Bargaining, a Case Study in the Steel Industry*, Pan, 1971, p 317

185 MARSH A I, *Disputes Procedures in British Industry*, Royal Commission Research Papers, 2, HMSO, 1966, p 2

186 Royal Commission on Trade Unions and Employers' Associations, 1965–68, Cmnd 3623, HMSO, 1968, p 54

187 Office of Manpower Economics, *Wage Drift*, HMSO, 1973, p 3

188 *Ibid*, p 22, The table from which the figures were extracted is on pages 58 and 59 of the report

189 BORASTON I, CLEGG H, RIMMER M, *Workplace and Union*, Heinemann, 1975, p 172
190 LUPTON and BOWEY, *op cit*, p 112
191 Royal Commission, 1968, *op cit*, p 262
192 CLEGG, 1970, *op cit*, p 466
193 *Ibid*, p 466
194 Royal Commission, *op cit*, p 108
195 BORASTON, CLEGG, RIMMER, *op cit*, p 176
196 Royal Commission, *op cit*, p 33
197 *Trade Unionism*, Trades Union Congress 1966
198 *British Labour Statistics Year Book* 1973, Department of Employment, HMSO, 1975, Table 22, p 54. NB The comparisons cannot be accurate. Wages Councils were excluded from the *Year Book*. The figure in brackets for Wages Councils under 1973 is additional and out of context; it is based on figures in the D E *Gazette*, April 1975. Further, the 1973 percentages are based on a sample and are proportions of a total sum of various types of collective agreement. The safest conclusion might be that there has been little change
199 National Board for Prices and Incomes, Report No 36
200 FLANDERS A, *The Fawley Productivity Agreements*, Faber, 1964
201 JONES K and GOLDING J, *Productivity Bargaining*, Fabian Research Series 257, 1966
202 THOMASON G F, Practical steps to productivity bargaining, Mimeographed
203 NBPI, Report No 123
204 CLIFF Tony, *The Employer's Offensive*, Pluto, 1970
205 NBPI, *Salary Structures*, Cmnd 4178, HMSO, 1969, p 7
206 *Industrial Relations Code of Practice*, Department of Employment, HMSO, 1972, p 11
207 See Barbara Wootton's argument in *The Social Foundations of Wage Policy*
208 This, at least, is the argument which has justified recent increases for mineworkers. It may well be a rationalization, for the compensation argument rarely applies to other groups (farmworkers, building workers, nurses) unless they happen to have access to negotiating power. The argument for mine-

workers' pay probably provides more by way of comfort for those who pay the increases than it does explanation for their extent

209 Pay Board Advisory Report No 2, *Problems of Pay Relativities*, Cmnd 5535, HMSO, 1974, p 15

210 Advisory Conciliation and Arbitration Service, Guide No 1, *Job Evaluation*, p 4

211 THOMASON G F, *Personnel Manager's Guide to Job Evaluation*, IPM, 1968, p 30

212 Pay Board Advisory Report No 2, *Relativities*, Cmnd 5535, HMSO, 1974, p 4

213 Office of Manpower Economics, *Incremental Payment Systems*, HMSO, 1973, p 6

214 *Ibid*, p 28

215 Incomes Data Services Ltd, *Staff Status for Manual Workers*, Part 2 June 1974, p 3

216 *The Attack on Inflation*, Cmnd 6151, HMSO, 1975, p 13

217 Quoted by Incomes Data Services Ltd, *Sick Pay*, March 1975, p 6

218 CLEGG, *op cit*, 1970, p 286

219 *Op cit*, p 200

220 Ministry of Labour, *Industrial Relations Handbook*, HMSO, 1961

221 *Report of the Royal Commission on Trade Unions and Employers' Associations*, 1965–68, HMSO, 1968, p 17

222 CLEGG, *op cit*, p 66

223 Royal Commission, *op cit*, p 110

224 CLEGG, *op cit*, p 247

225 The CIR Report on Hoover Ltd provides an example

226 CLEGG, *op cit*, p 255

227 STEVENS C M, *Strategy and Collective Bargaining Negotiations*, McGraw-Hill, 1963, p 2

228 WALTON R E and McKERSIE R B, *A Behavioural Theory of Labour Negotiations*, McGraw-Hill, 1965

229 STEVENS, *op cit*, p 3

230 FLANDERS A, *Collective Bargaining*, Penguin, 1969, p 15

231 *Ibid*, p 19

232 FLANDERS A and FOX A, The reform of collective bar-

gaining: from Donovan to Durkheim, *British Journal of Industrial Relations*, Vol VII, No 2, p 157

233 FLANDERS, *op cit*, p 21 (f)

234 GOODMAN, ARMSTRONG, WAGNER, DAVIS and WOOD, Rules in industrial theory, *Industrial Relations Journal*, Vol 6, No 1, Spring 1975, pp 22–23

235 BROWN W, A consideration of 'custom and practice', *British Journal of Industrial Relations*, Vol X, March 1972, p 45

236 *Ibid*, p 57

237 GOTTSCHALK A W, A behavioural analysis of bargaining, *The Sociology of the Workplace*, ed Warner M, Allen & Unwin 1973, p 70

238 LEVINSON H M, *Determining Forces in Collective Wage Bargaining*, John Wiley, 1966

239 CHAMBERLAIN N W and KUHN J W, Conjunctive and cooperative bargaining, *Collective Bargaining*, *op cit*, p 318

240 *Ibid*, p 323

241 DEUTSCH M, *The Resolution of Conflict*, Yale, 1973

242 WALTON and McKERSIE, *op cit*, pp 4–5

243 STEVENS, *op cit*, p 33

244 WALTON and McKERSIE, *op cit*, p 18

245 ANTHONY and CRICHTON, *op cit*, p 110

246 STEVENS, *op cit*, p 38

247 WALTON and McKERSIE, *op cit* , p 25

248 WALTON and McKERSIE, *op cit* , p 43

249 STEVENS, *op cit*, p 34

250 DEUTSCH, *op cit*, p 291

251 DEUTSCH, *op cit*, p 305

252 HARRIES Keith, unpublished thesis

253 WALTON and McKERSIE, *op cit*, p 42

254 The circumstances in which this statement is incorrect (that is, in which hostility may be preferred to mutual regulation) are worth mentioning. They can exist in what Professor Turner described as a situation of endemic conflict in which "disagreement, mistrust and detailed aggression or defense have become acquired attitudes." (Turner, Clack and Roberts, *Labour Relations in the Motor Industry*, Allen & Unwin, 1967, p. 289) and which "can only be securely resolved by the separation

of the leading personalities from them". The process may follow from a decision of one of the parties that considerable damage must be done to its opponent if only as a means of breaking out of endemic conflict. The damage intended by one is likely to be quite unacceptable to the other so that there is a deliberate escalation of conflict beyond the limits which collective bargaining is capable of containing. The costs of such conflicts are likely to be considerable and they are not lightly undertaken

255 DEUTSCH, *op cit*, p 87

256 DAHRENDORF R, *Class and Class Conflict in an Industrial Society*, Routledge & Kegan Paul, 1959, p 166

257 DEUTSCH, *op cit*, p 352

258 *Ibid*, p 353

259 WALTON and McKERSIE, *op cit*, p 56

260 HYMAN R, *Disputes Procedure in Action*, Heinemann, 1972, p 6

261 DEUTSCH, *op cit*, pp 131–132

262 SCHELLING T C, *The Strategy of Conflict*, Harvard, 1960

263 DEUTSCH, *op cit*, p 141

264 WALTON and McKERSIE, *op cit*, p 5

265 *Ibid*

266 HYMAN, *op cit*, p 5

267 *Ibid*, p 58

268 FRENCH J R P, *Power and Conflict in Organizations*, Kahn R L and Boulding E (eds), Tavistock, 1964

269 Workers participation in management in Poland, International Institute of Labour Studies, *Bulletin* No 5, November 1968, p 192

270 RAMSAY H, Participation: the shop floor view, *British Journal of Industrial Relations*, XIV, No 2, July 1976, p 137

271 DEUTSCH, *op cit*, p 141

272 WALTON and McKERSIE, *op cit*, p 60

273 ANTHONY and CRICHTON, *op cit*, p 113

274 WALTON and McKERSIE, *op cit*, p 65

275 HYMAN, *op cit*, p 59

276 DEUTSCH, *op cit*, p 136

277 HYMAN, *op cit*, p 55

278 WALTON and McKERSIE, *op cit*

279 HYMAN R, *op cit*, p 67
280 *Ibid*, p 66
281 Department of Employment *Gazette*, April 1975, p 314
282 THOMASON George, *A Textbook of Personnel Management*, IPM, 1976, p 148
283 DAHRENDORF, *op cit*, p 227
284 SINGLETON, *op cit*, p 62
285 Advisory Conciliation and Arbitration Service, Report No 1, 1975
286 SINGLETON N, *op cit*, p 85
287 DEUTSCH, *op cit*, p 379
288 *The Times*, 16 March 1972
289 PHELPS BROWN E H, *Collective Bargaining Reconsidered*, Athlone Press, 1971, p 6
290 *Ibid*, p 9
291 *Ibid*, p 10
292 *Ibid*, p 12
293 *Ibid*, p 12
294 DANIEL W W, *The PEP Survey on Inflation*, PEP, July 1975, p 7
295 The figures are taken from the Department of Employment *Gazette*. The Department's figures exclude stoppages involving fewer than 10 workers and those which lasted less than one day, except any in which the aggregate number of working days lost exceeded 100. Official stoppages are those which take place with the approval of the appropriate union executive
296 Department of Employment *Gazette*, November 1976, p 1220
297 Department of Employment *Gazette*, December 1975, p 1276. The figures given are selected from the 18 given in the *Gazette*
298 RICHARDSON T I, *The Guardian*, 3 June 1975
299 CLEGG, *op cit*, p 331
300 FOX Alan, *Beyond Contract: Work, Power and Trust Relations*, Faber and Faber, 1974, p 284
301 *Ibid*, p 293
302 *Ibid*, p 294
303 DANIEL, *op cit*, p 18
304 *Ibid*, p 24
305 *Ibid*, p 26
306 *Ibid*, p 28

307 PAHL R E and WINKLER J T, Corporatism in Britain: why protecting industry need not mean more bureaucracy, *The Times*, 26 March 1976, p 14 and
WINKLER J T, Law, State and economy: The Industry Act, *British Journal of Law and Society*, 2 (2) Winter, 1975, pp 103–128

308 Unprecedented, as far as I know, in any Western democracy. There are close similarities, however, to the 'transmission belt' role of the trade unions in the Soviet Union.

309 Report of the Committee of Inquiry on Industrial Democracy, HMSO 1977

310 THOMSON A W J and ENGELMAN R S, *The Industrial Relations Act, a review and an analysis*, Martin Robertson, 1975, p 154. In chapter 6 the authors engage in a thoughtful discussion of the issues that have only been touched on here

311 GOTTSCHALK A W, The management of industrial relations in a changing environment, *Industrial Relations in a Changing World*, Beesley M, Croom Helm, 1975.

312 McCARTHY W E J and ELLIS N D, *Management by Agreement, an Alternative to the Industrial Relations Act*, Hutchinson, 1973, p 98

BIBLIOGRAPHY

ADVISORY, CONCILIATION AND ARBITRATION SERVICE, Guide No 1, *Job Evaluation*

ADVISORY, CONCILIATION AND ARBITRATION SERVICE, Report No 1, 1975

ANTHONY P D, and CRICHTON A, *Industrial Relations and the Personnel Specialist*, Batsford, 1969

BAIN G S, *Trade Union Growth and Recognition*, HMSO, 1967

BAIN G S, and PRICE R, Union growth and employment trends in the United Kingdom, *British Journal of Industrial Relations*, November 1972

BAIN G S, and PRICE R, Who is a white-collar employee? *British Journal of Industrial Relations*, November 1972

BALDAMUS W, *Efficiency and Effort*, Tavistock, 1961

BALDAMUS W, Tedium and traction in industrial work, *Men and Work in Modern Britain*, ed Weir D, Fontana, 1973

BALFOUR C W, *Incomes Policy in the Public Sector*, Routledge & Kegan Paul, 1972

BENDIX R, *Work and Authority in Industry*, Wiley, 1956

BENSMAN J, and GERVER I, Crime and punishment in the factory, *American Sociological Review*, 1963

BERLE A, and MEANS G, *The Modern Corporation and Private Property*, Macmillan, 1932

BEYNON H, *Working for Ford*, Penguin, 1973

BLACKBURN R M, *Union Character and Social Class*, Batsford, 1967

BLAUNER R, Work satisfaction and industrial trends in modern society, *Class, Status and Power*, ed Bendix & Lipsett, Routledge & Kegan Paul, 1967

BORASTON I, CLEGG H, and RIMMER M, *Workplace and Union*, Heinemann, 1975

BOWEY A M, The impact of new management control techniques on industrial relations, unpublished

BROWN W A, consideration of custom and practice, *British Journal of Industrial Relations*, Vol X, March 1972, p 45
BUCKLEY, W *Sociology and Modern Systems Theory*, Prentice Hall, 1967
BURNHAM J, *The Managerial Revolution*, Putman, 1941
CHAMBERLAIN N W, and KUHN J W, Conjunctive and cooperative bargaining, *Collective Bargaining*, ed Flanders A
CHILD J, *The Business Enterprise in Modern Industrial Society*, Collier-Macmillan, 1969
CHILD J, *British Management Thought*, Allen & Unwin, 1969
CLEGG H A, *The System of Industrial Relations in Great Britain*, Blackwell, 1970
CLIFF T, *The Employers' Offensive*, Pluto, 1970
COMMISSION ON INDUSTRIAL RELATIONS, Report No 11, *Hoover Limited*, HMSO
COMMISSION ON INDUSTRIAL RELATIONS, Report No 17, *Facilities Afforded to Shop Stewards*, HMSO, 1971
COMMISSION ON INDUSTRIAL RELATIONS, Report No 34, *The Role of Management in Industrial Relations*, HMSO, 1973
COMMISSION ON INDUSTRIAL RELATIONS, Report No 39, *Communications and Collective Bargaining*, HMSO, 1973
COMMISSION ON INDUSTRIAL RELATIONS, Report No 69, *Small Firms and the Code of Industrial Relations Practice*, HMSO, 1974
COMMISSION ON INDUSTRIAL RELATIONS, Report No 85, *Industrial Relations in Multi-plant Undertakings*, HMSO, 1974
COMMISSION ON INDUSTRIAL RELATIONS, Report No 89, *Retail Distribution*, HMSO, 1974
COPEMAN G, *Employee Share Ownership and Industrial Stability*, Institute of Personnel Management, 1975
CRICHTON A, *Personnel Management in Context*, Batsford, 1968
DAHRENDORF R, *Class and Class Conflict in Industrial Society*, Routledge & Kegan Paul, 1959
DANIEL W W, *The PEP Survey on Inflation*, PEP, July 1975
DE VOS G, *Conflict in Society*, ed de Rueck & Knight, J & A Churchill, 1966
DEPARTMENT OF EMPLOYMENT, *British Labour Statistics Year Book, 1973*, HMSO, 1975
DEPARTMENT OF EMPLOYMENT, *Industrial Relations Code of Practice*,

HMSO, 1972
DEUTSCH M, *The Resolution of Conflict*, *Yale*, 1973
DICKENS L, UKAPE: a study of a professional union, *Industrial Relations Journal*, Autumn 1972
FELS A, *The British Prices and Incomes Board*, Cambridge, 1972
FLANDERS A, *The Fawley Productivity Agreements*, Faber, 1964
FLANDERS A, *Industrial Relations: What is Wrong with the System?* Faber, 1965
FLANDERS A, (ed), *Collective Bargaining*, Penguin, 1969
FLANDERS A, What are trade unions for? *Trade Unions*, ed McCarthy W E J, Penguin, 1972
FLANDERS A, and FOX A, The reform of collective bargaining: from Donovan to Durkheim, *British Journal of Industrial Relations*, Vol VII, No 2
FORD H, *My Life and Work*, Heinemann, 1922
FOX A, *Beyond Contract: Work, Power and Trust Relations*, Faber & Faber, 1974
FOX A, *Man Mismanagement*, Hutchinson, 1974
FRENCH J R P, *Power and Conflict in Organizations*, eds Kahn R L and Boulding E, Tavistock, 1964
GASKELL P, *Artisan and Machinery*, Cass, 1968
GENNARD J, and LASKO R J, Management behaviour towards strikers, unpublished
GOLDTHORPE J H, LOCKWOOD D, BECHOFER F and PLATT J, *The Affluent Worker: Industrial Attitudes and Behaviour*, Cambridge, 1968
GOODMAN, ARMSTRONG, WAGNER, DAVIS and WOOD, Rules in industrial relations theory, *Industrial Relations Journal*, Vol 6 No 1, Spring 1975
GOODMAN and WHITTINGHAM, *Shop Stewards in British Industry*, McGraw Hill, 1969
GOTTSCHALK A, A behavioural analysis of bargaining, *The Sociology of the Work Place*, ed Warner M, Allen & Unwin, 1973
GOTTSCHALK A, The management of industrial relations in a changing environment, Beesley M, Croom Helm, 1975
GOULDNER A W, *Patterns of Bureaucracy*, Free Press, 1964
GRANT MICHAEL, *The World of Rome*, Weidenfeld & Nicholson, 1960

HILTON W S, *Industrial Relations in Construction*, Pergamon, 1968
HMSO, *The Attack on Inflation, The Second Year*, Cmnd 6507, HMSO, 1976
HUMBLE J, Social responsibility audit, *Foundation for Business Responsibilities*
HYMAN R, *Disputes Procedure in Action*, Heinemann, 1972
Industrial Relations Review and Report, February 1976
JONES A, *The New Inflation*, Deutsch, 1973
JONES K, and GOULDING J, *Productivity Bargaining*, Fabian Research Series, 257, 1966
KAHN-FREUND O, *Labour and the Law*, Stevens, 1972
KENNY T P, Stating the case for welfare, *Personnel Management*, Vol 7, No 9, September 1975
LANE T, *The Union Makes Us Strong*, Arrow Books, 1974
LANE T, and ROBERTS K, *Strike at Pilkingtons*, Fontana, 1971
LEVINSON H M, *Determining Forces in Collective Wage Bargaining*, Wiley, 1966
LOCKWOOD D, *The Black Coated Worker*, Allen & Unwin, 1958
LOVERIDGE R, Occupational change and the development of interest groups among white collar workers in the United Kingdom, *British Journal of Industrial Relations*, Nov 1972
LUPTON T, *On The Shop Floor*, Pergamon, 1974
LUPTON T, and BOWEY A M, *Wages and Salaries*, Penguin, 1974
MCCARTHY W E J, *The Role of Shop Stewards in British Industrial Relations*, HMSO, 1968
MCCARTHY W E J, and ELLIS N D, *Management by Agreement: An Alternative to the Industrial Relations Act*, Hutchinson, 1973
MCCARTHY W E J, and PARKER S R, *Shop Stewards and Workplace Relations*, HMSO, 1968
MARSH A I, EVANS E O, and GARCIA P, *Workplace Industrial Relations in Engineering*, Kogan Page, 1971
MARTIN R, Union democracy: an explanatory framework, *Trade Unions*, ed MCCARTHY W E J, Penguin, 1971
MINISTRY OF LABOUR, *Industrial Relations Handbook*, HMSO, 1961
NATIONAL BOARD FOR PRICES AND INCOMES, Report No 123, *Productivity Agreements*, HMSO, 1969
NATIONAL BOARD FOR PRICES AND INCOMES, Report No 132, *Salary Structures*, HMSO, 1969

NICHOLLS T, *Ownership, Control and Ideology*, Allen & Unwin, 1969
OFFICE OF MANPOWER ECONOMICS, *Incremental Payment Systems*, HMSO, 1973
OFFICE OF MANPOWER ECONOMICS, *Wage Drift*, HMSO, 1973
PAHL R E, and Winkler J T, Corporatism in Britain, *The Times*, 26 March 1976, p 14
PAY BOARD, Advisory Report No 2, *Problems of Pay Relativities*, HMSO, 1974
PHELPS BROWN E H, *Collective Bargaining Considered*, Athlone Press, 1971
POLLARD S, *The Genesis of Modern Management*, Arnold, 1965
POOLE M, A back seat for personnel, *Personnel Management*, May 1973
RAMSAY H, Participation: the shop floor view, *British Journal of Industrial Relations*, Vol XIV, No 2, July 1976, p 137
REPORT OF THE COMMITTEE OF INQUIRY ON INDUSTRIAL DEMOCRACY, HMSO 1977
RICHARDSON T I, *The Guardian*, 3 June 1975
ROY D, Making-out: a counter system of workers' control of work situations and relationships, *Industrial Man*, ed Burns T, Penguin, 1969
ROYAL COMMISSION ON TRADE UNIONS AND EMPLOYERS' ASSOCIATIONS, HMSO, 1968
SALAMAN G, *Community and Occupation*, Oxford, 1974
SCHELLING T C, *The Strategy of Conflict*, Harvard, 1960
SILVERMAN D, *The Theory of Organizations*, Heinemann, 1970
SMILES S, *Self-Help*, Murray, 1908
SMITH E O, *Productivity Bargaining: A Case Study in the Steel Industry*, Pan, 1971
SPECTOR C, *Management in the Printing Industry*, Longmans, 1967
STEVENS C M, *Strategy and Collective Bargaining Negotiations*, McGraw-Hill, 1963
SUTTON, HARRIES, JAYSON and TOBIN, *The American Business Creed*, Harvard, 1965
THOMASON G F, *Personnel Manager's Guide to Job Evaluation*, Institute of Personnel Management, 1968
THOMASON GEORGE, *A Textbook of Personnel Management*, Institute of Personnel Management, 1976

THOMSON A W J, and ENGLEMAN R S, *The Industrial Relations Act, A review and an analysis*, Robertson, 1975

TRADES UNION CONGRESS, *Trade Unionism*, TUC, 1966

TURNER H A, *Trade Union Growth, Structure and Policy*, Allen & Unwin, 1962

TURNER H A, The morphology of trade unionism, *Trade Unions*, ed McCarthy W E J, Penguin, 1972

TURNER H A, CLACK G, and ROBERTS G, *Labour Relations in the Motor Industry* Allen & Unwin, 1967

UNOFFICIAL REFORM COMMITTEE, *The Miners' Next Step*, Tonypandy, 1912

WALTON R E, and MCKERSIE R B, *A Behavioural Theory of Labor Negotiation*, McGraw-Hill, 1963

WEBB S and B, *The History of Trade Unionism*, Longmans Green, 1920

WEDDERBURN K W, *The Worker and the Law*, Penguin, 1965

WINKLER J T, The ghost at the bargaining table, *British Journal of Industrial Relations*, Vol XII, No 2, July 1974

WINKLER J T, Law, State and economy, The Industry Act, *British Journal of Law and Society*, 2 (2), Winter, 1975, pp 103–128

BOOKS FROM IPM

The IPM produces a large number of books on a wide range of management issues. Some of these are described below. For a free catalogue giving details of all our 95 titles or if you wish to order any of our titles please write to IPM Distribution Centre, Publication Sales Office, Blackhorse Road, Letchworth, Hertfordshire SG6 1HN.

IPM books can be bought from your local bookseller or direct from IPM at the address on the contents page.

TRAINING IN INDUSTRY AND COMMERCE

Edwin J Singer

This revised edition which has been designed as an introduction to the subject reminds us that training is with us constantly and is far more pronounced in our modern society with mobility of labour, improvements, expansions, new techniques, mergers and reorganizations.

The whole purpose of the book can be summarized in its conclusion, 'Every firm can improve its training arrangements. The aim is not to maximize the grant from the Training Board, nor to introduce training schemes which meet some laid down standard of competence, but rather to create the environment in which every employee can master new skills in the shortest time at the lowest cost.'

'. . . useful . . . well written and worthy of a place in a student's or manager's bookshelf.' *Works Management.*

Revised edition 1977 160 pages

No Problems Here?

Keith Carby, Manab Thakur

The 1976 Race Relations Act has meant that there is no room for managerial complacency over race relations. After studying race relations in 22 British companies, the authors suggest that organizations will actually benefit by eliminating racial discrimination.

The book outlines positive steps which management can take to eliminate racial discrimination and disadvantage. Valuable data are provided which should help organizations separate fact from fiction as a first step in considering the case for action.

1977 160 pages

Statistics for Management

John Ashford

The intention of this book is not to produce an expert statistician but rather a person who is capable of taking an informed view of numerical problems and of thinking in a quantitative way.

Practical examples are given from the field of management with particular emphasis on personnel problems. Written by the current chief examiner of the IPM statistics course and Professor of Mathematical Statistics at Exeter University, this book provides essential reading for both management and students and is bound to become a standard text on the subject.

A Model Answers book is available in conjunction with this title.

Available in hardback and paperback

1977 416 pages.

Staff Status for All

Payment and Employment Conditions Committee Report

There is a trend within many European countries to integrate the conditions of employment for blue and white collar workers. This publication analyses the reasons for and methods of introducing staff status, discusses the problem areas and provides a checklist for action. A number of case studies provide company experience.

1977 70 pages.

A Textbook of Personnel Management

George Thomason

This much needed book was first published in October 1975 and sold out in nine months. The author has now revised the text.

When the original edition was first published, many major changes in public policy were under discussion in Britain and were mentioned only in passing. Since then, events such as the passing of the Employment Protection and Trade Union and Labour Relations (Amendment) Acts, and the development of the 'Social Contract' have changed the situation. The author has updated all such legislation and references to public policies and has made a number of other changes suggested by reviewers and colleagues.

The first edition was good; the second is even better, and still represents remarkable value. It provides ideal background reading and is indispensable for reference purposes.

Available in hardback and paperback

Revised edition 1976 540 pages

Negotiating in Practice

Keith Sisson

Negotiation as a decision-making process affects individuals and groups in every aspect of life. But nowhere is negotiation more significant than at the workplace where an increasing number of decisions are now being reached by collective bargaining with trade union representatives.

As well as describing the process of negotiation and the techniques involved, the book provides much needed case study material in the form of role-playing exercises. For the training officer who requires practical material in the subject of negotiating and for the non-student or student who wishes to make himself familiar with the pressures and constraints under which negotiators work, the book provides not only essential reading but a practical opportunity to gain experience in negotiating.

1977 193 pages